Categories and Experience:

Essays on Aristotelian Themes

by

John P. Anton

**Dowling Studies in the Humanities
and the Social Sciences**

Copyright © 1996 SSIPS

All rights reserved. No part of this publication may be duplicated in any way without the expressed written consent of the publisher, except in the form of brief excerpts for the purposes of review.

Published by:
Global Publications
Institute of Global Cultural Studies
Binghamton University, State University of New York
Binghamton, NY 13902-6000
Phone: (607) 777-4495 or 6104
Fax: (607) 777-6132 or 2642
E-mail: pmorewed@binghamton.edu

Imprint: DOWLING COLLEGE PRESS

Library of Congress Cataloging-in-Publication Data

John P. Anton, *Categories and Experience: Essays on Aristotelian Themes*

1. Aristotle 2. Philosophy 3. Ontology 4. Epistemology 5. Politics 6. Ethics

ISBN 1-883058-02-3

ANNOUNCEMENT

Dowling Studies in the Humanities and the Social Sciences (DSHSS) has been established to further research in the humanities and the social sciences. Manuscripts submitted undergo an external review and need not reflect the views of the Editorial Board.

On behalf of the Editorial Board, I am pleased to express appreciation for the support we have received from the Dowling College administration; we especially thank President Victor P. Meskill, Provost and College Secretary, Albert E. Donor, and Dean of Arts and Sciences, James E. Caraway.

Robert M. Berchman
Editor in Chief

DOWLING STUDIES IN THE HUMANITIES AND THE SOCIAL SCIENCES

―――――――――

Sponsor
Victor P. Meskill, ex officio

Editor in Chief
Robert M. Berchman

Managing Editor
Parviz Morewedge

Editors

Joseph Behar
James E. Caraway
Andrew Karp
Byron Roth
Martin Schoenhals

Joan Boyle
Jeffrey Cole
John D. Mullen
Susan Rosenstreich
James O. Tate

CATEGORIES AND EXPERIENCE:

ESSAYS ON ARISTOTELIAN THEMES

BY

JOHN P. ANTON

DOWLING COLLEGE PRESS

TABLE OF CONTENTS

1. Introduction 7

2. Aristotle's Principle of Contradiction:
   Its Ontological Foundations and
   Platonic Antecedents (1972) 31

3. The Meaning of *O Logos tēs Ousias*
   in *Categories* 1a (1968) 53

4. The Aristotelian Doctrine of
   Homonyma (1968) 75

5. Ancient Interpretations of Aristotle's
   Homonyma (1969) 99

6. Observations on Aristotle's Theory
   of Categories (1975) 131

7. On the Meaning of *Katēgoria* in
   Aristotle's *Categories* (1992) 151

8. Aristotle's Theory of Categories and
   Post-Classical Ontologies (1981) 175

9. The Unity of Scientific Inquiry:
   The Scope of *Ousia* (1989) 185

10. Revolutions and Reforms (1988) 205

11. *Politeia* and *Paideia*: The Structure
    of Constitutions (1988) 215

12. Aristotle on Justice and Equity (1989) 245

13. Ideal Values and Cultural Action (1991) 257

14. Aristotle's Architectonic of *Politike Techne* (1994) 269

15. Bibliography 285

16. Index 293

17. About the Author 299

ACKNOWLEDGMENTS

I am grateful to Professor P. Morewedge for the encouragement to prepare a collection of some of my publications on aspects of Aristotle's philosophy that have appeared over the years and which in certain cases are either accessible with difficulty or perhaps not at all. Where appropriate, I have indicated in the first endnote of each essay relevant information except for items that appear here for the first time. I wish to acknowledge appreciation for permission to reprint in this collection certain papers that were published over the years in the following journals: *The Journal of the History of Philosophy, The Monist, Diotima, Philosophia* (published by the Academy of Athens). I also want to express special thanks to the following publishers for permission to reprint articles that appeared in special volumes: The State University of New York Press, Fordham University Press, The Papazeses Publishers of Athens, Greece, for the article "Ideal Values and Cultural Values" in the *Festschrift in Honor of K. Despotopoulos*; to Dr. K. Boudouris, editor of the volume *On Justice*, 1981 Proceedings of the Greek Philosophical Society; and to Drs. R. Cohen and P. Nicolacopoulos, editors of the *Greek Studies in the Philosophy and History of Science: Boston Studies in the Philosophy of Science,* Kluwer Academic Publishers. The bibliography was compiled by Ms. Marianne Bell, in the office of the College of Arts and Sciences of the University of South Florida.

John P. Anton
Tampa, Florida

INTRODUCTION

I. The Early Background

This introduction is designed as a brief survey of Greek thought to provide in general outline the background against which the author could sketch the main features of Aristotle's philosophical inquiries and the problems he sought to solve. My purpose has been to draw attention to the broader context of the major themes discussed in the essays printed here. The student who wishes to learn more about Aristotle and the great tradition on which he built and to which he contributed, stands to gain more by consulting any of the standard works on the history of Greek philosophy and the excellent monographs on special Aristotelian topics that have appeared in recent decades. The introductory notes that follow will hopefully provide a needed focus for the present collection of essays, originally published in a variety of journals and volumes, some of which are no longer accessible.

Among the great thinkers who laid the intellectual foundations for the development of scientific cosmology and the study of nature were the members of the "School of Miletus," Thales, Anaximander and Anaximenes, who prepared the way for Pythagoras of Samos, Xenophanes, Parmenides and his Eleatic followers, Heraclitus, and the so-called "pluralists," Empedocles, Anaxagoras, Leucippus and Democritus.

Although this phase of Greek thought is mainly *natural* philosophy, seeking to explain *physis* as universal process and discover its origins, order and ultimate character, it is contiguous with that of the great poets of Greece. Some familiarity with the world of the poets and the religious traditions of the Greeks, e.g., the

Chthonian deities, the Olympian Pantheon, the Mystery Cults, is desirable if the reader wishes to explore the wider range of the theoretical achievements of the early thinkers.

Among the major ideas and distinctions which were treated during this period of Greek thought we find those of (1) Permanence and Change, (2) Appearance and Reality, (3) The One and the Many, (4) Nature and Art, (5) Reason and Sense-perception, and (6) The Limit and the Unlimited.

II. The Sophistic Movement and Socrates of Athens

The Sophistic movement, when it appeared in the second half of the fifth century, challenged the then current beliefs about (a) the nature of reality and (b) the reliance on reason for arriving at truth. The Sophists were attracted to Athens at a time when the religious political and economic values of the old aristocracy were under attack. They responded to the rising tide of new practical and social interests when it became apparent that the *possession* of knowledge was a powerful tool.

The leading Sophists were Protagoras of Abdera ("Man is the measure of all things"), an advocate of moral relativism, moderate tolerance of customary religion and utilitarian education; Thrasymachus (the leading discussant in Plato's *Republic* Bk. I), a defender of moral realism ("might makes right"), according to which view Justice is determined by the strongest man; Gorgias, who gave theoretical support to skepticism by demonstrating that universal moral principles are impossible to prove; Prodicus, whose lectures Socrates appears to have heard, known as "the master of definitions," who stressed the importance of practical knowledge and advocated a safe attitude toward conventional morality; Critias, who criticized religion and thought of the gods as inventions the powerful use to dominate the masses; Hippias, famous for his erudition, who took a skeptical view toward the absoluteness of laws and advocated a return to nature. The "fictional" Callicles (Socrates' adversary in the dialogue *Gorgias*) who asserted the extreme thesis that the principle "might makes right" is itself rooted in the nature of things.

The Sophistic movement contributed new ideas and assisted toward clarifying the following: (i) how the concept of human nature is central to political philosophy; (ii) why it is necessary to keep on re-examining all general assumptions; and (iii) how difficult it is to defend universal moral laws. The views the sophists held in all three areas ranged from radical skepticism toward all laws to a liberal attitude advocating reasonable reforms and social improvement.

Socrates of Athens met the sophistic challenge head-on by taking the questions it raised and providing new ways of rebutting the relativism and subjectivism of human values. He was the first to establish the practice of systematic induction and the method of inclusive definitions. His own teachings became controversial and led to serious accusations ("corrupting the youth and introducing new gods"); he was tried before the court of Athens and condemned to death in 399 B.C. Though not the founder of an official school of philosophy, his teachings provided new points of departure for the next generation.

III. The Philosophical Heritage of Plato

A number of philosophical schools claim to have been founded on the teachings of Socrates: the Megaric School of Euclid, the Cynic School of Antisthenes, and the Cyrenaic School of Aristippus. These leaders were contemporaries of Plato, and in their own way used the views of Socrates to arrive at solutions of their own.

Plato of Athens (his real name was Aristocles) became Socrates' most famous pupil and one of the world's greatest thinkers. He was born in 427 B.C. and lived during the most exciting yet unhappy period of Athens. He studied with Cratylus, a disciple of Heraclitus, probably wrote tragedies as a young intellectual, studied the views of the early philosophers, especially those of Parmenides and the Pythagoreans, established a school of his own, known as "the Academy," and wrote almost all his works in dialogue form. He is famous primarily as a philosopher. His dialogues, especially the early ones, make excellent use of dialogue and logical arguments to help the reader see the implications of the ordinary facts of life and how the fruits of philosophy can be had only through the pursuit of the ideals of the good life.

Plato extended further Socrates' method of question and answer, the *dialectic*, when he combined it with the uses of the dramatic method to perfect the art of the written dialogue. Although he touched on all sides and aspects of human life, his inquiries and investigations seem to have been organized around three basic themes: the problem of human excellence, the vision of politics and the ultimate ideal of knowledge. It is important to remember, while reading his works, that for Plato the tasks of ethics and politics are inseparable and that the pursuit of any single excellence or virtue involves us in the quest for the unity of all the virtues: Courage, Prudence, Wisdom and Justice. To the list we should add the virtue of piety.

Plato's theory of Forms is correctly regarded as the cornerstone of his philosophy and underlies every theme he explored. The Forms or Ideas are discussed in a number of Platonic dialogues, and even criticized occasionally as a theory (*Parmenides*). It assumes the basic distinction between sensible and intelligible things, the world of change and the realm of permanence. True knowledge is only of the Forms; the method which secures it is dialectic.

IV. Plato's Dialogues: The Basic Themes

Plato's criticisms of traditional religion are related to his intellectual passion to free religious beliefs and practices from impurities and irrational elements as well as to his concern for a perfect society. In the dialogue *Euthyphro*, he raises serious questions about the way in which people make claims on piety. He shows there how complex the religious attitude is and what demands it places upon those who claim to be pious. Plato discussed also such themes as the place of religion in the life of the *polis*, its relation to goodness and knowledge, and the relationship of God to the *cosmos*.

The nature of the universe and its creation is discussed in the *Timaeus* where Plato states in the magisterial manner of a "likely story" views comparable to the Presocratic cosmologies. The "myth" deals with the coming-to-be of the physical world, how this *cosmos* is the work of a Divine Intelligence and in accordance with an ideal pattern whereby the disorder of the original material is replaced with order and structure to emerge as a world creature endowed with soul and reason. This dialogue was widely read in antiquity and throughout the middle ages. The fascination it exerts continues to this day.

Plato's views on human nature can be organized around two central topics: (a) the theory of the soul and its parts, the appetitive, the spirited and the rational (mainly in the *Republic* and the *Phaedrus*); and (b) the immortality and destiny of the soul, which Plato presents as the grand topic Socrates discussed in the final hours of his life (*Phaedo*), and also in the celebrated dialogue, *Symposium*, where *eros* (love) is man's drive to generate in beauty by rising on the ladder of love to effect a vision of Beauty itself.

The theme of human fulfillment and the pursuit of excellence remained one of Plato central concerns. He wrote numerous dialogues in which he examines the virtues individually and collectively by raising all sorts of philosophical and practical questions, from the difficulties of defining them to the problem of their unity. Plato's chief motive is the pursuit of the good life for each human being and society as a whole. All the early dialogues can be seen as preludes to the full examination of how human happiness, peace, social order and the search for knowledge converge as aspects of the same basic theme: the philosophic life of love or wisdom and the just society.

Equally strong was Plato's interest in the contributions that the arts make to understanding the Good, including the art of legislation. Plato placed heavy demands upon the arts, calling for full appraisal of their place in society and in what service they are to the pursuit of truth, beauty, utility, justice and knowledge). He introduced novel evaluations in the arts, from the "fine" arts to those of medicine and education. Statesman-ship, the philosopher's highest art, recurs as the theme of his last but unfinished work, the *Laws*.

V. Aristotle: The Scope of his Work and Methodology

Aristotle (384–322) was born in Stagira (Chalkidiki). His father, Nicomachus, was physician to King Philip of Macedon. At the age of seventeen he went to Athens to study in Plato's Academy, and remained there for twenty years. After Plato's death (347) he and a few close associates went to Assos, then to Mitylene; later he returned to Athens to open his own center of learning, the Lyceum, and established what has become known as the Peripatetic school. In 342 he accepted Philip's invitation to become Alexander's tutor. He lived in Athens until Alexander's death; a year later, when the powerful anti-Macedonian party accused him of impiety, he decided to flee Athens. Aristotle died in 322 B.C. in the nearby city of Chalkis in the island of Euboea.

Aristotle is one of the greatest thinkers and scientists of all times and one of the most influential philosophers of the world. He systematized the available knowledge of his time and extended scientific research in new ways to become the founder of most of the branches of learning which antiquity bequeathed to modern times. He wrote on logic, rhetoric, literary theory, physics, botany, zoology, psychology, economics, ethics, politics, metaphysics, and astronomy. In his early period and while still under the influence of his teacher, Plato, he wrote a number of dialogues and essays, among them, "On Philosophy," the first attempt by an ancient author to deal with the origins of Greek "philosophizing," and a "Persuasion to Philosophy." His return to Athens marks his period of maturity and scientific investigations. His model of theoretical explanation remained that of Plato. He laid the foundations of scientific methodology for most of the sciences. He formulated his idea of science in the *Organon*, a collection of works that comprise the *Categories*, *De Interpretatione*, *Topics*, *Prior Analytics*, and *Posterior Analytics*.

The Aristotelian practice of science involves the determination of the object of investigation, the examination of previous opinions and established hypotheses, stating *what* is the case and *why* it is so, introducing the appropriate method in accordance with the nature of the subject matter itself, and explaining the facts of observation. The outcome or aim of science is definition: to state the structures of kinds. As method, science is formalized reasoning, demonstration and proof. It operates through syllogism, the premises of which are established by means of the powers of reason working with the facts of sense experience.

Most of the surviving writings of Aristotle are genuine. The ones he wrote for the wider public were lost; only the "esoteric" or "specialist" works survived. The first comprehensive "edition" of Aristotle's manuscripts was carried out in the middle of the first century B.C. by Andronikus of Rhodes. They are now divided into groups according to subject matter. (i) Logical works: to those already mentioned also belong the *Topics* and *Sophistic Refutations*. (ii) Natural science: *Physics* (8 books), *On Heavens* (4 books), *On*

Generation and Destruction, Meteorologica (4 books), *Botany* (spurious), *History of Animals* (10 books), *On the Parts of Animals* (5 books), *On the Locomotion of Animals.* (iii) Psychology: *On the Soul* (3 books), *Parva Naturalia*, including the writings *On Memory and Reminiscence*, and *On Dreams.* (iv) Metaphysics: a collection of 14 books dealing with "ultimate questions" and first principles. Aristotle did not use the expression "metaphysics." Andronikus added a title to the otherwise unclassified set of essays by dubbing the phrase "*ta meta ta physica*", meaning "the scrolls which come after the *Physika.*" (v) Ethics and politics: *Nicomachean Ethics* (10 books), *Eudemean Ethics, Magna Moralia, Politics* (8 books), *On the Constitution of Athens* (the only surviving study of the 150 ancient constitutions Aristotle compiled), *Economics.* (vi) Rhetoric and literary theory: *Rhetoric, Poetics* (only the portion which deals with dramatic poetry survived).

A definitive edition of the *Corpus Aristotelicum* was sponsored by the Berlin Academy (1831), under the supervision of J. Bekker, who edited the Greek text (volumes 1–2) and the Latin versions of the Renaissance (volume 3); C. A. Brandis and H. Usener edited the *Scholia* (volume 4), and H. Bonitz prepared the *Index Aristotelicus* (volume 5, [1870]). V. Rose edited the *Fragmenta* (Teubner, 1886).

VI. Aristotle's Philosophy of Life and Human Nature

In the brief treatise, titled *Categories*, Aristotle comes to grips with fundamental problems of classification and attribution. By the time he wrote this work, it seems that he had arrived at a solution of his own, different from that of Plato's, on the problem of the relationship between Form and Matter. In this work Aristotle states that there can be only ten inclusive genera of being (*ta genē tou ontos*): *ousia* (wrongly translated as "substance") quantity, quality, relatives, place, time, positions, state, action and passion. In meaningful discourse, that is when we make statements, which can be either true or false, we predicate something of something. The point is that in attributing x to y we are not simply referring to things; we want to talk correctly and truly about their connections. Hence only if we know what things exist and how they are related to each other can we in fact make true statements and have discourse on the nature of things. We sense, know, and talk on the basis of our natural ability to function *logically*. What then is the structure and function of human life?

In Aristotle's general theory of life the *empsycha*, existents endowed with life, *psychē*, are carefully distinguished from non-living types for their complexity of structure and activity. *Psychē* is Aristotle's general term for the determinate power by which living things are to be understood; it is an *archē*, a principle. Soul or *psychē* refers to the organizing principle of biological processes; it is the form of the living body as well as its controlling end or purpose (*entelecheia*). All functions or activities of living bodies are to be understood in terms of the ends to which they respond. The major characteristic which sets off the living organisms from other beings is that they are concrete individuals (*ousiai*) capable of growing, reproducing, sensing, and as the level of activities exhibits more complexity, also of judging, thinking and reasoning, powers that indicate possession of *logos* and *nous*. Organisms as purposive living existents have *psychē* as power and as operation (*dynamis-energeia*). Every operation is directed toward particular objectives; all activity is a response to a stimulus or a practical good, be it internal or external. According to Aristotle the three types of living things form a continuum of organic life. First there is the nutritive type of life, whose functions are reproduction and growth. Next on the scale is the sensitive life, endowed with reproductive, growing *and* sensing activities, enabling the *empsychon* being to discriminate at a distance and move toward a good. Finally, there is the thinking type of life, which includes all other activities under a principle of distinct organization of ends, aiming at *knowing* in action and theory.

All human action proceeds from *hormē*, a determinate drive, which in view of the *dynamis* which human beings have, enables them to respond through their senses to present and future needs; they can act intelligently in anticipation by choosing in advance with the aid of appropriate habits; they meet their complex problems successfully by developing prudence (*phronēsis*), the highest practical excellence. The human *psychē* possesses the power of intelligence; it has the power of *kritikon*, reflective and discriminatory response, and functions on two levels, sensing and intellecting. To the question "What makes us know?" Aristotle's answer is (a) the world, through its structured processes, i.e. the fact that it is an intelligible or knowable world, and (b) the nature of human intelligence, i.e. the natural endowment of logical and critical powers. From the point of view of psychology, Aristotle treats knowledge as a function of a cognizing organism responding to its environment. Thus *knowing* is at once a process of adaptation for the purpose of sustaining life and also a process of production and fulfillment, since knowledge can be put to practical uses and serve as the means to complete the actualization of the human *entelecheia*.

VII. Aristotle's Physics: the Principles of Process

Aristotle, the biologist and philosopher who formulated his views with the aid of biological concepts, has been increasingly appreciated since the middle of the nineteenth century. Though not an evolutionist, his model of analysis came from his studies of living things as presented in *De Partibus Animalium* I, ch. 5; *Historia Animalium* I, ch. 6, and other related works.

By natural things Aristotle means things which possess an internal principle of change; things which exist by nature are moved by an *hormē*, an inherent drive or power, and are capable of changing in determinate ways. Thus *natural science* is the inquiry that studies anything that possesses this power of change. Stated in a different way, this science is an inquiry into the general principles of process. Nature, *physis*, as this science understands the term, stands for the power or tendency things have to act; this power is implied in the definable essence and affords the explanatory principle of all processes. For instance, if the nature of man is stated in the essential definition (man is by nature a rational animal), the nature of human beings is expressed by the activities of thinking and knowing. Another way of understanding *physis*, as the internal principle of process, is in contrast with art, or *technē*. Whereas natural things have the principle of motion in themselves, the objects of art, viz. a house, a statue, a spear, etc. have no such internal principle, although the things out of which they are made do.

Kinēsis, process, in all its manifestations is always determinate. Any process of anything indicates a passage from *this* state to *that* state. It is a transition from the relative absence of formal completion to the eventual actualization of that completion. The important thing here is that what undergoes change is not the form or structure of X but its matter (*hylē*), the substratum. To understand any case of process or change, Aristotle holds, a minimum of three principles are needed: (a) the *matter* of a thing, i.e., that which undergoes change, the subject of process; (b) the structural identity of a thing, i.e. its form or *eidos*, which persists in the change toward its fulfillment; (c) a relative privation, that is a certain phase in the process which points to the fact that the structural completion is yet to be achieved. These three factors are distinguishable only in our talking about process, i.e. when we try to understand change.

Aristotle distinguishes carefully four basic types of change: (a) *substantive*, whose termini are *generation-destruction*; (b) *qualitative*, with a number of various contraries demarcating the limits of this type, viz. colors, tastes, sounds etc.; (c) *quantitative*, contained within *growth* and *diminution*; and (d) locomotion, change in *place*, within the contraries of natural *up* and *down*. Most important is the substantive type. It refers to the generation and destruction of existents. Generation, evidently, does not mean a mere combination of elements but the generation of a new instance of a natural and specific individual or its destruction. This is the background of Aristotle's insistence upon the permanence and continuity of natural forms (versus modern views of evolution). Within this framework, Aristotle discusses a set of fundamental concepts needed to understand process: chance, spontaneity, the infinite, place, void, time, contiguity, magnitude, extension, unity, diversity, eternal motion.

The great variety of natural things called for a theoretical explanation, a quest that goes back to the early Greek thinkers. Aristotle refers to the simple contrary qualities: the Hot and the Cold, the Wet and the Dry, and also to the four compounds which arise from the mixing of the elemental qualities: Earth (cold and dry), Water (cold and wet), Air (wet and hot), and Fire (hot and dry). The next level of *inanimate existents in the world* is the further mixture of compounds as seen in the diversity of minerals and other lifeless bodies. The elementary forms of life, analytically understood, are the homogeneous parts of plants and animals, *tissues and organs*, from the coordination of which constitutes *whole organisms*, plants and animals, ranging from sponges, plants, zoophytes and mollusks, to insects, crustacea, sea mammals, land animals and human beings.

VIII. Aristotle, the Founder of Metaphysics

The work titled *Metaphysics* is actually a collection of fourteen books on interrelated topics but not systematically organized to form a continuous whole. The secondary literature on this work is exceedingly extensive. The themes and problems treated in this work

Introduction

have been repeatedly discussed and investigated by ancient, medieval and modern authorities.

Aristotle defines the scope of this work as the science of the principles of existing things, "first philosophy," and in another context he states that its object is "knowledge about divine being." On the basis of the classification of human knowledge as discussed in the *Metaphysics*, this inquiry, in view of its scope and object, comes under *theoretical* knowledge, in line with other inquiries concerned with knowing for its own sake, e.g., mathematics, physics, biology and psychology. The other two kinds of knowledge form (a) the *practical* sciences, viz. ethics and politics, where knowing is pursued for the sake of action, followed by (b) the *productive* sciences, rhetoric and poetics, where knowing serves to produce something. To return to the first formulation of the problem of metaphysics, its objective is to determine, and to the extent that this is possible, *what it means for anything to be* and what is being *qua* being. It is precisely this highly abstract level of discussion and the subtlety of argument that makes the collection of essays known to us as *Metaphysics* rather difficult reading.

Ousia, we are told, is the central problem of "first philosophy". In the treatise called *Categories*, Aristotle presented the view that the term "being", *to on*, stands for ten distinct genera or irreducible types of existents and that the most fundamental of them all is that of *ousia*, (*substantia*, in Latin). In the *Metaphysics*, the main emphasis falls on a systematic exploration of *ousia*, its modes and ways, and how it can be understood in discourse. Thus, *ousia* as a collective noun denotes all beings, viz. all concretely existing individual things, be they elements, stars, minerals, plants, or animals. As such each existent involves some kind of motion, and this in turn raises the problem of what it is about each *ousia* that can be said to change while the structural identity of every *ousia* remains unaltered. In so far as all the instances of the other distinct genera or ways of being, viz. quantity, quality, etc., inhere in some individual *ousia* as its co-incidental properties, it is important to clear up the problems about the complex ways in which things and their properties are related so that our discourse, our *logos*, can state and communicate reality accurately and truthfully.

The doctrine of the Four Causes was worked out in order to give a full and satisfactory answer to the question What it is to be an *ousia*. It is expected of the inquirer to state precisely what is involved in the structural or formal perseverance as well as in the way change occurs in any existent. It is not enough to rely on accounts that say that a thing is a combination of matter and form. Aristotle insists that for an analysis to be a complete account, it should identify all the causes or determinative factors involved in change. Briefly put, there are four such causes: the material, the formal, the efficient, and the final. Thus, a complete account is not simply one which says what X is made of, but why it is X and not Y, what accounts for its being X and nothing else, and finally to what end or purpose.

In one sense, *nature* or *physis* is for Aristotle the sum total of individual existents in process, i.e., structured things in continuous motion; at least some of them exhibit purposive development, aiming at the completion of this movement (if this process is not violently interrupted). This inclusive collection of beings-in-process gives the impression of a dynamic system of reality; in a way this is true, for each *ousia* in the world is moving towards its completion along with everything else. But it is conceivable that there must be an "end", a final imaginable perfection of all purposive motions. This is what Aristotle called "the unmoved mover," pure Form, pure actuality, ideal perfection which moves other beings without itself being moved: God or Divine Intelligence (*nous*). This God or pure and perfect intelligence, is not only *ousia* complete, separate and unchanging, but ultimately what makes the best life possible; it is that which human beings try to envisage when they aspire to become god-like.

Introduction

IX. Aristotle and the Hellenic Ideal of Conduct

In writing his *Ethics*, (*Nicomachean* and *Eudemean*) Aristotle was addressing fundamental issues already present in the patterns and norms of the Greek institutions. Most of his subject matter and special problems are intimately related to the historical developments of classical Greece. The excellences or virtues he defends theoretically and recommends practically are the ideals of Greek society, of its outstanding citizens. Thus, in a sense, Aristotle's theory of ethics is a summation and clarification of the Hellenic ideal of human conduct. The general theme of the *Nicomachean Ethics* is how and why human beings should display intelligent conduct. The purpose is practical: how to know the good and how to attain it. In this respect, ethics as an *art* must not be confused with the *inquiry* related to it.

The inquiring attitude appropriate to ethical topics is basically connected with Aristotle's conception of method. Even if one were to disagree with the norms and ideals of conduct he recommends, still his method deserves special consideration. This is another way of saying that there is much in his ethics which is worked out systematically in the parts (e.g., *Nic. Eth.* Book VI) that deal with the intellectual excellences, parts that have an immediate bearing on the norms of the theoretical life. If properly extended, this aspect of Aristotle's philosophy reaches beyond the practical norms of Greek culture. It sets the foundations for the acceptance of universal criteria for theoretical pursuits, both as means and as ends. In the case of his own cultural context, Aristotle tries to strike a balance between understanding the facts of everyday life and showing what human life can be, ideally speaking. Although the *polis* and its institutions provide the pattern of norms, i.e. the current conceptions of the means and ends of life, this does not mean that institutionalized practices are necessarily in accord with what human nature demands for its genuine fulfillment. It is obvious that the prudent citizens will behave intelligently in adapting to prevailing norms as well as they can. But the most gifted of the citizens will go beyond adaptation; they will understand the facts, inquire into them and act to improve the accepted norms.

Aristotle always keeps in mind the social conditions of excellence. The conduct of citizens consists of habits or structured dispositions to act in certain ways in response to given situations. Yet the good citizen performs in an excellent way, for the habits involved are perfected, i.e. they are virtuous. A response can be *continuously* and not incidentally perfect only when character is stable and the right political environment to sustain it has been made secure. Hence, the good city, the well governed *polis* and the conduct of good citizens are interdependent.

The Good as "happiness" took on in Aristotle's writings the highly technical sense of *eudaimonia*, usually translated as Well-Being. It denotes in principle the good or the end toward which any directed activity strives. Each existent has its own good or native aim, and so it is with human beings. Their aim is the good life, which is something that can be found only through careful investigation. An analysis of the "continuity of goods" will show that that good is best which cannot be converted into a means to serve other ends. Such a good is human well-being, fulfillment or happiness as self-realization. Since human beings are basically logical and political animals, their good is tied to *acting intelligently in political communities.* In order to do so human beings need to develop their native capabilities for the sake of bringing about two sets of excellences, one relative to the desires, the *moral virtues*, and one relative to the rational powers, the *intellectual virtues*. To live the good life, human beings need both types of virtues, viz. intellectual cognition of the good and the performance of good acts. Still, extremes in conduct deviations are possible. An example of extreme deviation from the norm would be the case of a gifted individual who lacks the requisite excellences, one who can be more cruel than the most savage animal. At the other end there is the high-minded person of reason whose pursuit of wisdom coincides with sustained well-being, freely shared. The best life, to the extent that it is given to human beings to attain and enjoy, would be that of continuous *theoria* through which one partakes of deathlessness by understanding the ultimate and unchanging intelligibility of being.

X. Aristotle's Conception of Political Theory

It appears that Aristotle's *Politics* consists of three sets of lectures, interconnected yet overlapping. Books I–III, dealing with introductory themes, present his general theory of the state together with a classification of the various types of constitutions. Books IV–VI give his views on practical politics, introducing the reader to the nature of existing constitutions and the principles on which good government depends. Books VII–VIII are lectures on *ideal* politics and offer a theoretical discussion on the structure of the best state. The last book, outlining the educational policy of the curriculum for training children as prospective citizens, is unfinished.

Aristotle shows extraordinary analytical skills in treating the political facts of human life. He deals with the *polis* in all its aspects: the city, the citizens, the government. The first question he brings up for treatment is how to define what a *polis* is and how it differs from other types of human communities. Next comes the issue of what it means to be a citizen and how to define rights and obligations. After a brief analysis of constitutional changes and why revolutions take place, he proceeds to give his own views on what the *best state* is and how to sustain it through the *proper* education.

Aristotle's analysis of the *polis* as the highest form of community, shows that a constitution must be regarded from a number of perspectives before its complexity can be understood. The *polis* has functions which go beyond those of providing the bare necessities;

ultimately, it exists for the sake of the good life: the good of the community as a whole. By regarded it as a natural institution (*Politics* 1253a), Aristotle is able to define the human being as "a political animal by nature." Since the *polis* is a social organization whose purpose is to provide the external means and conditions for securing the development of human excellences, it becomes evident that for Aristotle, as it was for Plato, ethics and politics are converging sciences and interrelated arts. The individual human beings can reach the fulfillment of their *entelecheia*, their natural purposive endowment, only as citizens of a well-organized community with the complexity and opportunities of a *polis*. The *best polis* is one that successfully promotes all human excellences, moral as well as intellectual.

There are two sides to the science of politics: (a) the formulation of a conception of *polis* which satisfies the criterion of well-being (*eudaimonic polis*), an aspect that makes the theory of political life continuous with the inquiry needed to meet the demands of the art of ethics; and (b) the diagnosis and critique of deviant forms of constitutions, the pathology of governments, the purpose of which inquiry is to identify the causes of political *akrasia* and dysfunctions of institutions.

A distinction is made between rulers and the ruled, one that helps understand the functions of each in the respective varieties of constitutions. Aristotle considers the distinction between ruler and ruled to be a natural one in the sense that it is introduced into human political structures by way of the tasks that must be performed for the preservation of the community. Ultimately, the function of law is not "equality" (the elimination of all differences) but *good government*. The following diagram gives a simplified view of the classification of constitutions:

Introduction

Leadership Constitutions	Good Constitutions	Deviant
One Ruler	Monarchy	Tyranny
Few Rulers	Aristocracy	Oligarchy
Many Rulers	*Politeia* or Constitutional Government	Anarchic Democracy

Political responsibility and the pursuit of ethical fulfillment are interdependent activities. According to Aristotle, who extends the views of Plato on this issue, the citizen who can practice the excellences appropriate to the practice of statesmanship and the pursuit of philosophy is capable of happiness or well-being in the fullest sense. Not only is such a person an outstanding human being but also one who willingly shares his personal resources with his fellow-citizens for the sake of their own fulfillment. However, there are *practical limitations* to the political tasks; they are related to certain conditions such as the optimal number of citizens of given communities, the size of country, foreign relations, physical plan of the city, qualifications for citizenship, class relationships, dynamics of institutions, and the education of citizens.

XI. Aristotle's Poetics: the Principles of Tragedy

Aristotle wrote no single treatise on his general theory of art, as he did in the case of his philosophy of nature and psychology. His insights and observations on *technē* are to be found mainly in the *Metaphysics*, the *Physics*, the *Nicomachean Ethics*, and the *Politics*. These general observations are tied in with his treatment of other related philosophical problems on nature and human nature. What *technē* or art is and what tasks it calls for come under the *productive sciences*.

The *Poetics* belongs to the *esoteric* writings, and has survived in incomplete form. On the whole, it is more than a handbook to serve as a guide to aspiring dramatic poets. Actually, its aim is to set forth the right criteria, rules and canons a poet must consider in composing dramatic poetry. The method employed in the *Poetics* combines inductive procedures and syllogistic thinking from basic principles. Aristotle's concern is not to explain the creative process, or the nature of the creative genius; rather, his aim is to give a systematic exposition of certain general principles which tragic poetry employs. He builds his theory by starting out with a study of the available tragedies and offers the results of his analysis of the elements involved in the writing and enjoyment of dramatic poetry.

Poiesis, strictly speaking, means "doing" or "making" something, and in the case of a medium like language, it means creating in rhythmic discourse. Poetry is a case of *technē*; human art, however, is not an absolute production. In nature something is always being made from available materials. Both types of productive processes, by nature or from *technē*, make things by realizing forms which are potentially in certain materials. Art as human production completes what nature leaves incomplete, in the sense that it brings forth structural possibilities which could not have been achieved without the intentional activity of human art. Human beings imitate nature's productive ways, not its products. *Technē* as an activity works by abstracting forms from their initial setting in order to use them on other materials for the production of novel things. The artistic forms originate in nature but their deliberate application to new materials is the work of the artist. Since the abstractable forms are universals, and since nature works with forms, art illustrates the productive processes of nature and deliberately completes their possibilities.

Aristotle calls poetry an "imitation of human beings in action," by which he meant not literal mimicking but reenactment in discourse. Tragedy is a type of poetry; its function is to arouse pity and fear. In order to effect the *catharsis* and the intelligibility of the tragic emotions in the unfolding of the *mythos*, the plot, tragedy not only employs an array of facts and related passions, it also exhibits the rationale for the events that embody them. Thus, while in nature we *discover* universality and the intelligible aspects of facts, in art we *behold* them in their purposive construction. The poet depicts things as they ought to be, as fully realized and as universality demands. The aim of poetry is not to deceive but to convince intellectually and convey emotionally the scope and meaning of significant human actions.

A good tragedy must be based on a single and important action, complete in itself. It presents a "finished" process with a thorough design. Of the six elements of tragedy, Plot (*mythos*), Character and Thought are internal, while the other three, Scenery, Music, and Diction, are external. *Mythos* is the life-line, so to speak, of tragic poetry (ch. 6). The importance Aristotle assigned to Plot is anything but arbitrary; the extant works of Greek tragic poetry support this emphasis. The other ingredients of well-constructed tragedies are: (i) unity, (ii) logical sequence of events, and (iii) the elements of reversal, surprise and recognition. It should be noted that for Aristotle as well as the tragic poets and the spectators in general, the performances of tragedies were cultural events fraught with public significance and not occasions for casual entertainment.

XII. The Heritage of Greek Thought

Aristotle's contribution to human knowledge is part of that large body of human wisdom which constitutes the heritage of the Greek genius. One could single out for consideration Aristotle's writings on logic as the first systematization of procedures for scientific thinking. Regardless of the improvements, extension, and additions which subsequent generations of philosophers made to his logic, the important fact is that logic as an inquiry and an art became the fundamental way of stating and transmitting the intellectual attainments of our culture.

After the death of Alexander in 323 a new climate of opinion set in, but while the exciting intellectual life of Athens had entered its waning phase, the influence of the classical mind was far from over. The "Hellenistic age" with all its novelty, diversity, and the new attitudes and problems to which it gave rise, found it necessary to work with what it inherited from the Classical Age. Intellectually, the Hellenistic period stands in sharp contrast to the world of Athens and the other Greek cities. The "old" Greece was fresh, exciting, original; a marvel of human clarity and naturalness, whether it expressed itself as art, architecture, poetry, philosophy, science, or ethical ideas. Taken as a whole, it exhibited an organic integrity of cultural achievement; and it found in both Plato and Aristotle most gifted spokesmen who articulated its logical character and its perennial relevance to humanity. As the Hellenistic age advanced and political unrest, civil wars, military conquests, social instability and the rise of cosmopolitanism slowly became the defining features of the emerging social realities, the functions of philosophic reflection changed accordingly to meet different spiritual, political and cultural demands. Philosophy became a "way of life" and the pursuit of wisdom shifted its initial perspective to become the rationalized escape from loneliness, social chaos, cosmic turmoil, and also to serve the growing desire for individual salvation. When the Christian culture emerged as a distinct way of consolidating the available traditions, it marked the mode in which Western civilization was to select, alter and use the Greek heritage.

Whatever it is that the "modern mind" that has emerged from the demise of the medieval mentality has come to mean to the present generation many of its defining features are deeply rooted in the Hellenic heritage. And even if the prestigious position that philosophy enjoyed in the cultural affairs of the Greeks has ceased being central to the understanding of our own modalities of political conduct, the loss may be ours, not theirs. This, however, is a different theme for a different discourse. The essays that follow are offered as appreciations of certain select significant topics that this writer studied with the attention that close consideration of the classical Aristotelian heritage demands, confident that there is still much in his Aristotle's writings that is useful and enlightening.

ON ARISTOTLE'S PRINCIPLE OF CONTRADICTION AND ITS PLATONIC ANTECEDENTS[1]

> τὸν ἔλεγχον λεκτέον ἄρα ὡς μεγίστη
> καὶ κυριωτάτη τῶν καθάρσεων ἐστι.
> Plato, *Sophist* 230d

I

According to Aristotle, it belongs to the philosopher to study the ἀρχαὶ presupposed in all special inquiries. It falls within the philosopher's domain to examine thus the most certain principle, the principle of contradiction. In proceeding with this basic task, the philosopher can employ only dialectic, that is, can only unfold and discuss the consequences that follow the denial of this fundamental ἀρχή. In recommending and developing this approach, Aristotle was following and furthering the kind of reasoning Plato investigated in the *Theaetetus*. Both Plato and Aristotle argued against the theories that reality consists of nothing but things in constant change. As we shall see, such views, since they did not allow for states of constancy and formal determinants, led inescapably to the denial of the principle of contradiction (*Theaet.* 181c–183b). The relativism of Protagoras, resting as it did on a version of extreme Heracleitianism, denied the possibility of false judgments. It is a position that both Plato and Aristotle sought to discredit although on different epistemological and ontological grounds. This point will be discussed later in the paper. What is of central importance here is the fact that a theory which makes change ultimate not only denies all concepts of permanence but cannot be defended as a theory at all since it questions the grounds of the intelligibility of existence, change, and even discourse itself.

It is important for the purposes of our discussion to note that when Plato proposed the Forms as the ὄντα in the fullest meaning of permanent and changeless being, he did not mean to say that the sensible world was either unreal or totally unknowable. It is correct Platonic doctrine to say that we do in fact talk significantly about the sensible world and that in consequence do make true as well as false judgments about sensible objects. The veracity or lack of veracity of such judgments calls for serious investigations, and this is a problem for the philosopher to solve. However, no satisfactory solution can be reached if the sensible world is characterized either as unreal or if the power of sensation is taken to be totally illusory. The same holds if the world is seen as limited only to what is perceived through the senses or if the power of sensation is viewed as totally self-validating. Plato's own investigations, as the dialogues indicated, were carried out in an effort to resolve the absurdities and difficulties created by the theories of the leading philosophers of the sixth and fifth centuries, especially as these polarized around the more extreme positions of Parmenides and Heracleitus. But what brought the issues into focus were the challenging proposals worked out by the leading sophists who spared no effort to make their solutions applicable to ethics and politics.

When Protagoras made the bold claim that only sense perception is exclusively fundamental to making any judgment, his thesis carried with it the even more radical claim that all judgments are true and only true. Not only did he limit the scope of the world to the realm of the sensible, in total opposition to the Parmenidean view which denied veracity to the "way of opinion," but he cast a heavy shadow of doubt on the "way of reason" and its cognitive object, since it is not possible for the One to be perceived. Assuming as he did that the individual man is the sole agent to decide the truth claims of his opinions, it is necessarily the case that what seems real and true to him is so. No disagreements in judgments held by two individuals can render either person's belief false, for neither disputant can legitimate grounds for calling the other side wrong or false. Clearly, then, this type of epistemological relativism is committed to the view that all judgments are necessarily true just as it is tied to a position which limits knowledge to a sensible world in a state of constant change. Plato, regardless of his deep affinities with the Parmenidean insistence on the primacy of reason and the quest for permanent being, found himself in agreement with the Protagorean acceptance of the sensible world in flux. Again, while he agreed with the sophist that it is not sound doctrine to reject the sensible world because it does not afford true judgments of warranted permanence, he took issue with the sophistic position which limited the world to the sensible domain, particularly as one of total incessant change. But the *media via* called for a fresh approach to the nature of the sensible as well as a critical examination of the credentials of the judgments about sensed events. In pursuing this new course in the *Theaetetus*, Plato made certain discoveries that were to help Aristotle lay the foundations for his ontological approach to the principle of contradiction in *Metaphysics* bk. IV.

The assessment of the details of Plato's doctrines as they relate to our main topic requires separate treatment. We can deal in this paper only with those aspects that are of direct relevance to the theme under exploration. This we shall do in the next section. The main purpose of this paper is to exhibit the basic features of Aristotle's conception of the ontological basis of the principle of contradiction, its Platonic antecedents and his refutation of certain views which reject the principle.

II

In Plato's philosophy the theory of Forms is necessary for a complete account of sensible existence. Without this theory no satisfactory explanation of the possibility of knowledge, whatever its status, of the sensible world can be given. Unless we assume the Forms as being independent of change, the flux which characterizes the sensible domain will remain indeterminate and therefore beyond the grasp of cognition. Although the sensible object has change as its main feature, it also has constancy, deriving from the Forms and owing it to their existence.[2]

In the *Theaetetus* we are shown what consequences follow if we seriously entertain the hypothesis that all types of existence are reduced to instances of change. Plato argues that such a theory of absolute change: (a) not only rules out the possibility of quality and of sensation, but it necessarily goes against its own vital thesis that all judgments are true, on the ground that by not providing for referential constancy any true judgment becomes also a false judgment; (b) it cannot in any conceivable way introduce any notion of permanence without falsifying its central thesis; (c) by maintaining such a position about change it not only leads to the denial of the principle of contradiction, but also renders in retrospect any initial premises meaningless; (d) by resolving all sensible reality into one of absolute change, the hypothesis has to admit the existence of unchanging beings, for otherwise it cannot hold the view that everything is in process anymore than it can say that everything is at rest. Since these are interrelated issues they will be examined together in the remarks which follow.

It is not germane to our purposes to dwell on the diverse passages in the dialogues where Plato comes to grips with ethical, epistemological and metaphysical difficulties of the extreme version of relativism in theories of sense perception and the attendant ontologies of the sensible world. We need only concentrate on the implications these theories have for the truthfulness and applicability of the principle of contradiction to the extent that Plato was committed to the defense of the principle. First, we find in Plato a clear recognition of the problem relativism must face: the obliteration of differences in quality which necessarily follows if judgments about sensible objects claiming to attribute determinate properties and their contraries to an object are all indiscriminately true. The result will be that a given object is no more soft than it is hard, heavy than it is light, and the like. The attribution of contrary or contradictory properties to an object cancels the identity of the object. We read in *Theaetetus* 152d:

> ...Indeed the doctrine (Protagoras') is a remarkable one. It declares that nothing is one thing just by itself, nor can you rightly call it by some definite name, nor even say it is of any definite sort. On the contrary, if you call it "large," it will be found to be also small, if "heavy," to be also light, and so on all through, because nothing is one thing or some thing or of any definite sort. All the things we are pleased to say "are," really are in process of becoming, as a result of movement and change and of blending one with another. We are wrong to speak of them as "being", for none of them ever is; they are always becoming. In this matter let us take it that with the exception of Parmenides, the whole series of philosophers agree.[3]

The criticism is carried a step further. Not only does the identity of the sensible objects vanish, but on Heracleitean grounds the collapsing of opposites carries with it the rejection of any difference between seeing and not-seeing, and in general, perception and not-perception:

> [Seeing] has no right to be called seeing, any more than not-seeing, nor is any other perception entitled to be called perception rather than not-perception, if everything is changing in every kind of

way...(and since perception is knowledge) what knowledge is, did not mean knowledge any more than not-knowledge (*Theaet.*, 182e).

This way of talking which permits the interchanging of contradictory terms not only makes knowledge impossible but also undermines the ground for preferential choice, for in the last analysis, one thing is "no more" οὐ μᾶλλον, οὐδὲν μᾶλλον) than its opposite. Phillip De Lacy, in his study of the diverse uses of the expression οὐ μᾶλλον in ancient philosophy, points out how with Plato the expression begins to find its place in arguments and becomes a formula for refutation of self-contradictory views.[4] Commenting on the above passage in the *Theaetetus*, he remarks that "Plato's concern here is perhaps less with a violation of the law of contradiction than with the loss of identity that follows on the admission of contrary or contradictory predicates.[5] In support of what he believes Plato's concerns are he conjoins a passage from the *Cratylus* (439a–440a) and one from the *Timaeus* (49b). Now the issues, it would seem, cannot be so easily separated as to allow the comparison De Lacy suggests. The general tenor of the argument in the *Theaetetus* recommends a stronger stand. For the problem is not just to deal with a case which violates the principle of contradiction but the elaborate examination of an alternative philosophical thesis on the nature of knowledge, which, if shown to be irrefutable, will demand the suspension of the principle of contradiction itself. If so, it would follow that Plato is logically obligated to disprove such a thesis, not simply to reconstruct or improve it, but discredit it so that he may safeguard the intelligibility of the sensible world. The same vital concern preoccupied Aristotle as well who developed further the lessons contained in the *Theaetetus*.[6]

Plato's analysis of false judgments and error shows that it is impossible for sense perceptions, once their nature is correctly understood, to give rise to genuine contradictory judgments. Were it not so, the principle of contradiction would be true of the dialectic of the Forms but would not apply in sensible nature. To make the principle relevant to the intelligibles but not the sensibles leads to an absurd ontology and renders Plato open to the charge of a flagrant dualism. Assuming, with Plato, that judgments refer to real events and that commingling perceptions often cause confusion when they refer to contrary sensed events, it must be the case that not all such commingling judgments can be true. Confusion sets in when the power of sensing is trusted and representations are accepted as true. However, the intervening assistance from reason can and does clear up such confusions, for as *Republic* 436b declares, the same thing is never qualified simultaneously by contraries. Since this is an ontological stricture, confusions and ambiguities are to be found not in the processes of the sensible things but to be understood as due to the limitations of the power of sensing when its reports are taken at their face value without the illuminating benefit of reason. A distinction, therefore, must be made between the objective conditions of change and uncritical conjoining of perceptions of contrary occurrences.

A sceptical position which declares the sensible world beyond real comprehension, on the basis of a contention that its processes are governed by the simultaneous presence of contrary qualifications, is utterly incompatible with Plato's theory of Forms and participation. Against those who side with the skeptical position Plato demonstrates that to defend a theory that rejects the intelligibility of the sensible depends necessarily accepts the role of reason. But this is only a beginning, because once reason is employed in the dialectic of refutation it carries investigation to the substantive issues of the cause and the eventual removal of confusions in the operations of sensing. The sensible world is intelligible but it is reason that certifies perceptual truths, itself being as free of contradictoriness as is the world of the sensible.

It is idle doctrine for Plato as it is for Aristotle to say that we become aware of contradictoriness because we allegedly perceive instances of it in the world of change. Yet it is proper to raise the question, how is it that we can speak of the ontological grounds of the principle of contradiction, especially as regards the sensible world? The problem received no systematic treatment in Plato's writings. What he offered on the whole was a host of original insights and suggestions which Aristotle extended and elaborated as part of his broader investigations in his *Metaphysics*. According to Plato the principle of contradiction holds for the world of Forms as well as that of the sensibles.[7] Given the nature of sensation and the passions involved, we do in fact make true and false judgments, yet only through an appeal to reason can it be decided which is what. The dialectic of the Forms yields only true judgments, for in performing its highest tasks reason proceeds without encumbrance from sensations. Just as perceptual judgments depend on reason for the clearing of seemingly contradictory representations, which when removed restore order in *doxa*, so the sensible objects depend on the Forms for whatever structure, regularity and cohesiveness their processes display.[8]

The first clear formulation of the principle of contradiction is given in *Republic* 436b, where Plato uses the principle to prove the tripartite nature of the soul:

> It is plain that the same thing won't be willing at the same time to do or suffer opposites with respect to the same part and in relation to the same thing. So if we should ever find that happening in these things, we'll know they weren't the same but many.[9]

Since the passage refers to things capable of "willing" such as the soul and its parts, it forces the conclusion that the soul has parts. Other passages indicate that the principle obtains in external as well as internal events.[10]

III

Aristotle gave the principle its definitive formulation in *Metaphysics*, 1005b 20–23:

> The same attribute cannot at the same time belong and not belong to the same subject and in the same respect.

In order that we may understand why Aristotle regards the principle of contradiction a cornerstone in his discussion of the nature of existence, we must consider the following: what science examines this principle, what kind of principle it is, what method is appropriate, why it is necessary to refute the views which deny it, what sustains its truth, and why knowledge of its foundations involves a certain kind of science. In presenting Aristotle's views on these topics, our analysis will have to limit itself only to such aspects of his thought as bear directly on the issues involved. A few preliminary remarks are needed to set the context of his thinking on the subject, along with a few observations that indicate some points of difference with Plato's approach.

It should be noted that Aristotle, like Plato, was fully aware how the denial of the principle of contradiction follows from the acceptance of Protagoras' doctrines (*Met.* 1009a 6–12, 1008a 31–34) and the Heracleitean view of universal flux (1010a 10–15). The Protagorean position carries with it not only a rejection of the existence of intelligible entities, but also that of any significant distinction between qualitative and quantitative change. Aristotle's argument that the theory leads to the paradoxical conclusion that *all is rest* need not be discussed for the moment.[11] Aristotle sides with Plato in claiming that no meaningful analysis of the problem of change can be conducted without some conception of fixity and limits. Aristotle explicitly states that the intention of the theories which deny the principle of contradiction is not to deny the existence of the sensible world. The problem is that while affirming its existence they identify it in a way that makes existence hopelessly indeterminate and the seeking of truth about it a chase of flying game (*Met.* 1009b 13-38, 1010a 33-35).

On the positive side Plato and Aristotle agree on the presence of fixity in the world of sensible existence although they differ in their respective explanations. For Plato the fixity of sensible objects is ultimately due to the separate Forms but lack the eternality of the latter. For Aristotle the fixity is due to (a) the persistence of essential structure each existent has throughout its duration, and (b) the constant termini that delimit the changes an existent undergoes (*Phys.* 224b 1-16). Change for both Plato and Aristotle implies the presence of permanence. Whereas Plato asserted the existence of separate entities, the Forms, which are the ends of change (*Phil.*, 54c-d, 53d-e, *Phdo.*, 75b), Aristotle regarded the Forms as immanent principles defining the essential structures of things and the limits of substantial change (*Phys.* 224a 34-b 13; *Met.* 1015a 10-11, 1069b 35-1070a 4). The convergence of their views on the fundamental demand which recognizes principles of fixity that delimit all changes occurring in the sensible world, shows that both philosophers subscribed to ontological positions allowing for false statements and for affirming the material truth of the principle of contradiction. If Protagoras is right, the implications of his position are devastating, for the invalidation of the truth claim of the principle of contradiction carries with it the downfall of every ontology, including Protagoras' own, if it can be said that he had one. The controversy, therefore, when seen in this context, marked the highest crisis the philosophical mind encountered in antiquity.

IV

One of the main tasks of metaphysics is to inquire into the principles of being and knowledge. Since the principle of contradiction is regarded a fundamental truth, it is impossible to derive it from other truths without begging the question.[12] Since no direct proof can be given in the case of axioms, inquiry must proceed in the indirect way by exposing the paradoxes that follow from the denial of the truth of the principle. In fact this is precisely the method Aristotle follows in *Met.* bk. IV. Certain technical points need to be mentioned lest Aristotle's procedure be misunderstood. To ask for direct proof of an alleged true statement requires that the statement be deduced as a conclusion in one of the valid syllogistic schemata. This procedure of demonstrative reasoning does not apply in the case fundamental truths that are employed and presupposed by all other inquiries that secure their truths syllogistically. The principle of contraction, applicable as it is to every kind of inquiry, from physics and biology to ethics and poetics, is employed with equal force in the case of metaphysical inquiry, one of the functions of which is to discuss and establish this principle.

For Aristotle, it is not possible for metaphysics or any other inquiry to proceed with its tasks without assuming the truth of the principle. It may be objected that Aristotle is begging the question at this higher level; however, he anticipated the charge of circularity and sought to avoid it in two ways: first by arguing that the nature of inquiry and the architectonic of scientific knowledge cannot and do not require demonstrative proofs of the principles they use; secondly, by distinguishing carefully between the logic of proof and the psychological basis of the cognition of principles. His position on the problem of how we become aware of universals and form general statements and principles makes it clear that the problem of certainty cannot be decided solely in terms of the demands raised by an uncompromising theory of proof in the sciences.[13] The nature of perception as the background for induction, ἐπαγωγή, leading to the intuitive apprehension of principles by *nous*, is what establishes and validates the principles. In the last analysis, however, it is the nature of existing things that sustains the truth of all principles.

The absence of proof in the context of the logic of demonstration presents no threat to the claim of truth for the principle of contradiction from the point of view of ontology. Nor can the charge of circularity be levelled against metaphysics on the basis that, being an inquiry, it both uses and defends the truth of this principle. Aristotle conceived of *sophia* not as the demonstration but the study of the principles and causes of τὸ ὄν. Part of its subject matter are the essential attributes of all existents, including sameness, contrariety, otherness, genus, species, whole, part, unity and perfection (*Met.*, 982b 9, 1003a 26). On the whole, in his *Metaphysics* he defends the principle of contradiction with the aid of *elenchus*, and indirect proof. The remarks that follow are concerned with the place of refutation in the method of metaphysics rather than the details of the attack against the philosophers whose views imply the denial of the principle.

Actually, the purpose of the *elenchus* is to discredit alternative ontologies of the sensible world. Aristotle is not simply content to show that such alternative positions fail to do full justice to the facts, more importantly, they fail to qualify as ontological inquiries precisely because they render unintelligible the domain they claim to study. And this is a paradox of the first order. A few remarks on Aristotle's metaphysics must be made here. The science of being *qua* being while it studies existents and the attributes that belong to them by virtue of their own nature, is not a demonstrative science claiming that it can deduce syllogistically such attributes from the fact of a being. Metaphysics as the science of principles and common attributes of all existents is not a rival to the psychology of perception nor is its intention to replace it. Its subject matter is given, not deduced. Any science, he declares, starts with definitions, ὁρισμοί, and hypotheses, ὑποθέσεις, i.e., undemonstrated positing of relevant terms and unproved assumptions about the existents that such terms denote. Both are principles, ἀρχαί. In the case of metaphysics, the definitions must be of terms denoting existents and the attributes they must possess regardless of what special inquiry investigates them. Terms that are pervasive to all sciences but not treated by them, except in incidental ways, are form, matter, substance, accident, quality, quantity, potentiality, actuality, unity, plurality, and the like. One of the tasks of metaphysics is to remove, with the aid of elenchus, misconceptions about fundamental key terms. The hypotheses of metaphysics, no less than those of the special inquires, denote existents and their most general traits. In a broad sense, the principle of contradiction may come under the class of hypothesis as in *Post. An.*, 71a 13, since it points to ὅτι ἐστιν. More technically speaking, it is one of the axioms that are common to all inquiry but with the widest universality; it is better known without qualification; it extends to all beings without exception; it is non hypothetical, in Plato's sense as in *Rep.*, 510a–b. Being "the most certain of all principles," (*Met.*, 1005b 22–23), it is used as well as presupposed by all special inquires. No *elenchus* can ever succeed without this principle, including the case of *elenchus* that seeks to establish the certainty of the principle in *Metaphysics* IV.

The main thrust of the *elenchus* is targeted against all ontological and epistemological positions which invoke the primacy of indeterminateness. Here again Aristotle learned his lessons well from the teachings of Plato. It should be noted in advance that while pursuing the *elenchus*, Aristotle was also introducing cardinal doctrines of his own. It is not enough to say that his indirect proofs of the principle of contradiction expose the paradoxes of the alternative views. The paradoxes make sense on the condition that the positions that generate them cancel certain other theses indispensable to them or in conflict with certain true statements the relevance of which cannot be denied without loss of philosophical credibility. Aristotle misses no opportunity to carry his attack beyond the point of exhibiting of the internal inconsistencies of his opponents. On occasion the boundaries between his appeal to logical and ontological considerations become blurred. This can be readily understood since logic and ontology for him are not separate disciplines. On the whole, the refutation of views that deny the principle of contradiction through the use of indirect proof is carried out through a screening of the implications they have vis-à-vis his own doctrine. The correctness of his own position is a separate issue and need not concern us at this point, but the fact is that he presupposes it in the employment of the *elenchus*. Since our purpose is not to ascertain the logical merits of the *elenchus*, we must restrict our discussion to the identification of the doctrines used in the course of refutation of opposing views.

In *Metaphysics* IV, Chapter 4, Aristotle undertakes to probe into the difficulties involved in the denial of the principle and consider a position, extreme, to be sure, that does exactly that. His target seems to have been the school of Megara. The position maintains (a) the same thing can be and not be, and (b) it is possible so to judge. The implication is that the principle of contradiction holds neither in logic nor in ontology. The position, if its supporter can be brought to affirm or deny a statement which has some meaning both for himself and some others, can be denied. Once this procedure is accepted the opponent must assume the burden of proof, for to make a statement is to employ reason despite his denial. If the opponent refuses to make a statement it can be said that he is not intelligently in touch with himself. The cardinal point here is that *every judgment must have a definite meaning*. The seven indirect proofs that follow are founded on this Aristotelian rule. A judgment which does not meet this condition is ambiguous.[14] Words have definite meanings, and although single words like *is* can have a number of meanings, they cannot have an infinite number, for then discourse becomes impossible. The most that can be done with the statement *X is and is not the same thing*, where *is* has an indeterminate number of meanings, assuming that indeterminacy was not intended, is to declare the statement ambiguous, καθ' ὁμωνυμίαν (*Met.*, 1006b 18–19).

Principle of Contradiction

It is quite evident, then, that it is impossible for Aristotle to proceed with his indirect proofs and make a case against his opponents on the grounds of inconsistency without the rule of meaning. Since the conditions for observing the rule demand acceptance of the principle of contradiction, the refutation is valid only on Aristotelian principles and not by virtue of paradoxes drawn *exclusively* from the opponents' views. This much is admitted, but not fully acknowledged by Aristotle when he points out that his opponent will refute himself once he had made a statement which has met the rule of meaning. The case is very interesting because it shows two things: (a) the belief that words have infinite meanings is *per impossibile* irrefutable, and (b) either the belief is not a philosophical thesis at all, or if it is, it must be capable of reformulation in accord with the rule of meaning. Hence the paradoxes that follow from the view stated in 1005b 35–36, make sense only when the consequences are seen as incongruous with basic Aristotelian truths. It would make sense, then, to say that the aporetic method in his *Metaphysics* IV, as it pertains to the refutations, is not a pure case of indirect proof.

The fact remains that Aristotle uses a great number of doctrines in his refutations. He immediately introduces the doctrine of essence and attributes which, he claims, his opponents ignore. Insofar as they can be said to have a theory about attributes, it is one that converts all attributes, including the essential ones, into accidental. Next he mentions the necessity of an original substratum, ὑποκείμενον, in which accidental properties inhere and refers to the logic that governs the statements about accidents.[15] Along with the above comes the crucial principle of *ousia*:

> There must be something which denotes substance. And if this is so, it has been shown that contradictories cannot be predicated at the same time.[16]

The second proof, which shows that *if all contradictory statements are true of the same subject at the same time*, the plural character of the sensible world and all the differentiated existents that belong to distinct classes in it collapse, for one must conclude that all things are one. His doctrine of the existence of differences of degree in the nature of things is used in the seventh proof. The sixth proof is also of particular interest since it rests on Aristotle's view that truth in judgments of value involves the same as in judgments of fact.

Another set of basic beliefs is given in chapters 5 and 6, where Protagoras' position is being refuted. Once again, the paradoxes that result from the denial of the principle of contradiction make sense only when understood in conjunction with beliefs about the world which Aristotle holds to be true. As for Protagoras' own position, the implication is that it makes the world unintelligible since it leaves everything indeterminate. In carrying out his refutation, Aristotle appeals to the following truths about the world: (1) Things may have contrary qualities, but do so only potentially, not actually. (2) There are certain unchangeable substances which are not subject to generation and destruction. (3) Things maintain their essential identity while undergoing changes. (4) The distinctive types of change are not reducible to one kind.[17] In attacking the Protagorean theory of knowledge he draws from his own views on the nature and functions of the senses the following: (1) Not all appearances are true.[18] (2) The senses yield veridical appearances about their proper objects. (3) No single sense contradicts itself at the same object, nor at different moments with regard to the object itself.(4) The sensible objects exist even when there are no sensing beings; the objects are *hypokeimena*, subjects, with sensible properties which are the objective causes of sensations. (5) Sensation is not its own object; hence, the scepticism of the subjectivist is not an arguable position.[19]

Aristotle's interest in refuting Protagoras is a very serious one, and justifiably so. For, if the Protagorean position is philosophically sound in any conceivable way, the principle of contradiction must be surrendered, in which case none of Aristotle's ontological and epistemological theses can be true. It will not do for Aristotle to have his doctrine declared true on Protagorean grounds, to wit, that all judgments are true, including Aristotle's own. To yield on this point is tantamount to saying that one theory of knowledge is as good as any other, and one ontology as true as any other. If that were in fact the case, all *elenchus* would be but idle play on words and philosophical inquiry a sophisticated game of intellectual preferences with no significant consequences. If Protagoras is right, the paralysis of *logos* follows.

V

It has been correctly said that Aristotle is *fighting the indeterminate on several fronts*.[20] To which we must add: so is Plato. A limited attempt to discuss the issues involved in their respective theories of determinate being lie beyond the scope of this paper. Suffice it to say that in Aristotle's case I have give elsewhere a fuller discussion of how the principle of contradiction requires for its understanding the theory of genera of being and the contraries that correspond to each genus, also how his entire analysis of opposition presupposes that theory.[21]

The main goal of the present paper has been to exhibit in general outline the dialectic and basic tenets Plato and Aristotle employed in their defense of the truth of the principle of contradiction together with an examination of the consequences they thought its denial has for philosophical inquiry. Any attempt to go beyond these limits would have carried us too far afield. Thus, nothing was said about modern approaches to the principle of contradiction as *a law of thought* or *a law of logic*, as it came to be called in modern times. It appears that the classical formulations and solutions of the relevant problems have lost none of their significant features. Recent controversy on the nature of the principle reflects what new anomalies philosophy must face as the result of interpretations suggested by the methodology of sciences and linguistic theories. The implications they have for metaphysics constitute a problem that has engaged the attention of many thinkers.[22] Since they concern directly the possibility and nature of metaphysics, it would seem that the issues which Plato and Aristotle raised on the subject are still with us.

NOTES

1. First publication in *Philosophia*, Vol. II, 1972 Yearbook of the Academy of Athens, pp. 266–80. Reprinted here with minor revisions.

2. *Phdo.*, 78d–79a and *Symp.*, 207, *Phil.*, 59a–b; *Tim.*, 27d–28a.

3. Also at *Rep.* 524e: "so that a thing appears no more one than also its opposite."

4. "Οὐ μᾶλλον and the Antecedents of Ancient Scepticism," *Phronesis* 3 (1958), 59–71; reprinted in *Essays in Ancient Greek Philosophy*, edited by J. P. Anton with G. L. Kustas, (Albany, N. Y.: SUNY Press 1971), 593–606; references to this edition.

5. Ibid., 595.

6. See H. Cherniss, *Aristotle's Criticism of Plato and the Academy*, (Baltimore 1944), 214 ff. for key parallel passages from the *Theaetetus* and *Metaphysics* Bk. IV.

7. For a different interpretation on this important point see R. Demos, "Partly So and Partly Not So," in *Mind* 69 (N. S. 1959), 51–56. Demos proceeds from the examination of ordinary expressions like "partly so" and "partly not so", which also occur in attribute-statements in Plato to conclude that they make trouble for the law of contradiction. He tries to show that these expressions allow for indeterminateness, and insofar as Plato made use of them he gave no satisfactory answer to the issues they raise. Thus Plato found himself "obliged to admit contradiction in the area of attribute-statements, as when we assign a predicate to an empirical study" (53). He concludes that "the law of contradiction applies (without exception) to no language except that of mathematics;" in short, it applies only to what Plato called the realm of transcended forms. At least in the kingdom of ordinary language, the law of contradiction is far from being an absolute dictator; at best its authority is partly that of a reigning and partly that of a ruling monarch (56).

8. Consider, for instance, *Rep.*, 523a–524e.

9. Δῆλον ὅτι ταὐτὸν τἀναντία ποιεῖν ἢ πάσχειν κατὰ ταὐτὸν γε καὶ πρὸς ταὐτὸν οὐκ ἐθελήσει ἅμα, ὥστε ἄν που εὑρίσκομεν ἐν αὐτοῖς ταῦτα γιγνόμενα, εἰσόμεθα ὅτι οὐ ταὐτὸν ἦν ἀλλὰ πλείω. Translation by A. Bloom, *The Republic of Plato*, (New York: Basic Books, 1968), p. 115. Other translators e.g. F. M. Cornford (*The Republic of Plato*, Oxford 1945, p. 133), P. Shorey (Loeb edition) and H. D. P. Lee, *Plato, The Republic*, (Baltimore: Penguin Books, 1955, p. 187), either omit or alter significantly the expression ἐθελήσει; the context where the formulation occurs clearly intends the expression to pertain to cases that involve the soul and its parts.

10. Other versions of the principle are given at *Theaet.*, 188a, *Phdo.*, 102e and 103b, *Soph.*, 230b and *Rep.*, 602e.

11. Also *Met.*, 1010a 35–b1 and 1063a 17–21.

12. Aristotle regards anyone who would demand that the principle of contradiction be demonstrated ignorant of the fundamentals of scientific reasoning. The demand leads to infinite regress: *Met.*, 1006a 5–10.

13. Cf. *Post. An.* II 19; *Met.* I. 1–2, and *De An.* III.

14. Technical suggestions for the detection of ambiguity are found in *Top.*, 15; see also *De Int.*, passim.

15. The denial of an ultimate *hypokeimenon* makes accidents form an infinite regress, and this is impossible. An accident of an accident is properly handled only when both accidents are shown to belong to the same subject, but both must be brought back to *ousia*.

16. *Met.*, 1007b 16–17: ἔσται ἄρα τι καὶ οὐσίαν σημαῖνον. εἰ δὲ τοῦτο, δέδεικται ὅτι ἀδύνατον ἅμα κατηγορεῖσθαι τὰς ἀντιφάσεις.

17. What is meant here is that qualitative change cannot be reduced to quantitative change. Qualitative change in this connection is used in the sense of generation and destruction, that is, essential change, κατὰ τὸ εἶδος,

Principle of Contradiction 51

κατὰ τὴν οὐσίαν. For quality in the sense of essential difference, see *Metaphysics* 1020b 14, cf. *Categories* 3b 20 and *Sophistici elenchi* 178b 37.

18. The explanation is given in *Metaphysics* 1010b 1 ff. The belief that all appearances are true rests on the assumption that all things are relative and hence nothing is self-existent. It is also shown that the belief involves a confused theory of sensation. Aristotle's own position is that things do not in fact appear with contrary attributes to the same sense and in the same respect, manner and time.

19. This is presented in *Met.*, 1010b 30–1011a 1.

20. A. Edel, in his *Aristotle*, (New York: Dell Publishing Co. 1967), p. 89, points out that the principle of contradiction reveals a multitude of roles. It is a principle of (i) demonstrations, (ii) significance, (iii) limitation of meanings, (iv) essence, (v) pragmatic utility and (vi) determinate order in existence (90–91). He recognizes the richness in Aristotle's treatment of the principle but states that *it is possible to take issue with it in many if not all of his interpretations.* The critical issues he thinks that call for attention are states in the following: "Purely within demonstration there has been controversy about the possibility of formulating many-valued logics. With respect to essence and accident, there are other modes of specifying meaning, of a lesser sort, than his theory of definition allows. With respect to the fixity of existence, the Heraclitean tradition may have more evidence than the partisans of fixed order have believed—in any case, this is a problem of physical evidence. It is perhaps in dealing with the structure of system and communication that Aristotle's principle is most impregnable. Even three-valued logics may require a two-valued metalogic somewhere up the scale—if a proposition is given three possible values, then it either has a given one or the it doesn't. Communication requires some degree of determinateness in symbols. Action requires determinateness, too—although perhaps less than some of our cultural systems have embodied in their peremptory demands…All these are different issues requiring their own formulation of modes of solution" (91–92).

21. I have discussed these topics in my *Aristotle's Theory of Contrariety*, (London: Routledge and Kegan Paul, 1957), esp. Chapters 4 and 6.

22. See e.g., E. Mesthene, "On the Status of the Laws of Logic," *Philosophy and Phenomenological Research*, 10 (1950), 354–373. In agreement with Aristotle but without appealing to his ontological doctrines, Mesthene defends the principle of contradiction against recent interpretations which reduce it at best to an inductive generalization or a merely conventional logical rule. "Discovery of what exactly is the source, the status and the operations of these [logical principles] is the task of metaphysical inquiry." He defends the thesis that "they must enter into any description of the nature of existence as such, and function as the first principles of intelligible discourse" (368). For a fuller elaboration of his position see his *How Language makes us know*, (The Hague, 1964); also, J. Loewenberg, *Reason and the Nature of Things*, (La Salle, Illinois, 1959), esp. Ch. 2: "Faith in Reason."

THE MEANING OF Ο ΛΟΓΟΣ ΤΗΣ ΟΥΣΙΑΣ IN ARISTOTLE'S *CATEGORIES* 1a[1]

The purpose of this paper is to inquire into the meaning of the troublesome Aristotelian expression ὁ λόγος τῆς οὐσίας as it occurs at the very opening of *Categories* 1a 1–2, 7. That the passage has presented serious difficulties to commentators and translators alike can be easily ascertained through a survey and comparison of the relevant literature. It would seem from the disagreements among translators that the passage is either vague in the original Greek or that Aristotle did not have a special doctrine to put across at the very opening such that would require technical formulations that would comply with the ontology presented in this treatise.

The main body of this paper is given to an examination of the diverse difficulties the passage raises in connection with the doctrine of *homonymy* and the ontology which supports it. On the basis of this analysis, and after consideration of the available evidence, textual and historical, attention is given to the possibility of proving the thesis that ὁ λόγος τῆς οὐσίας (hereafter abbreviated as *L of O*, *L* for *logos* and *O* for *ousia*) has a special doctrinal meaning and is, therefore, free from terminological imprecision. Accordingly, the interpretation defended in this paper advocates a definite reading for *logos* and for *ousia*, and one that forbids a strict identification of *ousia* with the variant meaning of *tode ti* (individual existents or particular substances),[2] let alone taking liberties with the notion so that it may include in its denotation the *symbebēkota* (accidental properties). More pointedly, an argument is presented in favor of interpreting *ousia* to mean substance in the sense of species, on the ground that only in this sense is *ousia* definable.[3]

The thesis that the expression *L of O* has a precise and technical meaning can be put as follows: if we admit that *ousia* can occur as both subject and predicate, and that as ultimate subject it denotes individual substances whereas as predicate it ranges in denotation from *infima species* to *summa genera*, it can be shown that Aristotle means to say in this context that *ousia* must be understood in the sense of being (a) definable and (b) predicable. If so, then, it can only mean secondary substance, with the added restriction that the highest genera be excluded on account of their undefinability. The context of the first chapter is unmistakably one in which *homonymy* is presented and explained as a topic highly requisite to the exposition of the ontology that undergirds the general doctrine presented in the *Categories*.

Now, in order to establish the validity of our proposed thesis two things would have to be shown:

(a) *Logos* as it occurs in this passage must be understood as meaning strictly definition. This aspect of our problem has, admittedly, only antiquarian interest, since there is hardly any scholar today who is willing to propose alternative meanings. However, the issue must be raised if only because what is now universally agreed upon and constitutes accepted reading was an issue of high controversy among the ancient commentators. The expositors of Aristotle's doctrines on this issue, from Porphyry to Photius, made every effort to bend *logos* also to mean *description* of substance. The reasons why this additional reading was eagerly defended by every ancient commentator no doubt deserve the length of a separate paper but need not concern us here. Suffice it to say that our interpretation demands that such broadened views concerning the meaning of *logos* be rejected as non-Aristotelian. All that is needed to be said here is that if *logos* means both definition and description, then *ousia* has to be understood in the most inclusive sense, i.e., capable of denoting anything in any of the categories, which readily leads to the conclusion that the entire expression *L of O* is obviously lacking in

Logos tēs Ousias

terminological precision. The commentators completely missed the significance of this point.

(b) Our own proposed interpretation takes fully into account and is in agreement with Aristotle's views on definition as found in the *Topics* and the *Sophistici Elenchi*. The only assumption that is being made here is that the theory of definition present in these works holds true for the *Categories* and that the theory must have been formulated, even if not written down, prior to the actual composition of *Categories*.

We are now ready to undertake an examination of a number of translations from the Greek to determine whether the translators have actually succeeded in preserving the technical meaning we believe the passage has. If it can be shown that this is not the case, then we would be justified in drawing the inference that, like the commentators, the translators have similarly failed to see that Aristotle was putting across a strict doctrinal issue.

The contrast between the ancient commentators and the modern translators deserves further comment. The ancients apparently failed to appreciate the full technical import of the expression *L of O* mainly because they were over-explicating the two terms of the expression, *logos* and *ousia*. They discussed the terms in the light of considerations that more often than not were not those of Aristotle. This is especially true in the case of their reading into *logos* the sense of description. They extended *logos* to mean description mainly because they knew that under *homonyma* things one could include just about everything, from individual substances and accidents to secondary substances and the highest genera. But by repeatedly emphasizing this fact they developed an approach, quite broad to be sure, but one that did not alert them to the possibility that Aristotle might have used in this case a limited application of *homonyma*. In other words, the commentators give no indication that Aristotle might not have planned to discuss in the opening of the *Categories* all types of *homonyma* things.[4]

Evidently, the expression "homonyma things" is itself a homonymous expression, for it is used for things that are substantially different: accidents, substances, genera, principles. By applying Aristotle's own rules, it can be shown that if we were to give the definitions of the various sorts of things that are called *homonyma* we would have to give in each case a different definition. But again this is something the commentators knew quite well. It is also clear that Aristotle was well aware of this peculiarity. If so, then it is difficult to understand why Aristotle would want to state something as obvious as that and above all open the discussion in the *Categories* with an inclusive circumlocution of *homonyma* to refer unqualifiedly *to all cases of homonymy*. The wider scope of homonymy one has already learned from the other parts of the *Organon*, especially the treatises that deal with persuasion, rhetoric and fallacies due to the abuse of language. It is more reasonable to suppose that Aristotle in writing the first chapter of the *Categories* was not interested in restating familiar matters. Rather, he was concentrating on stating a technical doctrine with a restricted application of *homonyma* things. What is argued therefore in this paper is not that Aristotle did not know and thus could not have meant the broader meaning of *homonyma*; rather it is claimed that in the case of the *Categories* the need for such unqualified use does not arise and that the special demands of the topic are such that unless a technically restricted formulation of *homonyma* is given at the very beginning, unnecessary confusion about the doctrine of categories might result. Now, when we turn to our modern translators, our analysis shows that their error lies in their leaving *ousia* — not logos — so unspecified as to fail to convey the possibility that Aristotle might have meant the expression in the restricted way proposed in this paper. Finally, these translations do not by any means make it easy for the reader to suspect that there is a basic correlation between the nature of *homonyma* and the general theory of categories.

Logos tēs Ousias 57

We have sampled for discussion the following five translations (abbreviated T1...T5) of the key expression ὁ δὲ κατὰ τοὔνομα λόγος τῆς οὐσίας ἕτερος.

T1: 'The definition (of substance according to name) is different.'[5]

T2: 'The definition corresponding with the name differs in each case.'[6]

T3: 'The definition (or statement of essence) corresponding with the name being different.'[7]

T4: 'The definition given for the name in each case is different.'[8]

T5: 'The definition of being which corresponds to the name is different.'[9]

It is evident that not all translations agree. The reason must be sought in the fact that they are based on different textual traditions. Even those that follow the same tradition apparently do not derive the same meaning from their text. We are thus faced with two problems: (a) To identify the two textual traditions and decide in favor of that which is less confusing and closer to the doctrine the treatise intends. (b) To cut through the maze of the interpretations lurking behind the translations in order to determine, if possible, the exact meaning of the passage.

The first thing to note is that all translations accept *logos* as part of the expression, take it to mean definition, and hence no longer consider it important to discuss it as did the ancients. Secondly, the five versions form three different sets. The first set, consisting of T1 (Owen) and T3 (Cooke), accepts rather tentatively the *L of O* part and cautiously brackets the expression; the second set, T2 (Edghill) and T4 (Smith), openly rejects it.[10] Only the third, that is, T5 (Ackrill), gives it unreserved endorsement. Finally, none of the translations makes it unambiguously clear that the passage in which *L of O* occurs is embedded in a terminology highly pertinent to Aristotle's ontology and practice of scientific reasoning. Finally, all these renditions leave much to be desired in exactitude of meaning and clarity of thought.

Since T1 and T3 leave the textual matter in a state of suspense, the issue must be decided between T2, T4, and T5. The tradition supporting the set T2, T4 goes back to Boethus, and by way of modern authorities, to Waitz.[11] Boethus of Sidon (fl. c. 40 B.C.), a leading Peripatetic, who like his contemporary Andronicus, thought it unnecessary to preserve in his version of the *Categories* the τῆς οὐσίας part.[12] It appears that we might have to go further back to discover the antecedents of the shorter text. Georke, for instance, does not completely trust the critical and editorial abilities of Andronicus; he suggest that the critical notes pertaining to the reading of *Cat.* 1a 2, since they do not stand in all our copies, go back perhaps to the apparatus of Tyrannion.[13] Tyrannion, a contemporary of Cicero, is said to have brought to light and collected the works of Aristotle and Theophrastus, which Sulla had taken as his personal booty from the first Mythridatic war.[14] Simplicius in his commentary (*In Categ.* 29.5) mentions that Speusippus was the first to take the view that *homonyma* can be defined by saying simply ὁ δὲ λόγος ἕτερος. Thus, there is some ground for entertaining the hypothesis that the commentators who did not favor the *L of O* reading have been influenced by Speusippus' theory and definition of *homonyma*. Boethius (480–525) should be included in their ranks. Simplicius defends *L of O* and, furthermore, he chides Boethus and argues against the Speusippean approach to homonymy. Simplicius' argument, in summary, goes something like this: if Speusippus is right, then the distinction between *homonyma* and *synonyma* breaks down on the ground that on that definition all *synonyma* are *homonyma* and vice versa. Evidently, Simplicius remarks, Speusippus not only omitted τῆς οὐσίας but went as far as to reduce the definition to just ὁ δὲ λόγος ἕτερος. If Simplicius' testimony is reliable historical report, it would seem that the definition and theoretical explanation of *homonyma* were issues of considerable philosophic debate. The fact that Aristotle discusses many aspects of *homonyma* in his *Topics* should be regarded as additional evidence that such was the case.

Ancient opinion was divided on this issue, but the majority of commentators favored the reading *L of O*. Andronicus and Boethus are mentioned as being against it.[15] In favor of *L of O* were Nicostratus,[16] Herminus, Porphyry, Dexippus, Ammonius,[17] Philoponus, Simplicius, Olympiodorus, and Elias, and also Photius in his paraphrase of the *Categories*. The analysis of the arguments these commentators offer constitutes a separate matter and must be excluded from our present discussion. To return to our theme, the context of the *L of O* in *Cat.* ch. 1, is the doctrine of *homonyma*. Since for Aristotle scientific knowledge is not of individuals, and since the proper application of the syllogistic principle presupposes that the continuity from the major term to the minor is already made secure, it is imperative that homonymy of terms be decisively dealt with in order (a) to prevent logical error and (b) to determine under what conditions homonymy is acceptable and why. Whereas (a) is more fundamental to the *Categories*, (b) looms more significantly in other logical and metaphysical treatises. We know that Aristotle's ontology provides for legitimate cases of homonymy. Hence it is vital to his metaphysical investigation — the analyses that come under what will eventually be called πρώτη φιλοσοφία — that the sort of homonymy which pertains to principles be brought into the open. There are certain key terms in his categorial theory that clearly constitute cases of homonymy. We use 'genus,' for instance, to cover both secondary *ousia* and the other genera of being; similarly, 'category' to mean not only the predication of *ousia* but also of the remaining genera of being; again, we use '*ousia*' both in the case of the particular and the universal, though the two are far from identical; 'being' (*to on*) again, is an instance of homonymy;[18] it is a πολλαχῶς λεγόμενον.

If the doctrine of *homonyma* has a certain basic importance to it, then, the issue becomes one of ascertaining the relevance of the expression *L of O* in formulating the logical character of homonymy. The position this paper defends has been in its main features favored by the leading ancient commentators, though the interpretations they attached to it were conceived in the light of a number of non-Aristotelian considerations and philosophical commitments. But when we turn to the English translations of the passage, we are hardly given any instruction to suspect that there might be certain doctrinal and technical restrictions. For reasons given in the remainder of this paper, T2 and T4 must be dismissed as offering unacceptable readings. T1 and T3 are somewhat preferable but are still riding the fence. T5 falls short of the target for in using the term 'being' without any other qualification it does not distinguish between *ousia* and *on*, especially since *ta onta* is used homonymously later on in the text to refer to what all the genera of being denote.

Before presenting the grounds for our position, it behooves to state here what seems to be the function of the opening chapters of the *Categories*. If the main issue for Aristotle is to establish the meaning of *first ousia* and disentangle it from both secondary *ousia* (species and genera) and inhering accidental properties (the other genera), it would be proper to use the introductory chapters to clear up obscurities due to unphilosophical use of homonymy and illicit predication. But this issue is not merely a logical and terminological problem; it becomes one of ontology as well. Thus our thesis rests on the hypothesis that the *Categories* offers an earlier version of Aristotle's ontology and that *L of O* is part of its requisite terminological apparatus.[19] It may be objected that the opening part of the *Categories* offers no special clues as to doctrine, the reply may be given that the full import is realized only after the distinctions and concepts leading up to the ten genera of being and primary *ousia* as the ultimate subject of predication are fully presented.

Whatever else Aristotle might have meant by *L of O*, especially by *ousia*, for this is the debatable term, he could not have meant any of these: (i) first *ousia*, (ii) summa genera, (iii) differentia, (iv)

Logos tēs Ousias

accidental properties. Thus, we can only conclude that if Aristotle used the term in some technical sense, he must have meant secondary *ousia* as types and species, including the genera that are also species. Let us now consider the evidence.

The example of *homonyma* and the language Aristotle uses suggest that he is talking about types of secondary *ousia*. Of the two items named one is of the biological sort (man), the other from the world of artifacts (portrait). He seems to be talking about *sorts* of things. Three prima facie good reasons may be given here why *L of O* is used technically:

(a) The commentators discuss the expression at length and, on the whole, consider *ousia* more appropriate than *onta* for denoting the grounds Aristotle intends to cover: secondary *ousia*, primary *ousia* and their properties.

(b) Unless *ousia* has a technical meaning it would be difficult to defend *logos* in the sense of definition, and furthermore to explain why in the next few lines where he explains what we are expected to give when asked to provide the *L of O* in specific cases of *homonyma*, he uses idiomatic expressions characteristic of the technical terminology of formulating definitions of essences.[20]

(c) One has the impression that Aristotle is quite confident that his definition of *homonyma* is well stated, and the example much to the point. In fact he is quite certain that this case of *homonyma* cannot be reduced to one of *synonyma*; or, to put it differently, no definition of substance common to the sorts of things named in the example is forthcoming. Indeed, later on, when the list of the summa genera of predication is given, artifacts are not mentioned under the genus *ousia*.

However, the good reasons above do not prove conclusively the correctness of our thesis. Certain considerations, not to mention the fact that every ancient commentator extended *ousia* to cover individual men (Ajax, Achilleus, etc.), and that some of them went even further to include the accidentals as well, appear to militate against our interpretation. For instance, there is the problem of explaining why Aristotle referred to artifacts if he intended *ousia* to mean only definable secondary *ousia*. Since the problem points to certain difficult issues and appears germane to our quest, it is best, then, to proceed with its analysis before taking up a higher grade of evidence afforded by the texts. However, it should be clear by now that in so far as living beings, when considered in the light of appropriate classification, cannot under any circumstances be anything but cases of *synonyma*, it follows that in order to supply examples of *homonyma legomena*, which name *ousia*i, Aristotle had to select his instances from two distinct domains of existence, i.e., from incommensurate types. If so, only one of the *homonyma*, that is, one such instance, could be from the biological world or the domain of 'strict' necessity in general. Furthermore, in order to render the formulation of *homonyma* secure, the logic of Aristotle's categorial theory demanded that his examples of *homonyma* came not from items that fall within different genera of being, viz. *ousia* and, say, quality, but items denoted by the genus *ousia* only. The other domain of existence that could qualify to meet this condition is clearly that of *techne*: the artifacts *qua* substances. However the solution is not without difficulties.

The problem, however, is not so much whether we can speak of portraits and engines as cases of *ousia*, but rather whether they have the ontological status of individual entities and not of accidents. If the latter is actually the case, it follows that it makes good sense to speak of artifacts as having *logos tēs ousias*. The fact remains that though such things are not by nature (*physei*), but are brought about by art (*technei*), Aristotle's philosophy allows for the possibility of treating them as cases of *ousia* and that each may be viewed as a *tode ti*. Both are determined by *ti esti*, essentiality; both are formed according to *physis*, in the sense of *eidos* (*Met.* 1015a 13). However, the issue may be pursued a step further by asking "what is *ousia*?" The answer should state the conditions needed to serve as criteria for determining whether artifacts qualify to be considered *ousiai* in the full sense of the term. As W. D. Ross states the issue, "The substance of a thing is the principle of structure, the presence of which in a collection of materials makes them not a mere collection but an organized whole."[21] On this criterion, then, artifacts are not truly *ousiai*, for of perishable things, it is only those that are "held together by nature," unified by an inherent power of initiating movement, that are substances (*Met.* 1043b 21–23). Hence, only living things have nature in the full sense, and only these are in the full sense *ousiai*.

However, the important thing in all this is that despite this difference between living things and artifacts, the latter can still be considered *ousiai* in some special sense, and hence nonreducible to accidental beings. Even if the mode of artistic production is in fact different from that of natural generation, artifacts are not reducible to accidental properties. Producing a house or a portrait does not presuppose that the actual existence of the forms of such things be immattered, in a *tode ti*; what such production presupposes is that there be the form of the house or the portrait in the artist.[22] Suffice it to say that the ontological status of things brought about by art is in a serious sense that of *ousia*, even if buildings, ships, statues, portraits and the like, are not instances of necessary existence. The fact is that Aristotle insists that the artist is an efficient cause, and *qua* τεχνίτης he imparts to his selected materials the *eidos* or final cause appropriate to it. Aristotle is convinced of the naturalness of *technē*. He states that with regard to all things which involve production for an end "the product cannot come to be without things which have a necessary nature, but it is not due to these (except as its material); it comes to be for an end."[23] Again:

> Further, where a series has a completion, all the preceding are for the sake of that. Now surely as in intelligent action, so in nature; and as in nature, so it is in each action, if nothing interferes. Now intelligent action is for the sake of an end; therefore the nature of things also is so. Thus if a house e.g., had been a thing made by

nature, it would have been in the same way as it is now by art; and if things made by nature were made also by art, they would come to be in the same way by nature.[24]

Hence, in so far as individual things by *techne* are cases of *ousia* they are *loci* of properties. The fact that Aristotle uses the term *ousia* to cover in the opening passage of the *Categories* both domains of existence, is indicative that he held this view. Now if we turn to *Cat.* 2a 19–34, where Aristotle distinguishes between things that are predicated of a subject and things which are in a subject, the implication is that *ousia* as mentioned in *Cat.* 1a would exclude things which are in a subject, i.e., accidental beings. It is clear then that Aristotle could not have meant to refer to portraits as accidental beings and equate their mode of existence to that of accidental properties. Since portraits are not things that are said to be in a subject, they are included in the genus of *ousia*.

Now it must be emphasized here that nowhere in this paper do I insist to say that Aristotle meant to deny that qualities, accidental properties and anything else denoted by the other genera of being cannot constitute cases of *homonyma* things. On the contrary, Aristotle's works abound in examples of πολλαχῶς λεγόμενα from *ousia* and the other genera, concepts, names, terms and accidental properties. Consider what happens when we give examples of homonymous things which are homonymous not with reference to the *logos tēs ousias* but some accidental type of being, say white (*leukos*), an example used in *Top.* 107a 35–b5. Since both rats and horses can be white but both differ in essence, the things are *homonyma*. The peculiar thing here is that we do not have a strict case of *homonyma* things because it was not the *logos* of the essence that the word 'white' indicated. In the example of the *Categories*, however, clarification of the situation called for giving the definitions of the essences of the sorts of things that shared the same name and that different definitions were forthcoming for each type of thing. The relevant point, then, is not whether Aristotle recognizes the full range of *homonyma* things, but basically whether the opening passage of the *Categories* where the circumlocution of the basic or primary meaning of '*homonyma* things' is given, is also meant to denote this entire range. The thesis of this paper is that Aristotle purposely delimited the denotation to the case of *ousia* and furthermore that his expression *logos tēs ousias* purports to support a doctrinal point he is making. He is primarily concerned with homonymous classes and species of primary things, not the accidental properties of individuals and their names.

Part of the problem examined here is to make clear why it is that Aristotle is interpreted in this paper to have been concerned with *homonyma* species and sorts rather than individuals. Of course, there is no doubt that by analogy with what is said in *Cat.* 5, 3a 33-b 9, both the species and the individuals are *homonyma*. However it is not quite to the point to talk about the *logos tēs ousias* as the *logos* of a *named* individual *tode ti*. Rather, Aristotle prefers to direct attention to that by virtue of which a *tode ti* is what it is: the essence and form, *ousia* in the secondary sense, which alone is definable and by virtue of which the definition is predicable to all individuals of a species. Hence, it is doubtful that Aristotle was concerned in this particular context with *homonyma* things *qua* individual exemplars of an *ousia*; for to have done so would have led to broadening the circumlocution to denote all cases of homonymous accidental beings on the ground that two individuals of the same species can also be *homonyma* things either by means of something denoted by a secondary genus or because of naming. However such cases were not germane to the Aristotle concern of working out a doctrine that was basically free from the defects of the Speusippean formulation. We may now turn to the examination of the textual evidence in support of *L of O*.[25] It was mentioned before that Aristotle has repeatedly stated that the *homonyma* are incommensurable or not comparable things (*ou symblēta*).[26] Furthermore, he has made careful analysis of *legomena* that have many senses and are therefore *homonyma*. For instance, 'the good' and other such expressions are treated in what seems to be a basic chapter in the *Topics*.[27] He tells us there to look at the classes of predicates signified by a term and determine whether they are the same in all cases, and if not the same, to conclude that the term involved is a *homonymon*.[28] Another advice he gives to the same effect is this: look to discover whether the genera that come under the same name are at once different and not subaltern: τὰ γένη τῶν ὑπὸ τὸ αὐτὸ ὄνομα, εἰ ἕτερα καὶ μὴ ὑπ' ἄλληλα.

It is the passage in *Topics* A 15 to which this paper appeals as corroborative textual evidence that in *Cat.* 1a 2 Aristotle means by L of O (a) *logos*=definition and (b) *ousia*=definable secondary ousia. It should be noted that the example in the *Categories* parallels the one in the *Topics*. Thus, the *Topics* (A 15. 107a, 18–23):

> ...as (e.g.) 'donkey', which denotes both animal and the engine. For the definition of them that corresponds to the name is different: for the one will be declared to be animal of a certain kind, and the other to be an engine of a certain kind. If, however, the genera be subaltern, there is no necessity for the definitions to be different.[29]

Once again he mentions in this example two sorts of things, one living and one artificial.[30] However, two difficulties must be removed before it can be claimed that the evidence cited supports our interpretation.

(a) In the *Categories* the *homonyma* things are man and portraits of man; the common name is 'animal' or 'living' (*zoon*). In the *Topics*, they are given as animal and engine, and the common name is 'donkey.' The difference is that in the *Categories* example the class 'animal' includes man, whereas in the *Topics* the class 'donkey' is included in the class 'animal'. But this is not a real problem since homonymy does not depend on class inclusion but on *substantive incomparability* between the sorts of things sharing a given name. In the *Categories* example, *zoon* is shared by living things and artifacts, hence their respective definitions must differ. In the *Topics* example

Logos tēs Ousias

'donkey' is used as the name that applies to a sort of animal and a sort of artifact. The two sorts demand two different definitions. Actually, then, there is no logical difference between the *Categories* and the *Topics* examples. Aristotle could have used the *Topics* example in the *Categories* with the same results, though it must be conceded that the *Categories* example provides for better contrast in the discussion of the difference between *homonyma* and *synonyma* there. In any event, the examples are logically identical.

(b) In the *Categories* and the *Topics* respectively, we have the following formulations of *homonyma*:

ὁ δὲ κατὰ τοὔνομα λόγος τῆς οὐσίας ἕτερος (*Cat.* 1a 1–2.)

ἕτερος γὰρ ὁ κατὰ τοὔνομα λόγος αὐτῶν (*Top.* 107b 20.)

The *Topics* formulation is somewhat deceiving and hence might be regarded as supporting the Boethus-Waitz reading of the *Categories* which omits *tes ousias*. But, as we saw, unless this expression is retained in the text of the *Categories* the danger of misunderstanding the intent is a real one. Since the *Topics* passage leaves no doubt that the things referred to are definable genera and sorts, it follows that it corresponds in both language and meaning to the *Categories* passage, which this paper interprets to mean secondary *ousiai* as definable via *genus-differentia*.

Now, whereas the doctrine in the *Topics* A ch. 15 is clearly stated, this is not so when we read the opening of the *Categories*. Hence, to omit *tes ousias* is to make *logos* somewhat ambiguous, for if nothing else it might be taken to mean the definition of the name rather than the entities named. Since the word αὐτῶν in the *Topics* formulation is absent from its parallel one in *Categories*, and since what it refers to is clearly genera of sorts, we are permitted to conclude that the two passages are genuinely parallel in doctrine. Therefore, the expression *L of O* has a technical meaning. The main purpose of my paper has been to discuss the evidence that could meaningfully provide a key to appreciating the technical significance and function of the opening chapter. Evidently, the ancient commentators did not find *Categories,* Chapter 1 as deficient in clarity of intent as Owens does; their errors stem primarily from the liberties they took in overextending the meaning of the passage under consideration to cover both Aristotelian and non-Aristotelian teachings.[31]

NOTES

1. *The Monist* 52 (1968), 252–67. Copyright 1968, THE MONIST, la Salle, Illinois 61301. Reprinted by permission [with changes].

2. *Cat.* 3b 10; *Post. An.* 73b 7, 87b 29.

3. For *infima species, Post. An.* esp. *passim*; 73a 32. It must be remembered that unless *ousia* means species, *infima* or otherwise, it cannot be defined. *Post. An.* 83b 5.

4. This problem has been treated in a separate paper that has since appeared under the title "Ancient Interpretations of Aristotle's Doctrine of Homonyma" in the *Journal of the History of Philosophy*, VII/1 (1969), 1–18 (reprinted in this volume).

5. *The Organon, or Logical Treatises of Aristotle, with the Introduction of Porphyry.* Literally translated with notes, syllogistic examples, analysis, and introduction by Octavius Friere Owen. 2 vols., (London: 1882), pp. 1–2; "Things are termed homonymous, of which the name alone is common, but the definition (of substance according to the name) is different; thus 'man' and 'the picture of a man' are each termed 'animal,' since of these, the name alone is common, but the definition (of the substance according to the name) is different."

6. *The Works of Aristotle*, translated into English under the editorship of W. D. Ross. Vol. I, *Categoriae* and *De Interpretatione* (Oxford: Oxford University Press, 1928). The translation has been made from Bekker's text of 1831. The translator states in the Preface that "my chief authority in matters of interpretation has been Pacius; I have also consulted Waitz's commentary largely." E. M. Edghill translates the passage as follows: "Things are said to be named 'equivocally' when, though they have a common name, the definition corresponding with the name differs in each case. Thus a real man and a figure in a picture can both lay claim to the name 'animal'; yet these are equivocally so named, for, though they have a common name, the definition corresponding with the name differs for each."

7. Aristotle, *The Organon*, I.: *The Categories, On Interpretation*, translated by Harold P. Cooke (Cambridge, Mass.: Harvard University Press, Loeb, 1938), p. 13. It is stated in the "Preface" that the text printed in the present edition is Bekker's except for some slight deviations that are noted in the foot of the page. Cooke preserves the reading of *L of O*: "Things are equivocally named when they have the name only in common, the definition (or statement of essence) corresponding with the name being different. For instance, while a man and a portrait can properly both be called 'animals,' these are equivocally named. For they have the name only in common, the definitions (or statements of essence) corresponding with the name being different."

8. Aristotle, *Categories* and *Interpretation*, translated by Le Roy F. Smith (Fresno, California: Academy Guild Press, 1959). In a prefatory note, the translator states the following: "This is a new translation of the Greek text taking into account the scholastic tradition, the writings of St. Albert the Great, St. Thomas Aquinas and the latin version of William of Moerbeke. In a few instances some of the examples which Aristotle gives have been slightly altered to make them more easily understandable by an English reader." The edition of the Greek text is not specified. The translation runs as follows: "Things are named equivocally when they have only the name in common, but the definition given for the name is different in the two cases."

9. Aristotle's *Categories* and *De Interpretatione*. Translated with notes by J. L. Ackrill (Oxford, 1963), p. 3. In his Preface, the translator states: "The text translated is that of the best and most recent edition, L. Minio Paluello's edition in the Oxford Classical Text Series (1949, with corrections 1956)." Ackrill translates: "When things have only a name in common and the definition of being which corresponds to the name is different, they are called *homonymous*. Thus, for example, both a man and a picture are animals. These have only a name in common and the definition of being which corresponds to the name is different."

10. Tricot's French translation sides with T2 and T4. See, Aristotle *Organon*: I *Categories*, II *De l'Interpretation*. Nouvelle traduction et notes par J. Tricot (Librarie Philosophique, J. Vrin, 1946), p. 2. In p. v. the author writes: "[Nous avons utilisé de préférence le texte de Waitz, sauf

Logos tēs Ousias 71

dans un certain nombre de passages où nous avons préféré la leçon de Bekker; les principales variantes ont été indiquées dans les notes.]" The omission of *ousia* is indicated in p. 2., note 1. Tricot's translation of the passage has as follows: "On appelle homonymes les choses dont le nom seul est commun, trandis que la notion designée par ce nom est diverse." Despite the fact that Ackrill and Tricot translate from different editions, Ackrill calls Tricot's version of the *Categories* and *De Interpretatione* more reliable than either the Oxford (T2) or the Loeb (T3) versions. See Ackrill, *op. cit.,* 158.

11. *Aristotelis Organon graece*, edited with commentary by Th. Waitz (Leipzig 1844–1846), 2 vols; the scholia in Vol. I, 269–271.

12. Boethus, floruit circa 40 B.C. Philoponus informs us that Andronicus was the teacher of Boethus (*In Categ. Prooemium*, C.A.G. Vol. 13, 4, 15 ff.).

13. In Pauly-Wissowa, *Realencyclopaedie*, Vol. 1–2, Col. 2, 2166.

14. It is worth mentioning in this connection that Tyrannion is reported to have written a work on περὶ μερισμοῦ τῶν τοῦ λόγου μερῶν.

15. Simplicius reports that the expression does not occur in all the copies he has seen, but mentions only those of Boethus and Andronicus (*In Categ.* 30, 3–5). Dexippus also admits that this reading does not occur in all the copies, and mentions only those of Boethus and Andronicus as cases in point. He says the expression *L of O* is favored by most (παρὰ τοῖς πλείστοις) and adds that Aristotle did well to put it that way (*In Categ.* 21, 18–22).

16. Mentioned in Simplicius, *op. cit.*, 29, 25. Simplicius refers to Nicostratus; he draws attention to a special difficulty in the use of *ousia*, namely, whether it is proper to extend the term to include the accidents. Nicostratus, evidently, took the position that homonymy must be restricted to *ousia* only. Simplicius, arguing against him, points out that there is homonymy in the case of quality (white, color, voice), position, and other genera of being.

17. Ammonius' accounts present a special problem though by no means unsurmountable. In his commentary of Porphyry's *Isagoge*, *ousia* is not

mentioned in the scholium where he discusses the relationship of homonymy and synonymy to beings (*onta*, 84, 6–23). This omission is rather odd especially in view of the fact that the much admired Porphyry had been an ardent defender of *L of O*. As expected, in his commentary on the *Categories*, Ammonius supports as best he can the *L of O*. See his scholium on 1a 2 (*In Categ.* 20, 14–21, 2).

18. Dexippus remarks that the distinction between *homonyma* and *synonyma* is fundamental to the exposition of the doctrine of the categories; *to on*, 'being,' he points out, is a homonymous expression and refers to all the categories. This means that *to on* must not be taken to mean a *summum genus*. Grote correctly interprets Dexippus to mean (a) that *to on* does not comprehend the categories in the sense that these are "distinct species under it," and (b) that "each category is a genus in reference to its particulars." *Aristotle*, Vol. I, p. 82, note a; also p. 85, note a.

19. *N. b.* In a paper, published soon after the present, "The Aristotelian Doctrine of Homonyma in the *Categories* and its Platonic Antecedents," *Journal of the History of Philosophy*, VI/4 (1968), 315–26, (reprinted in this volume) I endeavored to treat the Platonic antecedents of Aristotle's doctrine of *homonyma*. Part of my argument is that Aristotle is offering in the opening chapter of the *Categories* a counter-formulation to the Speusippean conception of *homonyma*. We know that Speusippus had written works on division and classification, an enterprise that called for a technical use and formulation of the meaning of *homonyma*. I took the position that an important element in the proper context for understanding the opening chapters of the *Categories* is their anti-Speusippean logic and ontology.

20. Philoponus supplies the following definitions of the essences of the *homonyma* things in Aristotle's example (*In Categ.* 22, 18–19):

(a) ἄνθρωπος, οὐσία ἔμψυχος αἰσθητική.

(b) γεγραμμένον, μίμημα οὐσίας ἐμψύχου αἰσθητικῆς.

These two *legomena* constitute a case of homonyma for though they have the name 'living' in common, there is no definable *ousia* which inheres in both.

21. See his *Aristotle's Metaphysics* (Oxford, 1924), Vol. I, Introd., p. cxiii.

Logos tēs Ousias 73

22. Ross notes that "such a product is produced ἐξ ὁμωνύμου ἢ ἐκ μέρους ὁμωνύμου, for the house in the builder's mind is only part of — the formal element in — a house. In all artistic production there are implied two stages, one of νόησις, in which the artist works gradually back from the thought of the object he wishes to produce to that of the means necessary to its production, and one of ποίησις, in which, reversing the order, he successively brings these means into existence until he has fulfilled his purpose." *Op. cit.*, p. cxxi; also *Met.* 1032b 6–21; 1034a 9–32 and scholia on this passage, Vol. II, pp. 190–194.

23. *Phys.* 200a 7–10.

24. *Phys.* 199a 9–15. See also *Met.* 1034a 9–b 19. Ross correctly remarks that "this double action, final cause and necessity, is normally at work in natural substances as well as *artefacta*." *Aristotle's Metaphysics*, Vol. I, p. cxii.

25. This textual evidence, which occurs as a parallel passage in the *Topics*, is corroborative rather than definitive.

26. *Phys.* 248b 9, 17, 249a 4, 248a 11; *Top.* 107b 17; *Met.* 1080a 20, 1018a 5; *Nic. Eth.* 1133a 19.

27. *Top.* 15, 106a 9 ff.

28. *Top.* 107a 2–12.

29. Oxford translation. The Greek text reads: οἷον ὄνος τό τε ζῷον καὶ τό σκεῦος. ἕτερος γὰρ ὁ κατὰ τοὔνομα λόγος αὐτῶν. τὸ μὲν γὰρ ζῷον ποιόν τι ῥηθήσεται, τὸ δὲ σκεῦος ποιόν τι. ἐὰν δὲ ὑπ' ἄλληλα τὰ γένη ᾖ, οὐκ ἀναγκαῖον ἑτέρους τοὺς λόγους εἶναι.

30. Compare also the example given in *Nic. Eth.* II, 1129a 30: ὁμωνύμως καλεῖται ἡ κλεὶς ἥ τε ὑπὸ τὸν αὐχένα τῶν ζῴων καὶ ἡ τὰς θύρας κλείουσιν.

31. In defending this position I differ from J. Owens who writes: "The opening chapter of the *Categories* fails to reveal whether it is introducing a grammatical, a logical, or a metaphysical treatise. It deals with equivocals and univocals and ends with a definition of paronyms." See

also Owens' article "Aristotle on Categories," in *The Review of Metaphysics*, 14 (1960), No. 1, p. 74. Still I find myself in agreement with what he states in footnote 5: "For Aristotle, equivocals and univocals refer primarily to things, and only secondarily to conceptual expressions and words, as I have tried to show in *The Doctrine of Being in the Aristotelian Metaphysics* (Toronto: Pontifical Institute of Medieval Studies, 1951), pp. 49–63." Nevertheless Owens' view rests on the assumption that Aristotle is not stating any special doctrine in the "puzzling" chapter 1 of the *Categories*.

THE ARISTOTELIAN DOCTRINE OF *HOMONYMA* IN THE *CATEGORIES* AND ITS PLATONIC ANTECEDENTS[1]

The Aristotelian doctrine of *homonyma* is of particular historical interest at least for the following reasons: (1) It appears that the meaning of *homonyma* was seriously debated in Aristotle's times and that his own formulation was but one among many others. Evidently, there were other platonizing thinkers in the Academy who had formulated their own variants. According to ancient testimonies, the definition which Speusippus propounded proved to be quite influential in later times.[2] (2) The fact that Aristotle chose to open the *Categories* with a discussion, brief as it is, on the meaning of *homonyma*, *synonyma*, and *paronyma*, attests to the significance he attached to this preliminary chapter. Furthermore, there is general agreement among all the commentators on the relevance of the first chapter of the *Categories* to the doctrine of the categories. (3) The corpus affords ample internal evidence that the doctrine of *homonyma* figures largely in Aristotle's various discussions on the nature of first principles and his method of metaphysical analysis. This being the case, it is clear that Aristotle considered this part of his logical theory to have applications beyond the limited scope of what is said in the *Categories*.

Since we do not know the actual order of Aristotle's writings it is next to impossible to decide which formulation came first. It remains a fact that Aristotle discusses cases of *homonyma* and their causes as early as the *Sophistici Elenchi*. Special mention of the cause of *homonyma* is made in the very first chapter of this work. We find it again in the *Topics*, *de Interpretatione*, the *Analytics* and the other logical treatises. He opens the *Sophistici Elenchi* with a general distinction between genuine and apparent reasonings and refutations, and then proceeds to explain why some refutations fail to reach their goal, that is, establish the contradictory of the given conclusion.[3]

II

It would be an error to claim that Aristotle was the first to observe that homonymy constitutes a source of ambiguity. Plato had already made a diagnosis in the *Sophist*:

> At present, you see, all that you and I possess in common is the name. The thing to which each of us gives that name we may perhaps have privately before our eyes, but it is always desirable to have reached an agreement about the thing itself by means of explicit statements rather than be content to use the same word without formulating what it means.[4]

The Stranger is addressing Theaetetus in this passage; the issue before them is to hunt down "the troublesome sort of creature" that the sophist is. Plato is suggesting here that when two people embark on a conversation and are using names whose meaning they suspect is not the same for both, it is imperative that they settle their differences and decide upon a common and acceptable meaning of that name. In this particular case, the Stranger and Theaetetus happen to have private meanings on what it means to be a sophist. However, the Stranger suggests, the matter cannot be left to rest at this level of understanding. The discussion cannot continue and hope to bear some fruit unless an appropriate method is introduced to resolve the difference and affix with precision the meaning of the name in question. The warning is clear: one must not take it for granted that common names have common meanings. It is preferable to go on the assumption that two people who are using the same name actually have private meanings for it. The way to settle this matter and arrive at common meanings is by formulating explicit statements about the thing named. In the *Sophist*, Plato propounds the method of division. The main point here is that Plato identified the actual source of homonymy as follows: given a name which is commonly used by two persons, it is by no means certain that both entertain the same meaning.

When we turn to Aristotle, the context of the discussion on the nature of homonymy changes. In the *Topics* and the *Sophistici Elenchi* the tone is more Platonic, but less so in the *Categories*. Let us explain. In the *Categories*, we see Aristotle starting out with the fact that things have names; they are the *legomena*. There is no direct resemblance here to the Platonic context of the *Sophist* in which mention is made of two individuals who are said to have private meanings for the same name in their discussion. The first thing Aristotle mentions in this treatise is things that have common names. The issue that arises immediately is that of determining whether we have a case of *homonyma* or one of *synonyma*. The method to be followed here is not that of division as used by Plato in the *Sophist*, for it is not confused opinion about some subject that we wish to settle. Not our opinions, but how two things are related to a third thing whose name they have in common, is what must be clarified. Thus, the problem is not whether "sophist" means really this or that sort of thing to two different persons. The task is a new one: given that two things share the name of something else, we must ask by virtue of what pattern of relationships they come to share the name. The issue then is to find out whether the two things are essentially related to each other and to some third thing or not. What we are asked to do is to discover something about the claims things have to names of other things and by virtue of what properties. In the Aristotelian view we start out with things and with the natural fact of language whereby names of things happen to be common to certain other things. The ambiguities to be removed are not so much those of private opinion. The deeper issue has now become one whereby homonymy, if allowed to remain undetected, interferes with the validity of syllogistic thinking.[5] It is an obstacle to attaining scientific knowledge.

These two different approaches to homonymy point to the fact that Plato and Aristotle are not solving the same problem in their respective quests in the *Sophist* and the *Categories*, though it is true that both deal with some fundamental aspect of ambiguous talking. Just the same, one can readily notice how Aristotle is linguistically indebted to Plato for the formulation of his own definition of *homonyma*. Aristotle's formulation evidently owes much to Plato's choice of words. Compare for instance Aristotle's text in *Categories* 1a 1-2, with Plato's wording of the issue when he says: Τοὔνομα μόνον κοινῇ... συνομολογήσασθαι διὰ λόγων. The Aristotelian text runs as follows: Ὁμώνυμα λέγεται ὧν ὄνομα μόνον κοινόν, ὁ δὲ κατὰ τοὔνομα λόγος τῆς οὐσίας ἕτερος.[6]

We must pursue the difference between Plato and Aristotle on the meaning of *homonyma* a step further. In the *Phaedo*, Plato uses this expression to cover cases which normally Aristotle brings under the term *synonyma*.[7] Ὁμώνυμος, in other words, is regularly used by Plato to mean that which has not only the same name as something else but also shares with it the same formula of essence, λόγος τῆς οὐσίας.[8] Yet, it is of prime importance to note at this point that the expression *homonyma* did not receive in Plato's writings the full significance of a technical term. As A. E. Taylor has correctly remarked, "ὁμώνυμον is not, of course, used in the sense which had become technical in the next generation."[9]

Since the Platonic expression λόγος τῆς οὐσίας figures dominantly in the Aristotelian formulation of *homonyma*, and since one of the principal issues defended in this paper is the view that the Aristotelian use of *logos tēs ousias* has a special meaning in the opening chapter of the *Categories*, we must pause to examine some of the locutions in the Platonic dialogues in which it occurs.

In the *Sophist* 246c, Plato speaks of λαμβάνειν λόγον τῆς οὐσίας as in the sense of rendering an account of reality. It occurs in

Aristotelian Doctrine of Homonyma I 79

a statement the Stranger makes in the context of the celebrated epistemological battle between the Gods and the Giants, the Idealists and the Materialists, where the discussion the Stranger carries on with Theaetetus has reached the point where it has become necessary to "challenge each party in turn to render an account of the reality they assert." This usage of *logos tēs ousias* is also to be found in the *Republic* where Plato employs it to identify the task of dialectic, that is, to explore and articulate the nature of what he conceives to be the really real.[10] Comparably in the *Phaedo*:

> Then let us return to the same examples which we were discussing before. Does *this absolute reality which we depend in our discussions* remain always constant and invariable, or not? Does absolute equality or beauty or any other independent entity which really exists (αὐτὸ ἕκαστον ὃ ἔστιν, τὸ ὄν) ever admit change of any kind?[11]

Another key passage occurs in the *Laws*, where the Athenian says:

> You will grant, I presume, that there are three points to be noted about anything...I mean, for one, the reality of the thing, what it is, for another, the definition of this reality, for another, its name.[12]

The crucial point in this passage is the fact that Plato uses the term *logos* in the sense of definition, thus setting a precedent which will establish the context for subsequent formulations of the notion of *homonyma* so that the expression *logos tēs ousias,* especially in its Aristotelian usage, can take on terminological fixity. The ultimate object of the defining process will not change from Plato to Aristotle, that is, it will still be an *ousia*, but the fact that Plato meant by it the Forms and Aristotle restricted its *definable denotation* to the essences of things, must always be kept in mind in discussions of this sort. When we turn to *Epistle VII* we find another important passage that further illustrates the view we have taken here that *logos tēs ousias* has already received in Plato's writing a central doctrinal meaning. This passage leaves no doubt that *logos* means definition and that what is being defined is something which is an ideal object of knowledge, an *ousia*, γνωστόν τε καὶ ἀληθῶς ἐστιν ὄν:

> For every real being, there are three things that are necessary if knowledge of it is to be acquired: first, the name; second, the definition; third, the image; knowledge comes fourth and in fifth place we must put the object itself, the knowable and truly real being.[13]

The examination of the textual evidence we have presented shows that the Platonic antecedents of the theme under consideration are as follows: (1) Plato had made use of the linguistic elements that figure in Aristotle's formulation of *homonyma*, viz. the expressions "*homonyma*," "*koinos*," and "*logos tēs ousias*"; (2) he had employed the technical expression "*logos tēs ousias*" for logical, epistemological and metaphysical purposes, in a word, to convey specific philosophical convictions; and (3) Plato himself did not work out an explicit view of *homonyma* that seems to have called for a technical formulation of their logical properties. This last task and the debate over alternative ways of solving this problem were left to the next generation. The work was actually done by two of Plato's brightest students, Speusippus and Aristotle.

III

Speusippus discussed *homonyma* and *synonyma* and distinguished between words which express "the *logos* of an essence" and words which function simply as names. According to Speusippus, homonymous expressions do not stand for a common essence, whereas synonymous ones do so. Simplicius quotes Speusippus' version as follows: Σπεύσιππος δὲ, φασίν, ἠρκεῖτο λέγειν 'ὁ δὲ λόγος ἕτερος.'[14] The Speusippean notion, as H. Cherniss has aptly summarized it, is that "a name is ὁμώνυμον if it refers to several different concepts and συνώνυμον if it refers to one single and undifferentiated concept."[15] It is an established fact that Speusippus' formulation was essentially different from Aristotle's and also that the difference reflects the seriousness with which the attendant philosophical issues were debated. Cherniss has carefully discussed the doctrinal differences concerning homonymous names in the context of division as this methodological procedure was practiced by Speusippus and Aristotle.[16] The applications of this doctrine for settling questions of ambiguity also reflect the difference in the two formulations.[17] According to Hambruch, there is sufficient evidence to conclude that *Topics* I, 15, is closely related to issues discussed in a Speusippean treatise. Cherniss also cites relevant evidence to show that Aristotle responds to a Speusippean thesis in a much discussed passage of the *Sophistici Elenchi*.[18] Speusippus' mathematical conceptualism provided the appropriate framework within which he could formulate his doctrine of *homonyma* and the ontology where this doctrine could find application without residual problems. But once the Speusippean view is taken out of its initial context and is generalized to assist in the removal of ambiguities as these arise in discourse no longer governed by Speusippus' metaphysical assumptions, the thesis collapses for lack of elucidating efficacy. It has not been our purpose to debate here the logical merits of the Speusippean view of *homonyma* vis-a-vis that of Aristotle's, but simply to show that the issue was debated between the rival schools and that, as a result of such controversy, we find in the writings of these philosophers not only the first attempts to offer technical formulations of *homonyma* but also different conceptions of their status which were preserved in the copies of the commentators and often allowed to cause discrepancies in the textual traditions.

IV

The first issue that confronts us when we turn to an examination of Aristotle's theory is a serious textual problem. In fact the philosophical aspects of this theory cannot be decided unless the textual problem is successfully solved. Ancient and modern commentators, including editors, have expressed considerable disagreement over the opening lines of the text in *Categories*, ch. 1. Two substantially different versions of this passage, both claimed as genuine, have been recorded by ancient authorities.[19] We shall refer to them as V1 and V2. The available English translations of this passage are far from being in agreement, nor do they seem free from interpretation. A careful examination of the way in which they render the passage would lead one to infer that Aristotle did not intend it in a technical sense.[20] What partly explains the disagreements in the translations is the fact that they are based on different textual traditions. Even those that follow the same tradition do not derive the same meaning from the text. For a fuller explanation of the cause of such disagreements one would have to identify the interpretations that the translators bring with them when they try to render Aristotle's text in their own language. Another factor that should not be ignored is the availability of adequate terminological expressions in the translator's own language. In view of the difficulties attending the existing translations it is better not to supply one of our own. The extant versions of the opening passage in Aristotle's *Categories* have been preserved as follows:

V1. Ὁμώνυμα λέγεται ὧν ὄνομα μόνον κοινόν, ὁ δὲ κατὰ τοὔνομα λόγος τῆς οὐσίας ἕτερος.[21]

V2. Ὁμώνυμα λέγεται ὧν ὄνομα μόνον κοινόν, ὁ δὲ κατὰ τοὔνομα λόγος ἕτερος.[22]

Aristotelian Doctrine of Homonyma I

The difference between the two versions is that V2 omits the expression τῆς οὐσίας. Close discussion on this issue must be postponed until later. Suffice it to say here that once the expression is omitted, the entire passage takes on a different meaning, one that compromises its claims to terminological precision. But the real danger lies in the fact that without the expression the very doctrine which the passage is purported to convey lapses into doubtful Aristotelian theory. If so, then the intended meaning of the circumlocution of the nature of *homonyma* demands that the expression *tēs ousias* be kept in the text. Most of the commentators have argued for the inclusion of the expression, but for reasons that are invariably tied to their own favored interpretations. Of the ancient authorities only two are reported to have advocated the exclusion of the expression: Andronicus and Boethus. The commentator Dexippus mentions that Andronicus and Boethus omit the *tēs ousias* part and insists that the expression is found in most manuscripts *(para tois pleistois)*. In his opinion, Aristotle was right in stating the matter as given in V1.[23] Andronicus and Boethus are also mentioned by name in Ammonius' commentary as the ones whose copies (or editions) of the *Categories* omit *tēs ousias*, but there is also reference to others who did the same. Ammonius hastens to add that most manuscripts included the debatable expression. Simplicius reports that Porphyry, who had also discussed this matter, was of the opinion that Boethus was wrong to insist that *tēs ousias* did not appear in Aristotle's original text, even if Boethus had on his side no less an authority than that of his teacher Andronicus.[24]

In contrast, the defenders of V1 are: Nicostratus,[25] Herminus,[26] Porphyry, Dexippus, Ammonius,[27] Philoponus, Simplicius, Olympiodorus and Elias. Before we proceed to examine in detail why most of the commentators defended the *logos tēs ousias* (abbreviated hereafter as *L of O*) as essential to an adequate formulation of the nature of *homonyma*, and what meaning they assigned to the entire passage, we must first look closer into certain philosophical issues the passage raises and also state in advance what we believe to be the doctrine Aristotle intended.

Given the definition of *homonyma* as stated in V1, we must ask whether it is a good definition, and if so whether the expresion *L of O* is a requisite part of the circumlocution and with a technical meaning to it. Since the issue seems to depend largely on what *L of O* means, part of our problem is to determine the exact denotation of *ousia*. If it is true that the term *logos* is used technically here to mean definition, then the denotation of *ousia* has to be restricted to secondary substances on the ground that only these are at once definable and predicable. It is important here that we do not include the *summa genera* despite the fact that these also constitute cases of *homonyma*. Be this as it may, our proposed meaning of *ousia* is not without problems. More specifically:

(1) We still have to answer the question why there is an alternate reading of the text, which as a matter of fact omits the tes *ousias* part. In other words, there cannot be a conclusive defense of V1 unless it can be shown that if V2 is the genuine text it would not have been possible for Aristotle to state an integral part of his doctrine for lack of adequate terminology.

(2) Since it is a fact that Aristotle was aware of the wider range of application of *homonyma*, for *homonyma* range from *summa genera* to the accidental properties (*symbēbekota*), and since he seems to propose in this passage of the *Categories* a restricted use of the term, an explanation must be given for this phenomenon.

(3) There is the further problem of having to explain why it must be the case that Aristotle could not have meant to include in the meaning of *homonyma* the case of individual substances that have the same proper name. The examples of *homonyma* things he gives constitute irrefutable evidence that such is the case. However, this turns out to be a serious problem because all the extant commentaries interpret Aristotle's formulation of *homonyma* as designed to cover, above all else, the case of homonymous individuals with the same

proper name. The fact that all the commentators discuss at considerable length this special case of *homonyma* seems to militate strongly against our own interpretation.

(4) Since such things as *principle, genus, logos, one, common, being, element,* and the like, as πολλαχῶς λεγόμενα are instances of homonymy, there is again the problem of how they relate to the passage of *homonyma* things in the *Categories*. The issue here is to decide whether the definition of *homonyma* is designed to cover the case of abstract principles and concepts. Even the term *category*, as the commentators correctly saw, is open to homonymy. Whereas substance, quality, quantity, relation, etc., have the name "category" in common, they do not stand for the same sort of thing. It cannot be denied that Aristotle was aware of this peculiarity. Similarly, we cannot afford to ignore the possibility that the formulation of *homonyma* is intended in some technical sense. Evidently, then, this and the other problems mentioned above depend for their solution on the answers that are given to the question of the meaning of *logos tēs ousias*.

V

The position we have taken in this paper is based on the textual tradition which was highly favored by the leading commentators. There are philosophical reasons why it is necessary that we should retain the entire expression *L of 0,* reasons which are not discussed by the ancient commentators. To argue in favor of adopting V2 on the ground that it is doctrinally equivalent to V1 would lead to two serious and equally undesirable consequences: (1) It would make the Aristotelian position not only indistinguishable from other available formulations of the nature of *homonyma* but, even worse, it would lead to a surrender to the views of Speusippus and the pythagoreanizing Platonists.[28] (2) It would make the passage in

Categories 1a so imprecise as to render the distinction between *homonyma* and *synomyma* superfluous and even make it possible, especially when the *tēs ousias* part is omitted, to widen the denotation of *homonyma* beyond the point of usefulness. Curiously enough the ancient commentators did precisely something comparable to the second abuse of the passage without even omitting the *L of O* expression. The interpretations which the ancient commentators attached to the Aristotelian doctrine of *homonyma* were conceived in the light of a number of non-Aristotelian assumptions and commitments. The examination of this topic has been undertaken in a separate paper, sequel to the present, titled "Ancient interpretations of the Doctrine of *Homonyma*." However, the fact that the ancient commentators preserved the passage as given in V1, even if they misinterpreted its intent, can still be construed as positive evidence in favor of this version. More recent classical scholarship, again, has given unqualified preference to V1 over V2.[29]

Our own thesis rests on the hypothesis that the *Categories* offers an earlier version of Aristotle's ontology and that *L of O* in this context is part of a requisite terminological apparatus; furthermore, part of the background here is the issues involved in the controversy between Aristotle and Speusippus in their respective efforts to institute ways of dealing with problems that arise in the use of names and the effort to remove instances of ambiguity. It is further contended here that the first chapter of the *Categories* is not merely a place where Aristotle introduces distinctions which will prove to be useful in the subsequent discussion on substance, predication and the other categories, but that he is presenting his distinctions in formulations that are best understood as offering a distinctive alternative to the doctrine advanced by Speusippus and his followers.

Now, whatever else Aristotle might have meant by *L of 0,* especially by *ousia*, he could not have meant any of the following: first substance, *summum genus, differentia*, or accidental properties. The doctrinal meaning of *logos* in this passage demands that we

Aristotelian Doctrine of Homonyma I 87

interpret *ousia* in the light of the restricted sense of *homonyma*, that is, to mean only secondary substances which alone are both predicable and definable. Corroborative evidence in support of our thesis will be found in a parallel expression in *Topics*, A, ch. 15, 107b 20: ἕτερος γὰρ ὁ κατὰ τοὔνομα λόγος αὐτῶν, where αὐτῶν refers to things that are evidently definable genera, viz. species as secondary substances. Thus, it would be correct to mean the passage to read: αὐτῶν τῶν οὐσιῶν. But let us examine closer this piece of evidence. To begin with, Aristotle has repeatedly stated that the *homonyma* are not comparable *ou symblēta*.[30] Furthermore, he has made a careful analysis of *legomena* that have many senses and are therefore *homonyma*. For instance, "the good" and other such expressions are treated in what seems to be a basic chapter in the *Topics*.[31] He tells us there to look at the classes of predicates signified by a term and determine whether they are the same in all cases, and if not the same, to conclude that the term involved is a *homonymon*. Another advice he gives to the same effect is this: look to discover whether the genera that come under the same name are at once different and not subaltern: τὰ γένη τῶν ὑπὸ τὸ αὐτὸ ὄνομα, εἰ ἕτερα καὶ μὴ ὑπ' ἄλληλα. The corroborative evidence comes at this juncture.

It should be noted that the example in the *Categories* parallels the one in the *Topics*. Thus, the *Topics* (A 15, 107a, 18-23):

> ...as (e.g.) 'donkey', which denotes both animal and the engine. For the definition of them that corresponds to the name is different: for the one will be declared to be animal of a certain kind, and the other to be an engine of a certain kind. If, however, the genera be subaltern, there is no necessity for the definitions to be different.[32]

Once again he mentions in this example two sorts of things, one living and one artificial.[33] However, two difficulties must be removed before it can be claimed that the evidence cited supports our interpretation.

(1) In the *Categories* the *homonyma* things are man and portraits of man; the common name is "animal" or "living." In the *Topics*, they are given as animal and engine, and the common name is "donkey." The difference is that in the *Categories* example the class animal includes man, whereas in the *Topics* the class donkey is included in animal. But this is not a real problem since homonymy does not depend on class inclusion but on mutual *categorical exclusion* of the sorts of things sharing a given name. In the *Categories* example, *zoon* is shared by living things and artifacts, hence their respective definitions must differ. The *Topics* example uses "donkey" as the name that applies to both a sort of animal and a sort of artifact. The two sorts demand two different definitions. Actually, then, there is no logical difference between the *Categories* and the *Topics* examples. Aristotle could have used the *Topics* example in the *Categories* with the same results, though we must concede that the *Categories* example provides for better contrast in the discussion of the difference between *homonyma* and *synonyma* there. In any event, the examples are logically identical.

(2) In the *Categories* and the *Topics* respectively, we have the following formulations of *homonyma*:

ὁ δὲ κατὰ τοὔνομα λόγος τῆς οὐσίας ἕτερος (*Cat.* 1a 1–2).

ἕτερος γὰρ ὁ κατὰ τοὔνομα λόγος αὐτῶν (*Top.* 107b 20).

The *Topics* formulation is somewhat deceiving and hence might be regarded as supporting the Boethus-Waitz reading of the *Categories* which omits *tēs ousias*. But, as we saw, unless this expression is retained in the text of the *Categories* the danger of misunderstanding the intent is unavoidable. Since the *Topics* passage leaves no doubt that the things referred to are definable genera and sorts, it follows that it corresponds in both language and meaning to the *Categories* passage, which this paper interprets to mean secondary substances as definable via *genus-differentia*.

Now, whereas the doctrine in the *Topics* A, ch. 15 is clearly stated, this is not so when we read the opening of the *Categories*. Hence, to omit *tēs ousias* is to make *logos* somewhat ambiguous, for if nothing else it might be taken to mean the definition of the name rather than the entities named. Since the word αὐτῶν in the *Topics* formulation is absent from its parallel one in the *Categories,* and since what it refers to is clearly genera of sorts, we are permitted to conclude that the two passages are genuinely parallel in doctrine. The close examination of the *Topics* passage we have offered is not intended as definitive but primarily as illustrative of the comparable passages in other Aristotelian treatises that could be cited in favor of our interpretation.[34] However, one of the main reasons the *Topics* passage was singled out for commentary and citation is to offer evidence in favor of the apparent doctrinal affinity between this work and the *Categories.* If it can be maintained, for instance, that Aristotle had formed at the time he composed the *Topics* certain views which led him to explicit questioning of certain fundamental beliefs of the Platonic Academy, such could also be the case with the *Categories.* Cherniss has shown that by the time Aristotle had put forth the distinction between *homonyma* and *synonyma,* as this can be clearly gleaned through the relevant passages in the *Topics,* he had manifestly developed his criticism of the theory of ideas. Cherniss has also argued convincingly that Aristotle had maintained in the *Topics* that the Platonists cannot avoid certain difficulties unless they grant that "the ideas and the particulars are not συνώνυμα but ὁμώνυμα in Aristotle's sense."[35] In light, then, of the direct and indirect evidence we have presented, the following conclusions obtain: (1) the formulation of the meaning of *homonyma*, as defended in its V1 version, contains no superfluities; (2) the statement is a technical one and meant positively to assist in the exposition of the ontology that supports Aristotle's categorical theory; and (3) the doctrine is purported as part of the logical apparatus through which

Aristotle could criticize his Platonizing opponents and Speusippus, in particular.

Before closing, we must pursue one final point. Clearly, the expression "*homonyma things*" is itself a case of homonymy. The expression can be used for things substantially different: species and individuals, accidents and genera, principles and concepts. According to the Aristotelian rule, it can be shown that if we were to give the definition of the sorts of things that are presumably called *homonyma*, we would have to give in each case a different definition. The point is by now so obvious that it tends to lapse into a triviality. If so, then it is difficult to understand why Aristotle would want to state something as obvious as that and, furthermore, introduce his categorical theory with a circumlocution of *homonyma* that would refer unqualifiedly to all cases of *homonyma*. It is more reasonable to suppose that Aristotle, rather than making a trite point, was concentrating on a restricted application of the term for the purpose of bringing together certain aspects relevant to both his theory of syllogistic thinking and his ontology, especially in the form in which the latter is given in the *Categories*.

Basic to our thesis is our view that the meaning of *logos* must be understood in the strict sense of definition. Though this has not been a point of dispute among modern scholars, such was not the case with Aristotle's ancient interpreters. This pertains to all the commentators on the *Categories*, from Porphyry to Photius. *Logos* in the sense of description, which they insisted was part of what Aristotle meant by *logos*, must be rejected as non-Aristotelian, because failure to do so permits the meaning of *ousia* to become unduly broadened. The commentators missed the significance of this point. As I try to show in the sequel to this paper, "Ancient Interpretations of Aristotle's Doctrine of *Homonyma*," most of them were more interested in displaying their own special kind of erudition than in the relevance of their learning to the finer aspects of the doctrines under examination. Quite frequently they even ignored the strict theoretical issues that attended the Aristotelian approach to the problem of definition. Given their bold deviations from standard aspects of Aristotle's philosophy, it is small wonder that certain details in the system, significant though they were, when not completely overlooked, were grossly mishandled.

NOTES

1. Published in *The Journal of the History of Philosophy*, VI/4 (1968), 315–26. Reprinted in *Platon*, 21 (1969), 36–57.

2. See *De Speusippi Academici scriptis*, ed. P. Lang (Bonn, 1911), frag. 32. Simplicius comments that Speusippus defended this formulation and remarks that once the definition is granted, it could be shown that *homonyma* are also *synonyma*, and vice versa (*In Aristotelis Categorias commentarium*, ed. C. Kalbfleisch, *Commentaria in Aristotelis Graeca*, VIII [Berlin, 1907] 29, 5–6).

3. "It is impossible in a discussion to bring in the actual things discussed: we use their names as symbols instead of them; and, therefore, we suppose that what follows in the names, follows in the things as well, just as people who calculate suppose in regard to their counters. But the two cases (names and things) are not alike. For names are finite and so is the sum-total of formulae, while things are infinite in number. Inevitably, then, the same formulae, and a single name, have a number of meanings. Accordingly just as, in counting, those who are not clever in manipulating their counters are taken in by the experts, in the same way in arguments too those who are not well acquainted with the force of names misreason both in their own discussions and when they listen to others. For this reason, then, and for others to be mentioned later, there exists both reasoning and refutation that is apparent but not real" (165a 5–20, Oxford trans.).

4. At 218b-c (Cornford's trans.). This passage is mentioned by Simplicius as evidence to support the claim that Plato had anticipated the problem (*In Categ.*, 25,103). Plato's text reads: νῦν γὰρ δὴ σύ τε κἀγὼ τούτου πέρι τοὔνομα ἔχομεν κοινῇ, τὸ δὲ ἔργον, ἐφ' ᾧ καλοῦμεν ἑκάτερος τάχ' ἂν ἰδίᾳ παρ' ἡμῖν αὐτοῖς ἔχοιμεν· δεῖ δὲ ἀεὶ παντὸς πέρι τὸ πρᾶγμα αὐτὸ μᾶλλον διὰ λόγων ἢ τοὔνομα συνομολογήσασθαι χωρὶς λόγου. Earlier in his commentary, Simplicius refers to Plato's *Euthydemus* (277e, 295d), where Plato draws attention to the need for a proper method to distinguish between the various uses of names in order to meet the Sophistic nuisance and also to remove doubt. Simplicius reports that the need to deal with double meanings of names was one of the main reasons that led to the development of dialectic (22, 10-13).

Aristotelian Doctrine of Homonyma I					93

5. David in his commentary on Porphyry's *Isagoge* remarks that ὀφείλομεν μὲν τοίνυν διαστείλασθαι τὰ ὁμώνυμα πρὸς ἀναίρεσιν τῆς ἀμφιβολίας (123, 1415). However, the "removal of amphibole" is only part of the issue. Unless homonymy is dealt with in all its aspects, the connection that is needed to tie the major to the minor term in a syllogism could remain in doubt. The scholiast David failed to see how the detection of *homonyma* is vital to the validity of syllogistic thinking. Hence, the discussion on *homonyma* has broader implications than what David mentions in this passage. It might be said that his remark is related to the way in which he interprets the denotation of *homonyma*. Looking at this matter from a strict Aristotelian point of view, we could say that once this notion is allowed to mean individual substances of the sort that David mentions in his examples, then its relation to terms in syllogistic thinking becomes questionable on the ground that the terms in syllogistic premises are universals, not individuals.

6. It should be remembered that Aristotle distinguishes between ὁμωνυμία, τὰ ὁμώνυμα, and ἀμφιβολία. The first refers to the multiple use of a word (see *Topics*, esp. 106b 3–4, 106b 8, 107a 5, 107b 7); ἀμφιβολία refers to the multiple use of a whole phrase or a sentence, *logos* (*Topics*, 129b 31-32, 130a 9). G. E. L. Owen, in a recent essay observes: "Commonly, though not always, he [Aristotle] uses 'homonymous' and 'synonymous' to describe not words but the things to which a word is applied. Thus in the *Categories* (1a 1-11) he explains that two things (or kinds of things) are called '*syn*onymous' if they both answer to some such name as 'animal', and if the *logos* which corresponds to the name, i.e. the appropriate definition or paraphrase, is the same in each case. They are called *homo*nymous if both answer to the same name, but the appropriate *logos* differs in the two cases. By *logos* in such contexts he plainly does mean a definition or paraphrase: this is shown by the many examples in his logic" ("Aristotle on the Snares of Ontology," in *New Essay on Plato and Aristotle,* ed. R. Bambrough [London, 1965], p. 73). Owen correctly takes the view that *homonyma* is about things and not words. J. L. Ackrill, commenting on the opening chapter of the *Categories,* concurs and remarks that "it is important to recognize from the start that the *Categories* is not primarily or explicitly about names, but about the things that names signify" (*Aristotle's Categories and De Interpretatione,* trans. with notes and glossary [Oxford,

1963], p. 71, scholium on Cat. la 1). Also compare M. Grene, *A Portrait of Aristotle* (Chicago, 1963) pp. 70-73, who agrees that the discussion is about things and not words or terms, but still uses the Latin nomenclature: "things equivocally named" and "things univocally named." The history of this nomenclature and the interpretations lurking in the background have been appropriately exposed in H. W. B. Joseph's *An Introduction to Logic* (rev. 2nd ed.; Oxford, 1916), pp. 31, 46-47. The position we have adopted here understands the passage *L of O* not only in the sense that it refers to things, in this case, *homonyma* things, but also as intended to cover only special cases of *homonyma*, i.e., it has a restricted and technical application to kinds of things.

7. At 78e, τὰ παρ' ἡμῖν ταῦτα ὁμώνυμα ὄντα ἐκείνοις. For or other passages where the sensible things are called *homonyma* with regard to the intellectual objects, the forms, ὁμώνυμα τοῖς εἴδεσι, see *Timaeus* 52a, *Parmenides* 133d. H. Cherniss observes: " This Platonic use of ὁμώνυμον represented by Aristotle's συνώνυμον inasmuch as the ideas and particulars are understood to be 'specifically the same' (*Metaphysics* 1040b 32-34, 1059a 13-14, 1086b 10-11), although for Plato ὁμώνυμος when used of the relationship of sensibles and ideas meant not merely 'synonymous' in Aristotle's sense. The particular is ὁμώνυμον τῷ εἴδει, not *vice versa,* because it has its name and nature *derivatively* from the idea..., but apart from the relation of sensibles and ideas Plato uses the word of several things which, though more or less different, have the same name and belong to the same class" (*Aristotle's Criticism of Plato and the Academy* [Baltimore, 1944], p. 178, n. 102).

8. See *Timaeus* 41c, *Parmenides* 133d 2, *Sophist* 234b 7.

9. A. E. Taylor, *A Commentary on Plato's Timaeus* (Oxford, 1928), p. 342, schol. on 52a 5.

10. *Republic* III 534b: Ἡ καὶ διαλεκτικὸν καλεῖς τὸν λόγον ἑκάστου λαμβάνοντα τῆς οὐσίας ("And by master of dialectic do you also mean one who demands an account of the essence of each thing" [Cornford's trans.]). There is no doubt that Plato means by "each thing" the Forms.

11. *Phaedo* 78c (*The Last Days of Socrates,* tr. with Intro. Hugh Tredennick [Penguin Classics, 1954]): ἴωμεν δή, ἔφη...αὐτὴ ἡ οὐσία ἧς λόγον δίδομεν

Aristotelian Doctrine of Homonyma I

τοῦ εἶναι...

12. *Laws* X 895d (*The Laws of Plato*, trans. A. E. Taylor [London and New York, 1934]): ἓν μὲν οὐσίαν, ἓν δὲ τῆς οὐσίας τὸν λόγον, ἓν δὲ τὸ ὄνομα.

13. *Epistle VII* 342a–b (*The Laws of Plato*, trans. [with critical essays and notes] Glenn R. Morrow [The Liberal Arts Press, 1962]). In his "Introduction," Morrow makes a comment which supports our position. He states that "the list of things which we attempt to know by means of names, definition and image, is strongly suggestive of objects to which the theory of Ideas is applied in the dialogues" (p. 76). I should like to add here that though Plato does not use in the text of the passage quoted the more familiar words *idea, eidos* and *ousia*, he leaves no doubt as to the kinds of objects he intends. The phrase "knowable and truly real being," makes the meaning quite clear. The other passage from the *Laws* X 895, where *ousia, logos* and *onoma* are kept together as basic ingredients in any discussion of reality, corroborates and substantiates our proposed interpretation.

14. Lang, frag. 32.

15. Pp. 58–59, n. 47.

16. P. 57.

17. E. Hambruch, *Logische Regeln der platonischen Schule in der aristotelischen Topic* (Wissenschaftliche Beilage rum Jahresbericht des Askanischen Gymnasiums zu Berlin, 1904), pp. 27-29. Note the Speusippean usage in *Topics* 107b 4 and 17.

18. P. 58, n. 47. It is Speusippus to whom Aristotle refers when he denies that all refutations are παρὰ τὸ διττόν, καθάπερ τινές φασιν. See *Sophistici Elenchi* 177b 7-9. It was E. Poste (see his edition: *Sophistici Elenchi* [text, translation and commentary; London, 1866], p. 151) who made the first, not completely successful, effort to identify the opponent against whom Aristotle argues in *Sophistici Elenchi*, 170b 12-171b 2 as one who divided arguments into two classes πρὸς τοὔνομα and πρὸς τὴν διάνοιαν, the basis, as we have seen, for Speusippus' formulation of *homonyma* and *synonyma*. However, Cherniss corrected Poste's erroneous conclusion that this opponent was Plato by showing why Poste's conclusion fits only Speusippus.

19. According to Philoponus, there had been two different Aristotelian treatises on the same subject and with the same title: *Categories*. It is further reported that they resemble each other in almost every respect, including the introductory chapter. Philoponus quotes the opening sentence of the alternate "edition" which reads as follows: τῶν ὄντων τὰ μὲν ὁμώνυμά ἐστι, τὰ δὲ συνώνυμα. He appeals to this information as evidence to support his defense of the authenticity of the treatise (*In Categ.* 12.34–13.5). See also n. 20 below.

20. Consider, for instance, how the following five different translations leave undecided the question of the exact meaning of the passage: (1) "...the definition (of substance according to name) is different" (O. F. Owen, trans., *The Organon, or Logical Treaties of Aristotle, with the Introduction of Porphyry* [2 vols.; London, 1882]); (2) "...the definition corresponding with the name differs in each case" (E. M. Edghill, trans., *The Works of Aristotle*, ed. W. D. Ross, Vol. I [Oxford, 1928]); (3) "...the definition (or statement of essence) corresponding with the name being different" (H. P. Cooke, trans., *The Organon* [Cambridge, Mass.: Loeb, 1938]); (4) "...the definition given for the name in each case is different" (LeRoy F. Smith, trans., *Aristotle, Categories and Interpretation* [Fresno, Calif.: Academy Guild Press, 1959]); and (5)"...the definition of being which corresponds to the name is different" (J. L. Ackrill, trans., *Aristotle's Categories and De Interpretatione* [Oxford, 1963]).

21. As in L. Minio-Paluello, *Categoriae et Liber de Inter-pretatione*, (Oxford Classical Text Series, 1949, corr. 1956).

22. Boethus claims this version to be the one which Aristotle truly authored. See Simplicius, *In Categ.* 29, 30-31, 1. Comparably, Andronicus, paraphrasing Aristotle, gives the following version: τῶν ἄνευ συμπλοκῆς λεγομένων, ὁμώνυμα μὲν λέγεται ὧν ὄνομα μόνον ταὐτόν, ὁ δὲ λόγος ἕτερος. That Andronicus is taking liberties with the text should be evident from the following: (a) He introduces ἄνευ συμπλοκῆς well in advance of its actual place in our critically established text; doctrinally, there is no reason for such departure from the text since *ta legomena* clearly refers to named things. b) Andronicus incorrectly substitutes his expression *monon tauton* for Aristotle's *koinon*; by doing so he apparently assumes the equivalence of the two expressions, but neglects to discuss the

grounds on which this is permissible.

23. *In Categ.* 21, 18-22.

24. *In Categ.* 30, 3-5. Simplicius also informs us that the expression does not occur in all the copies he had examined and mentions again those of Boethus and Andronicus. It seems difficult to believe that Simplicius, a writer in the sixth century, had actually inspected the personal copies of Boethus and Andronicus. Rather, we must think of editions based on the versions of text which were used by those men in their teaching and writing.

25. Simplicius, *In Categ.* 29, 25.

26. Simplicius reports that Porphyry agreed with a certain Herminus and with "most of the others" who defended the view that *tēs ousias* appeared originally in the text (*In Categ.* 30, 7). Herminus flourished around the time of Adrian and is mentioned as the teacher of Alexander of Aphrodisias.

27. Ammonius' views of this issue present a difficulty, though by no means an unsurmountable one. In his *Commentary on Porphyry's Isagoge*, the word *ousia* is not mentioned in the discussion on *homonyma* and *onta* (84, 6–23). The omission is rather curious, especially in view of the fact that Porphyry is the most ardent defender of V1. However, when we turn to Ammonius' commentary on the *Categories*, we note that he quotes fully the text and includes the expression as integral to the formulation (*In Categ.* 20.21.2).

28. Simplicius who defended the *L of O* reading, argued also against those who deleted it, especially Boethus of Sidon who was, after all, a peripatetic. What is of special interest here is not only that he chides Boethus but also that he argues against the Speusippean approach to homonymy. The argument goes like this: if Speusippus is right, then the distinction between *homonyma* and *synonyma* breaks down on the ground that on that definition all *synonyma* are *homonyma* and vice versa; evidently, Simplicius remarks, Speusippus not only omitted *tēs ousias* but went as far as to reduce the definition to just ὁ δὲ λόγος ἕτερος. If Simplicius' testimony is reliable historical report, it would seem that the definition and theoretical

explanation of *homonyma* were issues of considerable philosophic debate. The fact that Aristotle discusses many aspects of *homonyma* in the *Topics* should be regarded as additional evidence that such was the case.

29. In n. 22, above. However, see *Aristotelis Organon Graece*, ed. (with commentary) Th. Waitz, 2 vols. (Leipzig, 1844-1846); cf. the *scholia* in v. 1, 269-271.

30. *Phys.* 248a 9-17, 249a 4, 248a 11; *Top.* 107b 17; *Met.* 1080a 20, 1018a 6; *Nic. Eth.* 1133a 19.

31. *Top.* A 15, 106a 9ff.

32. Oxford translation. The Greek text reads: οἷον ὄνος τό τε ζῷον καὶ τὸ σκεῦος· ἕτερος γὰρ ὁ κατὰ τοὔνομα λόγος αὐτῶν· τὸ μὲν γὰρ ζῷον ποιόν τι ῥηθήσεται, τὸ δὲ σκεῦος ποιόν τι. ἐὰν δὲ ὑπ' ἄλληλα τὰ γένη ᾖ, οὐκ ἀναγκαῖον ἑτέρους λόγους εἶναι.

33. Compare also the example given in *Nic. Eth.* 2, 1129a 30: ὁμωνύμως καλεῖται ἡ κλεὶς ἥ τε ὑπὸ τὸν αὐχένα τῶν ζῴων καὶ ᾗ τὰς θύρας κλείουσιν.

34. *Cat.* 2a 19-34, *Top.* 130b 25-28, where the *logos* which gives the *ousia* is compared with the *logos* that states the property, the former being parallel to the *L of O* in *Cat.* 1a; hence *L of O* does not refer to the definition of properties; *De Gen. An.* 715a 5 where *L of O* is used in the sense of formal cause and also *De Part. An.* 685b 12-16, *Met.* 1064a 22, 1028a 35, 1018a 10, 1054a 35, where *L of O* is the sense of essence and *to ti ēn einai*.

35. In *Aristotle's Criticism of Plato and the Academy* (op. cit. pp. 178-179, n. 102; the reference is to the following passages: *Top.* 99a 5-8, 1079a–3b 3, 154a 16–20 [cf. 148a 14–22].

ANCIENT INTERPRETATIONS OF ARISTOTLE'S DOCTRINE OF *HOMONYMA*

I

The main purpose of this paper is to offer an exposition and a critical examination of the ancient interpretations of Aristotle's doctrine of *homonyma*.[1] A circumlocution of what Aristotle means by *homonyma* things is given in *Categories*, ch. 1. The ancient interpretations with which we are concerned in this paper are to be found in the extant commentaries on this treatise. Evidently, more commentaries had been written on the *Categories* 1, 1a the vicissitudes of time allowed to survive, but we have only those of the following writers: Porphyrius (c. 233-303), Dexippus (fl. c. 350), Ammonius (fl. c. 485), Philoponus (c. 490-530), Olympiodorus (fl. c. 535), Simplicius (fl. c. 533), Elias (fl. c. 550). One might add here the relevant writings of John Damascene (675-749), Photius (820-891), and Michael Psellus (1018-1079), which are useful paraphrases rather than full commentaries; for that reason the interpretations they support are not discussed in this paper.

The main body of this paper is given to a discussion of the interpretations which the ancient commentators offered and to an analysis of the assumptions which underlie them. It can be stated here in anticipation of what follows that the commentators often attached to Aristotle's meaning of *homonyma* aspects that were quite foreign to his views and that by doing so these commentators were taking extensive liberties with the text at hand. As we hope to show, the commentators brought into their discussions of this particular portion of the *Categories* issues and views that were far more relevant to their own ontologies and logical theories than to Aristotle's doctrines. In order to show how this is the case, we must first give a summary of what we believe our text permits us to say about the meaning of *homonyma*, as given in the opening chapter of the Categories. Suffice it to add at this point that the interpretations of the doctrine of *homonyma* with which we are concerned here are only those that are discussed exclusively in the relevant commentaries on this work.

Textual tradition has preserved two versions, referred to here as V1 and V2, of Aristotle's formulation of *homonyma*. The difference between them is that while V1 preserves the key expression λόγος τῆς οὐσίας, the other, V2, omits it. V1, as established by modern textual criticism, reads:

Ὁμώνυμα λέγεται ὧν ὄνομα μόνον κοινόν, ὁ δὲ κατὰ τοὔνομα λόγος τῆς οὐσίας ἕτερος.

Not only did we defend the inclusion of the expression *logos tēs ousias* (hereafter abbreviated as *L of O*) as indispensable for distinguishing Aristotle's formulation from the one propounded by Speusippus, but we also found it necessary to advance the view that Aristotle used the expression *L of O* in a definitely technical sense. We showed why the deletion of the term *ousia* would make the passage open to misinterpretation, since by omitting it one could argue that Aristotle meant to include in the class of *homonyma* such things as accidental properties and individuals with proper names. We also argued in favor of a view that delimits the meaning of *ousia* to definable substance, i. e., in the sense of secondary substance as species. Textual evidence in favor of this reading was cited from other treatises and the case was further strengthened by arguing that the meaning of the term *logos* in the sense of "definition" left no doubt that the proper application of the term could only refer to *ousia* as essence. The conclusion we drew was that the formulation of *homonyma* in V1 suited perfectly the ontological doctrine put forth in the Categories and also that each term occurring in the total expression was employed in a precise terminological way.

When we turn to the philosophical value of the extant commentaries on the *Categories*, three special problems deserve attention: (1) We must know whether each commentator shows sufficient awareness of the technical terminology in which the doctrine of *homonyma* is couched and hence whether he phrases his interpretation of the doctrine in line with what seems to be the most acceptable reading of the text. (2) Given the way each commentator understands what is meant by *homonyma* things, it is imperative that we identify the implications each particular formulation has for a theory of substance and definition to which the commentators subscribe. (3) Since the miscellaneous materials which the commentators incorporate into their discussions are quite frequently alien to the issues at hand and since their expositions cover grounds not intended by Aristotle's own theory of *homonyma*, we must identify the intellectual affiliations of the commentators and uncover the logical and ontological views they seek to promote through Aristotle's authority.

The ancient commentators failed to appreciate the full technical import of the expression *L of O*. The reasons for this failure seem to be many. One of them is the tendency to over-explicate not merely each of the terms separately, but also the expression as a whole. In examining the non-Aristotelian considerations the commentators introduced in their discussion, we see that the outstanding example is that of taking *logos* to mean both definition and description. Now the latter is clearly an interpolation and is to be found nowhere in the *Categories*. However, by taking such liberties with the meaning of the term *logos*, the commentators were able to change the meaning of the whole expression and to force it to appear nontechnical. As a result, the denotation of the definiendum "*homonyma* things" became so wide as to include anything from accidental properties and first substances to highest genera, including the genera of prediction. By repeatedly emphasizing this broad interpretation of *homonyma*, the commentators turned their backs to the possibility that Aristotle could have intended the term in a limited sense and therefore given the expression L of o a technical meaning. Thus when we leave the commentaries to return to Aristotle's own text, we are hardly surprised to see that there was no plan on his part to discuss all types of *homonyma* things. Apparently Aristotle and the commentators were not doing the same thing.

II

1) *Porphyry's interpretation*: Porphyry begins his discussion by asking questions about the origin and function of *homonyma* and *synonyma*.[2] According to his theory, each thing has name, definition, and description. Now the relations that obtain between things and their names and definitions come under four types: (1) Things may have in common both the name and the definition of what the name signifies; when they do so these things are called *synonyma*. (2) Things may share the name, but if they cannot claim the definition in question, they are classified as *homonyma*. (3) When two things can actually claim a definition as common to both even if they do not have the same name, they are called *polyonyma*. (4) Things which have neither a name nor a definition in common are *heteronyma*. He also mentions a fifth type, *paronyma*, which refers to things whose names are the result of derivation; however, he considers it of little importance. Porphyry explains Aristotle's omission of (3) and (4) on the ground that he had no real use for either.

The next question he raises is addressed to the reason why Aristotle began the treatise with the statement on *homonyma* (61 4ff). It should be noted that the explanation he gives finds no support in the *Categories* and must be regarded as Porphyry's own invention. In any event, Porphyry claims that Aristotle believed that the categories

Aristotelian Doctrine of Homonyma II   103

themselves, when predicated of things, are used homonymously. His explanation is prefaced with the remark that Aristotle taught that being (*to on*) is homonymous.

> ...being is not the common genus of all things, nor, as Aristotle says, are all things of the same genus with respect to one summum genus. Still, let the first ten genera be arranged, as in the *Categories*, as ten first principles and even if a person should call all things beings, yet he will call them, as he says, equivocally, but not synonymously, for if being were the one common genus of all things, all things would be synonymously styled beings, but the first principles being ten, the community is in name only, yet not in the definition also belonging to the name: there are then ten most generic genera.[3]

Hence, Porphyry argues, Aristotle should have begun with the notion of homonymy rather than *homonyma* things.

Porphyry's explanation is interesting and deserves notice. Beginning with line 13, he proceeds to explain his views which may be summarized as follows: Since there is a distinction between homonymy as a notion (*phōnē*) and things (*pragmata*) which are *homonyma*, we cannot really talk about homonymy unless the claim can be made that we already know that things are ordered in a variety of ways and that all do not partake in the same definition. The cause of homonymy, then, lies in the fact that things are found to be different and that they are such that do not share the same name. Without this sort of knowledge, Porphyry remarks, we cannot conceive of homonymy.[4] He takes *logos* in the sense of definition (*horistikos*), and justifies the inclusion of *L of O* by means of an argument. The term *logos*, he claims, has many meanings (definition, oral speech, reckoning, seminal reason, etc.), and if we fail to make *ousia* part of the expression, the real meaning of *logos*, i.e., in the sense of definition, becomes obscure (64 28-65 11).

In a preceding comment on the inadmissibility of the elliptical variant *logos heteros*, vis-a-vis that of *kata tounoma logos... heteros*, he correctly defends the fuller version (contra Speusippus?) by pointing out that the accuracy of meaning demands it be made clear here that it is not the name which is the referent, but something else in conjunction with the name.[5] What he means is that only the fuller version expresses Aristotle's point: the denotation of a name used and the denotation of the definition of the substance named must be the same. Porphyry offers the following examples of the two definitions of the substance denoted by the name "man":

1) ἄνθρωπος ζῷον λογικὸν θνητόν.
2) ἄνθρωπος οὐσία ἔμψυχος αἰσθητική.

The problem now becomes one of determining whether the two definitions have the same denotation. Since definition 2 denotes not only men but also other things such as oxen and the like, the equivalence is canceled, and one of the two definitions is declared too wide.[6]

The first sign of Porphyry's deviation from Aristotle's meaning appears with the listing of the diverse uses of *logos*. It is obvious that some of them are totally foreign to Aristotle. But the initial suspicion we form that Porphyry is about to misinterpret the text is eventually confirmed when he proceeds to give the example which illustrates his discussion of the logic of homonymy. The point is that theory and example are incompatible. The illustration he mentions is two human beings with the same name: Ajax (son of Telamon) and Ajax (son of Oileus). The definition of "man" applies to both, and though they have the same (proper) name they are not the same entities. Still the definition of the substance underlying the name 'man' is true for both Ajaxes. Next Porphyry tells us that the only way we can logically differentiate between the two is by resorting to different descriptions. By advocating this solution Porphyry abandons the strict approach to *homonyma* and in effect widens the term to denote also such things as the homonymous accidental properties. The terminology is shifted to accommodate a very special case: homonymous individuals. I f our thesis is correct, it follows that Aristotle's doctrine was not intended to cover homonymy due to proper names. If so, Porphyry is illicitly extending the initial use of the theory. The departure is so radical that it permits the term *homonyma* to refer to named species as well as individuals with proper names. Once the two views, Aristotle's and Porphyry's, are allowed to come under the formulation of *homonyma* as stated in the *Categories*, that formulation becomes at once imprecise and inconsistent; imprecise, on the ground that L of O is no longer a technical expression, and inconsistent because the term *logos*, in the sense of definition, is now taken to apply to both definable and non-definable things.

Porphyry's special *scholium* on L of O is quite revealing. He admits that in view of the many uses of *logos* the expression *tēs ousias* is needed in order to make clear that it is the defining sense of *logos* that concerns Aristotle (64 28-11). Thus, he infers, the defining *logos* (*horistikos*) which refers to the name and *logos* which indicates substance (*ousias dēlōtikos*) are the same thing, except in the case of *homonyma* things where the definition of substance must be different in each case. Two critical reservations must be made at this point. (1) Porphyry is simply assuming that Aristotle had in mind the problem of the homonymy of the term *logos* and that *ousia* was made part of the expression primarily to avoid this particular ambiguity. Aside from the obvious anachronism about the Stoic seminal reason as one of the senses of *logos*, the list of meanings is too elementary if not irrelevant to the discussion. As a result, the explication appears contrived, and the conclusions drawn far from acceptable. (2) Though Porphyry is correct in taking *logos* to mean definition, he is far from clear as to the meaning of pragmata. Strict Aristotelian doctrine would demand identification of pragmata with definable species. However, Porphyry shows no sign of having detected here that a real ontological issue arises when the emphasis is shifted from species to individuals, an issue which touches on the very philosophical framework of syllogistic thinking. As we said in the previous section, the referents to *homonyma* and *synonyma* are substances which are both definable and predicable; they are the things which normally serve as terms in the premises of the syllogism.

Just the same, confident that he has settled the problem of the meaning of *homonyma*, he proceeds next to consider the issue of their tropes. His list of tropes (65 12ff) has many merits to it, but again it turns out that it is geared to the discussion on the homonymy which is due to proper names. He lists two main types:[7] *homonyma* by accident (*apo tychēs*), and *homonyma* by intention (*apo dianoias*). The latter is further divided into four classes: from (1) similarity, (2) analogy, (3) unity to multiplicity, (4) multiplicity to unity. Once again, the examples used to illustrate *homonyma* by accident leave no doubt that he was thinking of *homonyma* pragmata not in terms of Aristotelian secondary substances but in the light of the paradigmatic case of individuals with proper names.[8] What he failed to realize here is that his proposed tropes, though theoretically interesting, were explained with the aid of illustrations that could not be accommodated within the strict Aristotelian context of *L of O*, which, as Porphyry himself admits, requires that *logos* be taken in the sense of definition.

Porphyry's illustrations of each type within the trope of intentional *homonyma* are particularly suited to his classifications. The type of intentional trope which is of special interest to Porphyry is that from similarity. According to his interpretation, Aristotle's own examples mentioned in *Categories*, 1a, are based on the trope from similarity (66 22-8). Man and painting of man are *homonyma* by virtue of the fact that both are called "living," except that the painting of man is called so from similarity. This is also reflected in the language in which Porphyry couched the definitions of these *homonyma* things: (a) ἄνθρωπος, οὐσία ἔμψυχος αἰσθητική (human being, *ousia* ensouled, sensible), (b) γεγραμμένον, ὁμοίωμα οὐσίας αἰσθητικῆς (drawing, likeness of sensible *ousia*). It is the kind of examples he offers that leads us to conclude that Porphyry did not suspect he was actually taking liberties with the text before him and that he was expressing views that violated the intent of the Aristotelian doctrine. It seems really strange that he did not observe that his and Aristotle's paradigms were at odds, nor for that reason did any of the subsequent commentators. They all repeated Porphyry's error. Throughout the history of the ancient commentary practice, the source of misinterpretation remained unidentified and the error was never removed, let alone suspected.

2) *Dexippus' interpretation*:[9] He prefaces his comments on *homonyma* with a discussion on what can be legitimately considered a "category," and proposes that the following sorts of expressions be disqualified: (1) metaphors, (2) tropes, e.g., necessity, possibility, subsistence, and (3) modifiers, e.g., all, none, no one in particular, etc. The criterion he employs for rejecting such expressions is that the things they stand for have no determinate nature of their own (12 20-25).[10] Next he proceeds to show why certain principles which cannot be subsumed under any of the categories are nevertheless highly relevant to categorical theory; since they have as many uses as there are categories, such principles are cases of homonymy.[11] The third problem he considers before presenting his interpretation of *homonyma* concerns is the reason why Aristotle chose to discuss *homonyma*, *synonyma*, and *paronyma* rather than proceed directly with the theory of categories. In giving an answer to this question he allows the discussion to sidetrack to what turns out to be an interesting bit of linguistic theory.

He remarks that things and names of things, considered as quantitative collections, are not commensurable. In some cases we have more words for the same thing, whereas in others we have more things than names available for them. Hence in considering any given simple or non-composite word, it is necessary to determine under which of the categories it should be classified. It is on account of this peculiar relationship between words and things that, according to Dexippus, Aristotle prefaced his treatise with a brief analysis on *homonyma* and *synonyma*. Unfortunately Dexippus does not discuss the issue in any detail. Instead he returns to his previous point and offers the peculiar hypothesis that the real reason Aristotle opened the *Categories* with a formulation of the nature of *homonyma* is because the ten categories are themselves instances of *homonyma* (17 25-29). His point is that each category is predicated synonymously of the species subsumed under it, and that the categories, if taken absolutely, are used homonymously. Ignoring for a moment Dexippus' numerous irrelevancies, we must pause to mention that, like Porphyry, he also gives serious attention to *homonyma* in the context of individual substances with the same proper name. This is readily seen in his paradigm of the two Ajaxes. Notwithstanding his uncritical adoption of Porphyry's interpretation, it should be noted that Dexippus was quicker in accepting the implications of that approach for the total widening of the denotation of *homonyma* pragmata. Thus Dexippus promptly included the accidental properties. Evidently this is in agreement with the theory that homonymy is obtainable in all the categories. However what is not clear from his discussion is the extent to which he was aware of the liberties he was taking with the text.

Though Dexippus defends the reading *L of O*, he does not hesitate to interfere with the Aristotelian way of phrasing the nature of *homonyma*. He does so when he asks why it is that Aristotle did not say ὁ δὲ κατὰ τοὔνομα ὅρος ὁ αὐτός. No doubt, he knows that *logos* is a wider term than *horos*. According to his explanation, Aristotle wrote *logos tēs ousias* rather than *horos tēs ousias* simply because not all things are signified through definitions: some are signified only through descriptions (20 28-31). The explanation assumes that Aristotle was actually interested in all types of *homonyma*. Though it has an ingenious side to it, the explanation is not really original. It simply states the Porphyrian thesis in a fresh way. Since he knows that individuals are undefinable and, like Porphyry, insists on including them in *ousia*, the only way to meet the difficulty which the term '*horos*' poses is by (1) saying that Aristotle never meant to use '*horos*', and (2) arguing that *logos* means both definition (*horos*) and description (*hypographē*) and that Aristotle intended *logos* in this inclusive way. What is simply amazing about all this is that the term *hypographē*, description, is to be found nowhere in the *Categories*. Just the same, he criticizes Aristotle for phrasing elliptically, i.e., not saying *hypographē tōn homonymōn*. His argument is that since Aristotle knew that homonymy obtains in the case of genera as well as in the other categories, he should not have said "*logos tēs ousias*."

He suggests that a good way out of this problem would be a textual reading like that of Boethus and Andronicus which omits *tēs ousias*. But he admits that this will not really do for a number of reasons, chiefly because the term *logos* is itself a homonymous expression and has different senses. It is at this point that Dexippus states his main reason for defending the acceptability of *L of O*: it is the only adequate way of showing that all things can be *homonyma*, for when we speak of *logos* we think of beings, such as substances and genera, and when we speak of *ousia* we know we can signify through this term individuals and their accidents (21 11-29). All that can be said about the argument is that while it is a good attempt to defend VI, it fails completely as interpretation to recapture Aristotle's thought.

3) *Ammonius' interpretation*: Ammonius is deeply indebted to Porphyry for his views on the subject. It is also evident that he was familiar with Dexippus' commentary. He has worked out, on his own, two formulations of *homonyma*, neither of which compares favorably to Aristotle's for brevity or precision.[12] Like his predecessors he defends the reading *L of O*, and offers extensive

comments on each of these key terms: (1) He contends that Aristotle used *logos* and not *horismos* because he knew that all things cannot be defined, as for instance in the case of the highest genera (20 15-16). Since individuals are not exempted from being *homonyma* and are not capable of being defined but only described, Aristotle had to use the term *logos* in order to cover all cases. The argument is a familiar one. It assumes that Aristotle intended to include in his theory homonymous individuals, and also that *logos* meant for Aristotle both definition and description. (2) In his special comment on *ousia*, he argues for its textual adoption in a way that pushes Dexippus' position a step further but in the wrong direction. First, he says, we must ask whether homonymy applies to accidental properties. Evidently, such is the case, for we do say "sharp taste" and "sharp knife." This being so and because of the fact that accidents subsist in beings, Aristotle must have used the term *ousia* to show that he meant to cover both substances and their accidents under the denotation of *homonyma*. The surprising element in Ammonius' argument is the facility with which he abuses the meaning of *ousia* and ignores its restricted categorical sense.[13] In effect he mistakes *ousia* for *onta*. It is clear that Ammonius is convinced that in this context Aristotle did not mean *ousia* in the sense in which it is contrasted to accidents (συμβεβηκότα), but rather in the wider sense that would permit us to include particular existents, that is, primary *ousiai*. It follows from this, his argument goes, that Aristotle's view of *homonyma* must be understood as designed to cover the accidental properties as well. If Aristotle did not mean his theory to cover that case, he would have said φύσεως ἑκάστου καθ' ἓν ὑφέστηκεν... rather than *tēs ousias*. Ammonius' speculations receive no support from the text. We are dealing here with a strained interpretation, but one that enables Ammonius to take *logos* to mean *hypographē*, description, and *ousia* to stand for accidental properties as well.

However when Ammonius is not speculating or following another commentator, he shows good judgment. For instance, despite the fact that he took *logos* to mean both definition and description in his discussion on *Categories* 1a 4, he equates it exclusively with definition. *Logos* means *horismos*. He interprets the passage correctly and suggests that *homonyma* things refers to species.

Our discussion on Ammonius could have ended on this happy note if it were not for the fact that his treatment of *homonyma* appears in two different works. his commentary on the *Categories* and in his treatise *On Porphyry's Introduction*. Our account would have been pronouncedly incomplete without at least some elementary effort to correlate what is said in these two works. The respective treatments on *homonyma* are connected by means of an extensive discussion on the relationship between definition and description. We have already seen what he said in the commentary on the *Categories*. Before turning to his analysis of Porphyry's Isagoge, we must point out that we are confronted here with a special difficulty, since we are dealing with a commentary on another highly interpretive commentary. For this reason it is often a most cumbersome task to decide whose views it is that Ammonius is expounding. However, the fact that he is exploring the relationship between definition and description as two uses of *logos* is sufficient to alert us that he is working with a Porphyrian issue. The key to his understanding of Aristotle's views on this matter lies in what he has to say on definition. He begins by explaining that things are signified in two ways: name and definition (54 5ff).[14] Discourse which is indicative of things (*logos sēmantikos*) is of two kinds: with reference to what things are according to essence and with reference to accidental properties. The former gives us the definition, the latter the description. However, he argues, accidents accompany the essential nature, say, of man, even if they do not complement the essence. Next he explains what description is. It is *hypographē*, a sort of drawing, an imitation of likeness which succeeds in signifying something without articulating it with precision. The analogy he uses is interesting. Definition is to description what life-like painting is to drawing.

So far he has said nothing to justify the relevance of the discussion on description to Aristotle's text. What controls the analysis is Porphyry's insistence that description is part of the meaning of *logos*. One suspects here that Ammonius is accommodating Aristotle to Porphyry's theories rather than the reverse. He quotes Porphyry's dictum to the effect that "Things we cannot signify through definition we like to indicate through description" (55 12-13). No sooner do we ask what are the things to which Porphyry's dictum refers than we discover that included in the class of such "undefinables" are, next to the accidental properties, the highest genera. Hence Ammonius agrees with Porphyry, they are accessible only through description. But the point of real interest is that he explains the undefinability of highest genera on the familiar grounds that there is no genus higher to them and that they are cases of *homonyma* (56 1). It is reasonable to conclude that Ammonius did not see that the position which he took in his *In Porph. Isag.* contradicted what he said in the *In Categ.* In the *Isagoge* he asserted the undefinability of all *homonyma*, and this, he insisted, holds true of Aristotle's own categorical theory where it deals with *homonyma*. If so, then he should have said that *logos*, since it refers to *homonyma pragmata*, can mean only description. In other words, Ammonius commits a contradiction when, on the one hand, he asserts the undefinability of all *homonyma* and, on the other, that *logos* in the context of the *Categories* can mean both description and definition.

The syllogism is clear: Since all *homonyma* are undefinable, and highest genera are *homonyma*, all such genera are undefinable.[15] But the significant thing here is that the undefinability of all *homonyma* was never defended by Aristotle. The only alternative is to conclude that Ammonius is expounding on Porphyry's doctrines. If his thesis claims to cover Aristotle's view on *homonyma* as well, the consequence is that it degenerates into a contradictory explanation of two incompatible theories. It is unfortunate that Ammonius neglected to state the difference between Porphyry's and Aristotle's respective approaches to *homonyma*. There are other special features in Ammonius' theory of description, but they cannot be included in this study. Had this been done we could have shown how Ammonius' Neoplantonic idealism prevented him from cutting through the maze of Porphyry's philosophical assumptions to determine for himself whether Aristotle's text permitted the expansion of the meaning of *homonyma* to suit Porphyry's non-Aristotelian ontology.

4) *Philoponus' interpretation:* He opens his discussion on *homonyma* with a pious bit of theological epistemology. Had we been blessed, he remarks, with the being only naked souls have and were free from the bondage of our bodies, we would be able to signify everything by means of concepts only. However, bodies act like clouds, cover the intelligible and intervene with our seeing them directly. This is the reason why we need names (*In Categ.* 14 1ff.). Since it is not given to us to signify through concepts, we enlist the help of names and definitions (*horismoi*). Next he proceeds to give a brief account of *homonyma, synonyma, polyonyma,* and *heteronyma* and states that he means by *homonyma* things which "share the name but differ according to the definition." He makes an effort to explain why Aristotle did not refer to all four kinds of signified things. The answer he gives is that Aristotle "potentially" spoke of the other two as well, because to know a *homonymon*, for instance, is to know potentially its opposite, the *polyonymon* (14 24ff.). He also has an answer to the much discussed question why Aristotle decided to begin this work with a statement on *homonyma*. These things, he informs us, are actually the simplest sort, for they share one aspect only—the name; therefore, they are by nature (*physei*) prior to the *synonyma*. In fact, being (*to on*) is predicated of the categories homonymously, not synonymously.

Philoponus, following the example of the preceding commentators, is asking questions for which he has pat answers. The explanations he provides are at once debatable and irrelevant. Philoponus' explanation is not the only one that can be given to the last question, and more significantly, it is not basically related to the logical context of Aristotle's formulation of *homonyma*. One can not escape forming the impression that Philoponus is misled into believing that Aristotle is referring indiscriminately to all instances of *homonyma*, including "being" as a *homonymōs legomenon*. Be that as it may, Philoponus burdens his discussion with a number of trivial themes (15 11ff.), only to tell what the real meaning of the opening lines is:

> Let it be understood that Aristotle tells us directly in the opening statement what the purpose of the book is. He says '*homonyma legetai*'... What he means by '*homonyma*' is things, and by '*legetai*,' significant sounds (*phōnai*). We know things with the aid of conceptual meanings (*noēmata*).[16]

That Philoponus is straining the intent of the passage is evident from his insistence upon making the homonymy of a concept, including the concept of homonymy, a foremost and necessary part of the formulation of *homonyma pragmata*. If we keep in mind that it is this interest that dominates his itemized kind of commentary, we are in a better position to understand why he takes special pain to explicate *homonymon* as being itself a homonymous expression. The point is that Philoponus purports to alert his reader to the fact that the term '*homonymon*' has many senses. He adopts Porphyry's two main tropes of *homonyma* and introduces certain minor changes in the types of intentional *homonyma*. Actually, all he does is to replace Porphyry's class of *homonyma* from similarity with two sub-classes, each related to a different underlying motive: intention to commemorate, viz., a father who names his son after himself, and intention to indicate expectation, viz., a man who names his son after Plato.[17]

Aristotelian Doctrine of Homonyma II

More pertinent to our discussion is his comment on "legetai." His interpretation is that the subject of the verb is *pragmata*. The point is that Aristotle is actually referring to things, not concepts. Aside from the problem Philoponus has in tying this pointed explication to his previous tangential remarks on homonymy in general, he falls into the serious and repeated error of offering the Ajax paradigm (17 26ff.), and to make matters worse, he tries to support it through a remarkable showpiece of irrelevant erudition: a line from Plato's *Phaedrus*.[18] Since most of the comments on the itemized textual expressions are rather trivial, it is best that we give some attention to what is basic to our theme: his understanding of *pragmata*. Once again, the paradigm is individuals with the same proper name. The discussion is tied to the reasons he gives for preserving in the text the expression *kata tounoma*. The reading is justified, he thinks, because certain things which are *homonyma* with regard to one name are not so with regard to another name. Since two things may have more than one name in common, such things may turn out to be now *homonyma*, now *synonyma*. Hence it should be plain, Philoponus argues, that Aristotle specifically meant to alert us to the need for restricting the definition called for only to that common name by virtue of which the things are *homonyma* and not any other. It would be tedious to give here the details of his analysis of the example of the two Ajaxes. What matters really is the nature of the paradigm. Aside from his questionable interpretation of the intent of the aforementioned part of the total passage, there is the further issue of the paradigm. It is here where Philoponus misunderstands the meaning of the passage. What strikes the reader is Philoponus' reluctance to as much as mention Aristotle's own examples. Instead he follows the previous commentators and supplies the illicit example of individuals with the same proper name. We have already seen what consequences follow from this sort of interpretation of *pragmata*. What we should look for next is the inconsistent view

Philoponus is inadvertently forced to adopt. This matter hinges on his understanding of *logos*.

Like the other commentators, Philoponus' answer is part of his broader treatment of *L of O*. He defends the expression but interprets it as follows. Aristotle said *logos* and not *horismos* in order to cover cases of *homonyma* which are beyond proper definitions (19 21ff.). He repeats the familiar theory of descriptions as the only avenue to signification of *summa genera* and accidental properties. In short, *logos* means here definition and description of substance. He argues that since Aristotle used "substance" to mean something self-existent, in contrast to accidents, and also any "absolutely existing entity," the accidents are thereby part the meaning of *ousia* in the passage. The surprising aspect of his discussion comes with his comment on *Cat.* 1a 4, for he gives there the impression he has forgotten what was already said about *logos*, and unaware of the inconsistency into which he is about to fall, he declares that Aristotle is asking in this passage for the definition of the species. In this respect he is doing nothing substantially different from what Ammonius did before him. What is of real interest, however, is the fact that he did not perceive the inconsistency in his interpretation, an inconsistency which would have been easier for him to detect, since it did not originate with him. For all these reasons, Philoponus' commentary on the problem of *homonyma* is pronouncedly inferior to that of Ammonius.

5) *Olympiodorus' interpretation:* What he says on the subject is not radically different from any previous treatment of *homonyma*, but his commentary is interesting as a variant misinterpretation. He also defends the reading of *L of O* and comparably takes *logos* to mean both definition and description. In a general introductory comment (26 5ff.), he tells us that *homonyma* arise from the fact that each thing is at once one and many; as unity it has a name, as plurality it is signified through *logos*, which is of two kinds. By combining name and *logos*, we arrive at four classes of things: *homonyma, synonyma,*

heteronyma, polyonyma. His treatment of *homonyma* presents no novel features, and the illustrations are the standard ones of the two Ajaxes (27 10-20). What is of particular interest is the facility with which he ignores his own terminology. For instance, after mentioning his example of the two Ajaxes as cases of *homonyma*, he does not hesitate to use the term definition (*horismos*), despite the fact that these are individuals. He seems convinced that he is actually giving definitions when he says, e.g., Ajax, son of Telamon: "from Salamis, who fought a duel with Hector and committed suicide." For his answer to why Aristotle treated only *homonyma* and *synonyma* but began with the former, he borrows heavily from Philoponus (27 25ff.). His main points are that the categories are the most inclusive genera (*genikōtata*), that the species which come under them are all synonyma, and that "being" is predicated homonymously of all the categories. There are two sorts of confusion in this portion of Olympiodorus' commentary: (1) While emphasizing the synonymous character of the kinds of things subsumed under each category, he loses sight of the real differences between the sub-categorical sets. Olympiodorus the grammarian has evidently misled the ontologist. (2) Like the others he also assumes that Aristotle's starting point and main concern of the chapter is "being" as *pollachōs legomenon*. The reason, he says, Aristotle begins with the *homonyma* is because they are the simplest things, meaning that they have only one thing in common, unlike the *synonyma* which have two. This, he argues, is as it should be, for the simple must always precede the complex. Furthermore it just so happens that the most general thing is itself a *homonymon*: "I speak here of *to on*..., [hence] the theory of *homonyma* must have priority."[19]

Beginning with 31 5, Olympiodorus offers a general treatment of the Aristotelian formulation as a whole. What he says there presents an aspect of special interest. His first question is whether the formulation contains superfluous expressions, especially in view of Aristotle's love for brevity. He draws attention to the importance of each word for the sake of clarity (*saphēneias heneka*), and also to the fact that Aristotle means to be technical: ὡς τεχνικὸς ᾿Αριστοτέλης τοῦτο πεποίηκεν (31 15). Olympiodorus' justification of his claim is not without disappointments. He says that the real reason why Aristotle did not confine his definiens to ὧν ὄνομα μόνον κοινόν was to prevent us from attributing to him the view that all *homonyma* are also in some sense non-*homonyma* and all *synonyma*, non-*synonyma*. Consider how Plato and Alcibiades, not being *synonyma,* become so when "man" is predicated of both. Again, if Aristotle had limited his formulation only to "things whose definition is different," then it would be possible to show that it permits us to say absurd things. Consider, e.g., the following: Since genera are predicated synonymously of subordinate species, and since we can give two distinctive accounts of the same individual, say Socrates — (1) "Socrates animal logical and mortal," (2) "Socrates bald-headed, philosopher with a protruding belly" — it would turn out that by virtue of the first account Socrates and Alcibiades are *synonymous* and by force of the second *homonymous.*

The intriguing thing about all this is that Olympiodorus should call Aristotle's formulation systematic and technical for reasons so foreign to Aristotle's logic and theory of definition. It did not occur to Olympiodorus that Aristotle perhaps did not mean to include as part of his denotation of *homonyma* the commentators' individuals and their accidental properties. Furthermore it is evident that Olympiodorus did not see that it was only his loose talking about *ousia* that permitted an indiscriminate passing back and forth from *logos* as definition to *logos* as description. He is simply committing an error typical of the rest of the commentators. He is on better grounds when he argues in favor of keeping the *tēs ousias* part in the expression. Without it, he points out, Aristotle would have compromised precision, and the reader would not have been able to say whether the passage is about things or words. Thus in order to avoid any misunderstanding Aristotle distinguishes between words

Aristotelian Doctrine of Homonyma II

and their definitions, on the one hand, and things signified by words and the definitions of such substantive things, on the other (32 2ff.).

Olympiodorus' point is well taken but for one item: his implication that Aristotle is talking about all things in general, for to say so is to cancel the possibility that Aristotle's formulation has a technical side to it. But to return to Philoponus' defense of *L of O*, we must admit that it is subtle and ingenious but brings to the foreground issues which, even if not irrelevant to the broader aspects of the problem, cannot be shown to have figured originally in Aristotle's discussion. Finally it must be recognized that his comment on *Categories*, 1a 4, indicates that for once he understood correctly the intent of the formulation (37 16-30). Suddenly in this comment all the grammatical trivia, the preoccupation with individuals, proper names, accidental properties, theory of description, and other such notions withdraw to make room for a pointed answer to the real problem. He responds to Aristotle's own illustrations and offers appropriate essential definitions for the kinds of things that are *homonyma*. Correct though he is on this point, it cannot be said that his approach, when seen as a whole, is either unaffected by misconceptions or free from non-Aristotelian presuppositions.

6) *Simplicius' interpretation*: Simplicius never doubts the usefulness of the discussion on *homonyma*. He quotes from Iamblichus and Plato's *Euthydemus* to show the seriousness of the subject (*In Categ.* 22 1-9). Plato, according to Simplicius, had to deal with ambiguity which is due to the lack of proper distinctions in the use of names (22 9-13). The important thing is that Simplicius depends rather heavily on Iamblichus' lost commentary (*In Categ.* Proemiun, 2 10f.) and also refers to Porphyry's work which had already exerted considerable influence on Iamblichus. Simplicius credits Iamblichus for being the first to observe that *to katēgorein* is homonymously predicated of the ten categories and that they have the name "category" in common only as a homonymously predicated

name. Iamblichus is further reported to have taught that it was only proper for Aristotle to open the *Categories* with a brief discussion on the nature of *homonyma*. Simplicius is also eager to inform us that there were certain commentators, like Nicostratus and his followers, who had expressed serious reservations about the relevance of the first chapter of the *Categories* to the main doctrine presented in this treatise.[20]

Simplicius opens his valuable and in many ways highly informative commentary with a remark on the importance of making appropriate distinctions that enable us to classify things signified by words under the right category. Since it is often the case that two different things may share the same signifying word, we need criteria to distinguish one thing from another and to focus attention to the kinds of words that give rise to ambiguity (*In Categ.* 21 1-10). He observes that if each thing had only one name, then it would come under only one category. But had this been the case, there would have to be as many categories as there are things. However, we know that one and the same name is frequently used to signify a number of substantively different things. Hence the need arises for categorical classifications. He mentions as an example the name "animal" and points out how it is used to signify a man and a horse, or again, Socrates and a painting of Socrates. The manner in which Simplicius discusses the examples is quite significant. He prefers to start with homonymously predicated names rather than *homonyma pragmata*. Thus since man and horse partake in the substance of animal, the substance is predicated synonymously, and the two things are brought under the same category. But since Socrates and his portrait do not partake of the same substance, Socrates must come under the category of *ousia*, whereas his portrait under that of quality. In order to account for such cases, Simplicius insists, Aristotle found it necessary to begin his treatise with *homonyma*.

Three things must be pointed out here: First, the readiness with which he substitutes his own examples of individual substances for

Aristotle's specific ones. Second, his interesting speculation about *homonyma* as the key to categorical ambiguity, and how this was considered by Aristotle an item of priority. Third, his diagnostic treatment of the categorical identity of the two *homonyma*, particularly his prompt classification of the portrait of Socrates under the category of quality, despite the fact that Aristotle's text does not permit such inferences. Evidently by placing the portrait example under quality, Simplicius gives the impression that he is presupposing that Aristotle is using *homonyma* in the broadest sense — hence non-technically — and *ousia* in a very loose sense to mean anything from substance to accidental properties. It is not certain whether Simplicius would have openly endorsed these implications. Regardless of what his reaction would have been, the point is that his treatment of the subject allows such inferences.

When Simplicius turns to examine "the nature of *homonyma*" (22 14ff.), he repeats the well known views of his predecessors how each thing can be signified through either name or *logos*, and how the latter means either definition or description. Since names in their symbolic capacity can symbolize substantially different things for which different *logoi* can be given, and since things which are essentially the same can have a variety of names, we arrive at five types of things; Aristotle, however, treated only three: *homonyma, synonyma, paronyma*. The other two, *polyonyma* and *heteronyma*, were omitted for two reasons: (1) knowledge of them is easily attained as opposites of the first two types; and (2) Aristotle actually had in mind the preparation for speech-making (*lektika*), rather than an inventory of real things. In offering the second explanation, Simplicius admits he is following Syrianus. His endorsement of that position is intimately related to a more basic issue. He tells us that he agrees with Iamblichus who taught that Aristotle opened the *Categories* with the *homonyma*, not only because these are the simplest of expressions, but primarily because the expression "category" is homonymously predicated of the categories (23 25-24

5). One begins to suspect here that the Neoplatonic concern for the stratification of species and genera, with the highest genera at the top, is at the back of Simplicius' explanation. What seems also to be true is his interest in pointing out that Aristotle did not assign any reality to the expression "category" or to "being." By doing so, Simplicius, like Iamblichus from whom he derives this approach, is able to contrast Aristotle's ontology from the Neoplatonic theory of Being.

Faithful to the tradition he follows, Simplicius interprets *L of O* not in the strict sense of definition of *ousia*. He speculates that Aristotle purposely used the term *logos*, a broader term, to include in his formulation both the summa genera and the individuals. Only by means of description can we render the property of some substance (29 16-24). We have already seen how this has become the standard treatment of *L of O*; hence it would only surprise us to read in Simplicius' account something different on the subject. But in view of his unusual erudition and familiarity with the *Categories*, we wonder why it never occurred to him to peruse the text merely for the sake of discovering the passages to which he could have appealed for his support of the interpolated meaning of *logos* as description. Nor did he realize that in order to accommodate this meaning, he was simply following the other commentators when he supplied the very examples which alone could make *logos*, in the sense of description, applicable to this non-Aristotelian situation. True, Simplicius defends the reading *L of O*, but he does so for reasons of his own. He appeals to such authorities as Porphyry, Herminus, and "the majority of scholars," but instead of arguing on his own he quotes Porphyry's full approval.[21]

Even more disappointing is the comment on an *aporia* that was raised by Nicostratus and Atticus and has to do with the claim that all *synonyma* are *homonyma*, and vice versa. Consider, for instance, the fact that there is a sense in which we can say that all *homonyma* have in common the name by virtue of which they are *homonyma*, and the definition of the homonymous name. Thus, they are *homonyma* in that sense. But in so far as they are essentially different things, they are also *synonyma*. Simplicius informs us that Porphyry resolved the difficulty by pointing out that there is nothing paradoxical about things being *synonyma* in some context and *homonyma* in another. Against this background, conspicuously unrelated to Aristotle's major theme, Simplicius proceeds to discuss Porphyry's answer by using the two Ajaxes example. Even later in the next comment, where the opportunity presents itself to focus attention on Aristotle's own examples and identify them correctly, as Ammonius and Olympiodorus at least were able to do, he forgoes it in favor of rehashing such commonplaces of the tropes of *homonyma*. All he is able to offer there is to explain why he thinks the Aristotelian examples come under the class of "intended" *homonyma* due to similarity (31 22-32). Simplicius is not even original when he misinterprets Aristotle. Aside from depending blindly on Porphyry and repeating characteristic Neoplatonic misrepresentations of Aristotle's views, he shows no signs whatever of having suspected the extent to which the doctrine of *homonyma* was strained to suit the commentators' own intellectual loyalties.

7) *Elias' interpretation:* There is hardly anything in Elias' treatment of *homonyma* that has not been said by one of the previous commentators. He shares most of their misconceptions about Aristotle and repeats the same standard errors. Like the others, he defends the reading *L of O* and assumes that *logos* means both definition and description. He begins his commentary by saying why he thinks Aristotle was right in distinguishing between *homonyma* and *synonyma*. He argues against certain unnamed thinkers who claimed that all cases of *homonyma* are reducible to *synonyma*. He appears familiar with Simplicius' work and echoes the new emphasis this old Porphyrian problem was given by Simplicius. In fact he offers two arguments against the "reductionists," but they present little philosophical interest and have nothing to do with Aristotle's

logical views. More interesting is the way in which he understands the *Categories*. He writes:

> Since the main objective is to discuss the categories, and since *homonyma* is predicated of them, whereas each category is predicated synonymously of the species which come under it in the manner of the genus,...for these reasons Aristotle begins his treatise with the doctrine of *homonyma* and *synonyma*. If he gives priority to the former, this is because unity precedes duality" (*In Categ.* 135 3-7).

His comments abound in speculations of the sort. His is a pat explanation, typically Neoplatonic and altogether unoriginal. He also ignores Aristotle's examples of *homonyma* and replaces them with the celebrated ones of the two Ajaxes. But instead of discussing any further the repetitious character of his misinterpretation, we may conclude this account with a note on Elias' original inconsistency.

Elsewhere, viz., in his *In Porphyrii Isagogen* (56 11-14 and 4 5-11), he explains in the familiar cliches the difference between definition and description: the former is done with reference to substance, the latter to accidental properties, and is therefore inferior to definition. His discussion of the example of the two Ajaxes as instances of homonymous substances is peculiar, to say the least. He is presumably talking about individual substances, knows that in such cases we cannot have definitions, yet uses the terms description and definition interchangeably as if there were no problem at all (138 19-139 6). The same careless use of terminology we find in his comment on Aristotle's examples. He has just admitted that *logos* in Aristotle's text means definition and yet writes the following:

> The real man is living substance endowed with sensation whereas the portrayed man is not substance but *symbebēkos*, not living but lifeless, not sensing but lacking in such faculty; the latter is called

'alive' in the sense of being a representation of a living and sensing substance (139 25-28).

Why the portrait is not a substance but an accidental thing and why he prefers to ignore Aristotle's text which leaves no doubt that only definitions should be given for both instances of *homonyma* mentioned, Elias' commentary offers no explanation. The inconsistency remained unnoticed.

III

When we view in retrospect the tradition of Aristotle's interpreters, starting from Elias and going back to the earlier commentators, certain major themes begin to stand out even more pronounced than when we look at these thinkers in the normal chronological order. It seems that these commentators honestly believed they were discussing and logically extending Aristotelian doctrines even after they had seriously departed from Aristotle's thoughts and had in essence abandoned some of his principal views. Whether these thinkers could have developed their philosophies without the use of the method of expounding through commentaries on major texts of the classical period is something that need not be considered here. What has been of concern was the correctness of their interpretations of an Aristotelian issue.

In general, the commentators we discussed were all Platonizing thinkers and, on the whole, well-known professors and teachers. Some of them, like Elias, taught Aristotle as a preliminary to Plato (123 9-11).[22] Common to all the commentators on the *Categories* is the noted discrepancy between their ardent defense of the fuller version of the Aristotelian formulation of the nature of *homonyma*, one which preserves the L of O textual reading, and their misunderstanding of the intent of the passage. What is striking about the entire tradition that goes back to Porphyry, if not to others before him, is a common and serious effort to extend Aristotle's views and, in this particular case, to promote the belief that *logos* meant for Aristotle something more than definition. The persistent preoccupation with the meaning of *logos* in the sense of description calls for an explanation.

The new meaning the term took was appended to Aristotle's *logos* with a facility that leads one to infer that the commentators were less interested in correctness and more in using some significant text in order to bring to the foreground of their exposition certain concepts of their own. One might venture here the opinion that even more important than the extended meaning of *logos* was their eagerness to assert the view that would permit *ousia*, in the sense of individual substances, to become an object of "knowledge" even if admittedly undefinable in terms of Aristotle's logic. This view was asserted, as we saw, by means of an interpretation that rested on certain liberties the commentators took with Aristotle's text. It is difficult to know whether the commentators had actually realized the significance Aristotle had apparently attached to his way of formulating the nature of *homonyma*. The fact is that we are allowed to infer that they either ignored or suppressed the ontological and logical aspects of the doctrine and by the same token overlooked the possibility that Aristotle had conceivably stated his case through the aid of technical expressions.

It is not easy to say what it was that led the commentators to insist upon treating the two concepts, *ousia* and *logos*, in so obviously a non-Aristotelian manner. A fuller explanation of this treatment might eventually reveal that what we have here is doctrinal innovation in late Hellenistic logical theory and comparable developments in ontology. However all we are permitted to say at this point is that no matter what new views the commentators had developed on their own, it is still a fact that they failed to distinguish their own concepts from what their texts permitted.

The interpretation that takes *ousia*, as it occurs in the first chapter of the *Categories*, to mean individual substances and that such substances, if they happen to have the same proper name, are cases of *homonyma pragmata,* goes back, as far as our documents permit us to tell, to the writings of Porphyry and his pupil Iamblichus. We have no extant commentary on the *Categories* that antedates that of Porphyry. If we had the commentaries from which he was able to draw we might have been in a position to trace the origins of this misinterpretation of Aristotle's text. The way matters now stand, all we can say is that the available evidence points to the fact that the misinterpretation originates with the early Neoplatonists, it is transmitted through Neoplatonist writers, and becomes an established approach which is shared by all the commentators whose Neoplatonic affiliations cannot be doubted. Perhaps the long interpretive tradition from Porphyry to Photius and Psellus which preserved a correct textual reading only to distort its meaning and allow an error to go unnoticed for centuries, is as curious a phenomenon as is the fact that the only commentaries we have on Aristotle's *Categories* are those that were written by Neoplatonists.

NOTES

1. This essay, the second of a two-part article, was originally published in *The Journal of the History of Philosophy*, VII/1 (1969), 36–57, and is reprinted with minor changes. It was based on an invited paper presented at the annual meeting of the Society for Ancient Greek Philosophy in New York City, Dec. 27, 1965. For a full discussion of the doctrine of *homonyma* and the background against which it can be understood, see my "The Aristotelian Doctrine of *homonyma* in the *Categories* and its Platonic Antecedents," also in *The Journal of the History of Philosophy* VI, 4 (Oct., 1968), 315-326). I tried to show in that paper how Aristotle's formulation is indebted linguistically to Plato but was worked out not in response to Plato's usage but to his own philosophical position and as part of his logical apparatus to attack the Speusippean wing of the Academy. On the whole, the textual evidence from the Platonic writings indicates clearly that Plato had not proposed a technical use of *homonyma*. Speusippus and Aristotle, however, offered two different and opposing technical formulations intended to fit their respective ontologies.

2. *In Categ.*, beginning with 60 11.

3. *Isagoge* (6 5–11). *The Organon, or Logical Treatises of Aristotle* [with Porphyry's *Introduction*, tr. O. F. Owen (London, 1883), II, 615-616). Dexippus (*In Categ.* 13 3) is in complete agreement with Porphyry. Of special interest is also the fact that Ammonius has constructed an argument of his own to support Porphyry thesis. Also Ammonii, *In Porph. Isag.* 81 16ff.

4. It is against this background that he proceeds with his support of Vl (62 35).

5. Comp. Simplicii, *In Categ.* 30 7.

6. Porphyry's rule is that a term is correctly rendered not only when properly named but also when defined in conjunction with the proper denotation of the name.

7. The same division is adopted by Olympiodorus (*In Categ.* 34ff.).

8. An example of accidental *homonyma* is the case of two unrelated individuals who have been given the same proper name but without any design or planning on the part of those who gave them the name. Consider, e.g., the case of two Alexanders: Alexander, the son of Priamus, and Alexander, the son of Philippus.

9. Simplicius expresses serious reservations about the originality of Dexippus' commentary (*In Categ.* 2 25-9). He remarks that the problem which Dexippus raises had been anticipated by Plotinus, and that his solutions offer nothing beyond what Porphyry and Iamblichus had already said on the subject.

10. οὐδὲν...ἔχει ἀφωρισμένην ἰδέαν πραγμάτων φύσιν.

11. He emphasizes the following principles: being (*on*), one (*hen*), plurality (*plēthos*), non-being (*mē on*), essence (*ti esti*), identity (*tauton*), otherness (*heteron*), category (*katēgoria*), definition (*horos*), genus (*genos*), and difference (*diaphora*) (*In Categ.* 13 3-15 13).

12. Ammonius' two definitions of *homonyma* will be found in *In Porph. Isag.* 6 8 ff. and in *In Categ.* 17 6-7.

13. Evidently Elias is following almost to the letter both Porphyry and Ammonius when he states with unusual succinctness the difference between definition and description: τὸ δὲ τί ἐστιν τοῦ ὁρισμοῦ πρόσρημα ἢ ὑπογραφῆς· διαφέρει δὲ ταῦτα ἀλλήλων, ὅτι ὁ μὲν ὁρισμὸς ἐκ τῶν κατ' οὐσίαν λαμβάνεται, ἡ δὲ ὑπογραφὴ ἐκ τῶν κατὰ συμβεβηκότων· χείρω δὲ ἡ ὑπογραφὴ τοῦ ὁρισμοῦ. Eliae, *In Porph. Isag.* 56 11–14; also *Prolegomena Philosophiae* 4 5-32.

14. The definition of man, which is the illustration he uses, is taken word for word from Porphyry as in *In Categ.* 60 17-8.

15. He states in the *Isagoge*: τῶν δὲ ὁμωνύμων οὐκ ἔστι ὅρους ἀποδοῦναι...ὁ δὲ ὁρισμὸς οὐσίαν σημαίνει· ὧν δὲ οἱ ὁρισμοὶ οἱ αὐτοί, τούτων καὶ τὰ πράγματα τὰ αὐτά· οὐκ ἄρα ἐνδέχεται τῶν ὁμωνύμων ἕνα κοινὸν ὁρισμὸν ἀποδοῦναι (56 2–6).

16. Philoponi, *In Categ.* 16 15-8.

17. *In Categ.* 16 20-17 25.

18. At 206A: ἴσον θυμὸν ἔχοντες ὁμώνυμοι.

19. *In Categ.* 28 8ff. Olympiodorus abounds in such irrelevancies and speculations. For his comment on the phrase "*homonyma legetai*," he borrows heavily, according to his own admission, from Iamblichus' lost commentary. More often that not, Olympiodorus fails to keep his discussion within the boundaries of basic issues. His irrelevancies run the gamut from a Homeric verse to Attic syntax.

20. Since we have no reason to doubt the historical accuracy of this information, it is reasonable to say that we can speak with certainty about the existence of two schools opposing each other on the issue of the relevance of the doctrine of *homonyma* to the rest of Aristotle's categorical theory: the school of Nicostratus on the negative side and the Neoplatonists Porphyry and Iamblichus defending the other.

21. *In Categ.* 30 5-15. The quotation is most likely from Porphyry's lost work *Tois pros Gedaleion*. Porphyry argues that Aristotle added *tēs ousias* in order to leave no doubt about the exact meaning of *logos*, i.e., definition and description. Without *ousia*, *logos* might have also been taken to mean such things as eduction, syllogism, an affirmation, or a denial.

22. Elias states that it is necessary for the exegete of Aristotle to πάντα εἰδέναι τὰ Πλάτωνος, ἵνα σύμφωνον ἑαυτῷ τὸν Πλάτωνα ἀποδείξῃ τὰ Ἀριστοτέλους τῶν Πλάτωνος εἰσαγωγὴν ποιούμενος (cf. 11O 28-30). See L. G. Westerink, *Anonymous Prolegomena to Platonic Philosophy* (Amsterdam, 1962), p. xx.

OBSERVATIONS ON ARISTOTLE'S THEORY OF CATEGORIES[1]

I

This paper deals with what seems to be a rather small topic but one, as I hope to show, which has significant implications. As many interpreters before me have said, the treatise titled *Categories* brings together certain basic logical and ontological views of Aristotle. I find myself in agreement with this interpretation but I take it a step further to say that the treatise contains enough evidence to support the view that Aristotle intended and in fact did make a basic distinction between a theory of being and a theory of categories, and even more sharply than has been hitherto recognized.

I will argue that this distinction has been largely overlooked and even ignored by every major interpreter of Aristotle, with the subsequent result that these two basic doctrines as presented in the *Categories*, instead of being kept apart, have been treated as identical theories. One of the most serious consequences of the tendency to collapse the meanings of the key terms "being" and "category" is not so much that they have been used interchangeably, but more importantly, that their fusion obscures our understanding of that treatise. I propose to show that Aristotle's intent was to correlate the ultimate genera of being, *ta genē tou ontos*, and the logically fundamental modes of predication, *ta schēmata tēs katēgorias*. I do not contend that scholars have been remiss to notice the fact that Aristotle has a theory which deals with these modes of predication but only that they have been misled by the prevailing tendency to overlook the difference between the two concepts, "being" and "category."

The well-established tradition of viewing the categories as ultimate predicates, or ultimate types of being, or as with Iamblichus, "expressions signifying things by means of concepts" (Olympiodorus, *Proleg. in Categ.* 9, 14–15), is systematically misleading. I will not deny that there are passages in the Aristotelian texts that permit such identifications. In fact Bonitz' *Index Aristotelicum* lists a variety of usages which should be consulted for a full scale investigation of this broad theme. The point I wish to emphasize is that in connection with the text of the treatise *Categories* there is more to the theory as presented there than is usually admitted, and also that failure to bring forth its full meaning leads to serious distortions. The purpose of this paper is to make an attempt to restore the distinction between genera of being and genera of categories, and also to suggest what the function of the theory of categories is in its original setting. Before proceeding with the argument I feel obligated to acknowledge that my discussion is only a preliminary presentation of a problem and that its fuller treatment can only be done in a much longer essay than this paper.

It has been generally recognized that the term 'category' was initially a legal expression deriving from *katēgorein*, to accuse.[2] Aristotle was the first to assign to the term 'category' its technical use; '*katēgorēma*' means predicate; *katēgoria* means predication, and in certain contexts, predicate; and the verb *katēgorein*, has the technical meaning "to predicate" or "to assert something of something." *Katēgoria* is also used as an abbreviated expression for modes of predication, that is *schēmata tēs katēgorias*. Such modes are arrived at by means of careful sorting of the basic kinds of assertions made of the instances of the genera of being as subjects. In the *Categories* Aristotle settles for a list of ten such modes, in correspondence to the ten *summa genera* of being. E. Kapp, explaining the problem to which Aristotle was responding, writes:

> ...in the philosophy of the first half of the fourth century B.C., confusion was the result of too few rather than too many

distinctions. From this point of view Aristotle's distinctions of as many as ten different classes or forms of predication was certainly a step forward in the development of logic and philosophy.[3]

I will not dispute Kapp's point, for it is well taken. The evidence from the *Topics* and other works supports it. But I should like to emphasize here that the restriction of the list to ten *schēmata* is intimately related to Aristotle's investigations in ontology, and to be more precise, his search for ultimate types of being. In the terminology of the *Categories*, *ta onta* are given as *ousia*, primary and secondary, and as *symbebēkota*. This is not the place to discuss Aristotle's account on how we come to grasp or form the most inclusive concepts, universals and principles, and therefore, how we arrive at the highest genera of being. Nor is there any special need to repeat here the list of meanings of such basic terms as *on* (being) and *genos* (genus, for they are readily given in the *lexicon*, *Metaphysics* Book IV. I will restrict our discussion to the difference between two expressions: *genē tou ontos* and *genē tēs katēgorias*. The objective is to show that Aristotle meant to keep their respective meanings separate and that the primary meaning he assigned to the categories as "modes of predication" is a precise and technical one. Furthermore, it is part of our thesis that Aristotle employed this technical use of the categories in all his investigations and that in the psychological works, the *De Anima* in particular, not only did he employ it but also gave it further theoretical support in his analysis of the faculty of sensation.

In the remainder of this paper I will first present a criticism of W. D. Ross' interpretation as a typical case of misidentifying the categories, and then I will proceed with my own alternative explanation. In the conclusion I will briefly indicate the support which the *De Anima* lends to the theory of predication.

II

First we must clear up some terminological matters. By so doing we will be able to see how important it is to keep separate the two senses of the term *katēgoria*, i.e. predication and predicate. As I will argue in the sequel, it is not enough to say that the meaning of *katēgoria* as predication is all that Aristotle meant to convey, for Aristotle proposed a more controlled and therefore technical use than our translation of *katēgoria* as predication is able to convey. But more of this later. W. D. Ross has listed the relevant passages in which *katēgoria* means (a) predication, (b) predicate and (c) both of these senses.[4] I will challenge his claim that *Cat.* 3a 33–37 supports the meaning of predicate. The full passage reads:

> It is the mark of substances and differentiae that, in all propositions of which they form the predicate, they are predicated (*legesthai*) univocally. For all such propositions (*apo toutōn katēgorias*) have for their subject either the individual or the species (*katēgorountai*). It is true that, inasmuch as a primary substance is not predicable of anything (*oudemia esti katēgoria*), it can never form the predicate of any proposition (*kat' oudenos...legetai*). But of secondary substances, the species, the species is predicated (*katēgoreitai*) of the individual, the genus both of the species and the individual.[5]

In the Oxford translation by Edgehill, of *Cat.* 3a 33–37 there is a hopeless mingling of expressions rendering *katēgoria* and related terms, despite the fact that all of them do not occur in the text. Other translations are comparably inaccurate.[6] It would be more to the point to say that Aristotle's formulation of the issues is quite condensed in this passage, in which case we could substitute in the translation "predication" for "predicate" when *katēgoria* is explicitly used, without loss of meaning or danger of confusion. The same procedure obtains with reference to *Topics* 109b 5, where *katēgoria* means clearly predication or attribution. Part of the difficulty in the cited

Aristotle's Theory of Categories

translation is the indiscriminate interchange of *legetai* and *katēgorein*. Further discussion of the issues involved must wait until we have examined Ross' interpretation of the doctrine of categories.

III

W. D. Ross, in the Introduction to his edition of Aristotle's *Metaphysics* states:

> The doctrine of the categories is a peculiarly puzzling one, partly from the lack of any definite information as to Aristotle's precise object in formulating it, partly from our ignorance of the relative dates of the works in which various aspects of it are presented. (lxxxii)

Ross' remarks are well taken, except for one important point regarding what he says about Aristotle's precise object in formulating the doctrine. It may well be the case that Aristotle does in fact give that information in the treatise *Categories*. I shall try to explain how this is so. But first I must proceed with an issue that has caused considerable confusion and misidentification of the doctrine. Ross' views provide a good illustration of the problem. The doctrine in the *Categories*, he writes,

> ...is introduced as a classification of the meanings of τὰ μὴ κατὰ συμπλοκὴν λεγόμενα, i.e., of such expressions as 'man', 'ox', 'runs', 'wins' in opposition to 'man runs', 'man wins', which are κατὰ συμπλοκὴν λεγόμενα. In other words it is a classification of the meanings of words and phrases in opposition to sentences and judgements. Aristotle's interest is not logical, not grammatical, but he approaches the classification of objects of thought by a consideration of the words by which we symbolize them. (lxxxii–lxxxiii)

So far Ross' view is clear, although it is difficult to understand what he means by "classification of objects of thought." Then, in the next paragraph he says "The *Categories* refers to the categories by the general word γένη," and cites as evidence 11a 38 and 11b 15. But he misreads the text, for neither passage supports this claim that Aristotle calls the categories "genera." The term "genera" in both passages refers to τὰ γένη τῶν ὄντων. The substitution of *katēgoria* for *on* is permissible only if the reader is bent on adopting the view that the categories are "a classification of the meanings of words and phrases," that is, as τὰ κατὰ μηδεμίαν συμπλοκὴν λεγόμενα.

However, Ross makes an attempt to clear up the issue and defend his approach by saying that the classification in the *Categories* is not a classification of predicates (lxxxiii), and claims that this is indicated by two facts:

(1) Aristotle's instances quoted above show that τὰ κατὰ μηδεμίαν συμπλοκὴν λεγόμενα include the subjects of propositions no less than the predicates; and (2) the first category, that of substance, is divided into two parts, and substance in the most proper, primary, and complete sense is said to be that which is neither asserted of a subject nor present in a subject. (lxxxiii)

What Ross is defending is that the term "category" is wider than "predicate" since it covers the case of substance which is not a predicate. Ross is right in this connection but it is still debatable whether what he calls the "technical sense of the word" is sufficiently identified. Ross proceeds to argue against Bonitz who took the position that Aristotle moved from the ordinary use of *katēgoria*, where the term meant 'names' or 'designations' rather than 'predicate' to a technical sense of the word, and states that "it is undesirable to divorce the technical sense of the word from its natural meaning of 'predicates,' and it is not necessary to do so" (lxxxiv). The technical use Bonitz spoke of, Ross summarizes as follows:

Aristotle's Theory of Categories

The categories would then be a classification of the meanings of names, i.e. a classification of nameable objects of thought, and among these would naturally be included individual substances as well as those entities which can stand as predicates. (ibid.)

Ross objects that since secondary substances are predicates we can rightfully include that meaning of substance within the meaning of the term 'predicate' and thus avoid the divorce between the ordinary and technical uses of *katēgoria*. Ross' position is that the names of the categories are not just predicates, but indeed predicates *par excellence*. He cites *Categories* 10b 17–23 to show how the transition from the ordinary to the technical sense of the word took place, and concludes: "The categories are simply the predicates *par excellence*." (lxxxiv)

What is left out of Ross' interpretation is the meaning of *katēgoria* as *predication*. Thus he overlooks the possibility that the technical meaning of *katēgoria* may hinge in a serious way on its other meaning, i.e. assertive judgment. I intend to propose a different reading of the term *katēgoria*, one which will keep the term within the context of the logical syntax of predicative statements, i.e. of κατὰ συμπλοκὴν λεγόμενα, but not of μὴ κατὰ συμπλοκήν, as Ross insists. My view is that the doctrine of the categories is one which deals with the rules of correct and ultimate types of assertions, *kataphaseis*, on the ground that the genera or types of such assertions are in correspondence and agreement with the ontology of the γένη τῶν ὄντων. Failure to keep *onta* and *katēgoriai* apart leads (a) to a narrow view of the doctrine of categories, such as that put forward by Ross and others who see it as dealing with the classification of the names of things or objects of thought; and (b) to the error of redundancy which seems to result from identifying the genera of categories with genera of being, one which makes the two interchangeable, except insofar as the former is a list of the highest types of names whereas the latter is a list of the highest types of being. To return to Ross' approach, it seems to me that he reads every passage in which the term "category" appears as supportive of his view, namely that "the categories are simply the predicates *par excellence*." As he says:

> The expressions τὰ σχήματα (or τὰ γένη) τῶν κατηγοριῶν (or τῆς κατηγορίας) emphasize the fact that the categories are the highest types or classes under which all predicates fall. So too κατηγορίαι τοῦ ὄντος, σχήματα κατηγορίας τοῦ ὄντος mean 'predicates of being, types of predicates of being,' i.e., the highest predicates under one or other of which falls everything that is. (lxxxiv–lxxxv)

Ross' difficulty is further compounded by his insistence that Aristotle in the later works introduced "another mode of reference to the categories." He mentions the *Metaphysics* as a case in point where the substitute expressions are πολλαχῶς λέγεται τὸ ὄν, ποσαχῶς τὸ ὄν σημαίνει, οἷς ὥρισται τὸ ὄν, and he adds:

> The assumption in fact is made that to these various classes of entity there answer as many senses of 'be.' To be means one thing for a substance, another for a quality, a quantity, etc. This appears to be a later phase of the theory; indeed the difference between the senses of 'be' is announced as a conclusion which follows from the difference between the main types of 'what things are.' καθ' αὑτὰ δὲ εἶναι λέγεται ὅσαπερ σημαίνει τὰ σχήματα τῆς κατηγορίας· ὁσαχῶς γὰρ λέγεται τοσαυταχῶς τὸ εἶναι σημαίνει. ἐπεὶ οὖν τῶν κατηγορουμένων τὰ μὲν τί ἐστι σημαίνει, τὰ δὲ ποιόν, τὰ δὲ ποσόν, τὰ δὲ πρός τι, τὰ δὲ ποιεῖν ἢ πάσχειν, τὰ δὲ ποτὲ, ἑκάστῳ τούτων εἶναί τ' αὐτὸ σημαίνει. ('being has a different meaning corresponding to each of these kinds of predicate'). (lxxxv)

The passage Ross quotes is from *Met.* IV, 1017 a 22. In the footnote he mentions that further support will be found in a passage from VII, 1030a 21. His reading of these passages is not without problems. Even the passage in *De Anima* 402a 22–25 does not give the needed support since the expression *katēgoria* is clearly tied to the

Aristotle's Theory of Categories

quest for a *definition* of the soul, a task which calls for selecting the correct *katēgoria*; in other words the passage directs attention to the need to bring in line the kind of thing the soul is with the appropriate *katēgoria* or correct predicative assertion, so that the definition will be logically and ontologically proper. More literally the passage calls for identification of what it is precisely to be predicated (*katēgoroito*).

By the time Aristotle came to discuss the theme of the categories in the *Metaphysics* and the *De Anima* he had clarified the technical problems of correct attribution. Thus he had little difficulty in bringing together the genera of being and genera of category. For instance, when Aristotle uses the expression τῶν διαιρεθεισῶν κατηγοριῶν (*De Anima* 402a 25 and 410a 15) he can mean, as Hicks puts it in his commentary, that

> ...the table of the ten categories [is] at once a classification of predications or attributes predicated of a subject and the *summa genera* of all that exists (γένη τοῦ ὄντος). Ultimately these ten *summa genera* may be reduced to two, viz. substance on the one hand, and its appendages, quality, quantity, relation etc. on the other. (182–83)

Hicks gives three related passages in the *Metaphysics* which seem to support the expression "categories of being": VII, 1028a 10–b7; IX, 1045b 27–32; and XII, 1069a 18–24. The second one seems most pertinent to our topic:

> We have treated of that which *is* primarily and to which all the other categories of being are referred i.e. of substance. For it is in virtue of the concept of substance that the others are also said to be—quality and quantity and the like; for all will be found to involve the concept of substance, as we said in the first part of our work.[7]

I find nothing incompatible in this passage with my interpretation. The subtle distinction between γένη τοῦ ὄντος and γένη τῆς κατηγορίας is kept. The expression κατηγορίαι τοῦ ὄντος means the genera of predication of being, all, πᾶσαι αἱ ἄλλαι except that of πρῶτον ὄν, οὐσία. What I think Aristotle means here is that all correct predications asserting genus of being ultimately refer to *ousia*. The Oxford translation is done by W. D. Ross. It should be noted that the original reads *logos* for what Ross translates as "concept." Furthermore, where the text reads "ta alla onta" Ross renders simply as "and the like." One is led to infer that he means "the other concepts" and if so then "category" and "concept" cover the same grounds. But this is puzzling, especially in view of what Ross states in the aforementioned Introduction: "In other words it (the doctrine in the *Categories*) is a classification of the meanings of words and phrases in opposition to sentences or judgements," and then repeats in a note: "Of words and phrases rather of terms, for the latter are essentially the termini of propositions, while Aristotle is here thinking of objects of thought and the names for them, apart from the proposition" (lxxxii, note 7). Ross' thesis is thus abundantly clear. He means to exclude from the technical meaning of categories that of proper and irreducible modes of correct predication.

My own thesis is not that Ross is completely wrong but rather that he has arbitrarily limited the technical meaning of the doctrine. Positively stated, my interpretation advocates *the inclusion* of the part of the theory that Ross leaves out. On this basis, the so-called "classification of things and their attributes" belongs mainly to the "genera of being" part of the theory. Once this is established, the part which deals with the "genera of category" comes in to formulate the canons of correct types of *kataphasis*, assertion, so that the κατὰ συμπλοκὴν λεγόμενα will reflect the basic types of being, i.e. the things or beings signified by the ὀνόματα, the meaningful expressions, the ordered μὴ κατὰ συμπλοκὴν λεγόμενα.

Aristotle's view in the *Categories* is quite clear. Unless we know the genera of being and how they are connected, how their instances constitute types and how some inhere while others do not, how they

Aristotle's Theory of Categories

can be divided into *ousiai* and properties of *ousiai*, we cannot talk correctly, i.e. make systematically correct statements. Naturally and inevitably, we do make statements because we are logical animals, but we do not necessarily make correct and precise statements according to the order that prevails in the genera of beings and their instances. It is not uncommon to mistake quality for *ousia* or quantity for relation, etc. A proper *kataphasis*, then, not only must take into account the order of things but must also satisfy the syntactical demands of the κατὰ συμπλοκὴν λεγόμενα in accordance with the canons of correct predication. The logical function of a theory of categories is to specify the schemata and rules of correct attribution and predication. The task calls for the careful identification of the *genera of being* in order to exhibit their legitimate function as predicates. For Aristotle, the outcome of this enterprise had to be what his theory of ultimate types or genera of being demanded: a set of *schēmata tēs katēgorias*, modes or schemes of attribution, corresponding to the complex connectedness of the genera of beings: a categorial scheme for each kind of *on*, substance, quantity, quality, etc. Hence the "theory of categories" is a theory of classification of logically correct statements of attribution made according to canons which also regulate in advance the corrigibility of proposed *kataphaseis*.

IV

Two things need to be noted: (a) that the technical use of *legetai* must be clearly distinguished from that of *katēgoreitai*, the two are not interchangeable as technical terms; (b) that the verbal expression *katēgoreitai* appears for the first time in *Categories*, in chapter 3, and only after the following distinctions have been introduced:

(1) "Things that are said" are (i) *homōnyma* (ii) *synōnyma* and (iii) *heterōnyma*.

(2) "Things that are said" are said (i) either in combination (*kata symplokēn*) or (ii) without combination (*aneu symplokēs*).

(3) "Things that are," beings, are said in any of the following ways, depending on what they are.

Thus: (i) Some are said of a subject but are not in any subject—this is the case of secondary substance being said of primary substance. (ii) Some are in a subject but are not said of any subject—this is the case of a qualium as being in a subject, the case of inherence. (iii) Some are both said of a subject and are in a subject—the case of an effected thing such as knowledge which in one respect can be said to be in a subject, the soul, and in another respect be said of a subject, such as grammar. (iv) Some are neither in a subject nor said of a subject—the case of primary substance. The basic distinction which controls these four cases is that between "being said of a subject" and "being in a subject" —*kath' hypokeimenou legetai and en hypokeimenō einai*. The distinction is needed for a number of reasons. First there is the need to bring together with as much clarity as possible the ways of talking and the kinds of being. Secondly, there is the troublesome problem of finding rules to distinguish between two senses of the term "subject" in order

Aristotle's Theory of Categories 143

to know which is ontological and which logical, and if the former, in which of the many senses of "being" the logical subject is meant. The problem is not merely one of identifying the referents of our various kinds of uncombined expressions, but mainly how to conjoin correctly the referential or reliable uncombined expressions in a statement of attribution.

Chapter 3 discusses a special canon of attribution or predication by introducing the term *katēgorein* in connection with the clear-cut case of predicating secondary substances of a primary *ousia*—these terms are introduced later, especially in chapter 5. The example is properly chosen because its *uncombined expressions* here are cases of *synōnyma*, i.e., they share in the name and the definition of the substance. The canon reads:

> When one thing is predicated (*katēgoreitai*) of another all that which is predicable of the predicate will be predicable also of the subject. (1b 10–12)

We have a series of judgments or assertions here related syllogistically. Each assertoric act conjoins expressions *aneu symplokēs*, which is precisely what the function of *katēgorein* is. At this point we have moved from *legetai*, saying or designating meanings and distinctions, to more controlled verbal acts of attribution or predication. The *designata* of the example to which the canon is applied are already cleared of ambiguities, for the predicates which are attributed to the first predicate are *synōnyma*. But before Aristotle can take up other cases of attribution, he finds it necessary to present us with his inventory of the ultimate genera of being which uncombined expressions with referential meaning signify. He informs us in chapter 4 that each of the κατὰ μηδεμίαν συμπλοκὴν λεγόμενα signifies (σημαίνει) one of the following: an *ousia*, a quantity, a quality, a relative something, "where" something is, or "when" it is, position, having, doing, being affected. And concludes the brief section on the following note (translation mine):

Each of these aforesaid, in and by itself, cannot be taken as an assertion or affirmation; it is only by the combination of one with another that an affirmation is made. For every affirmation (κατάφασις) it seems, is either true or false; whereas in the case of uncombined expressions none is either true or false. (2a 4–10)

In chapter 4, Aristotle considers the case of *ousia* and after screening it as an uncombined designation against the clearing house of the fourfold distinction of relationships between *legetai-einai-hypokeimenon*, he proceeds to place it in the context of *kategorein*, beginning with line 2a 15. Once again, *kategorein* is clearly the verbal act which provides a *kataphasis*. So far we have encountered nothing that would justify Ross' or anyone else's interpretation which advocates converting the genera of being, to which the uncombined signifiers are tied, into categories of being. The textual evidence does not permit it. In fact the only transitional term we have in order to move from *ta legomena* to the act of *kategorein* is the performance of a *kataphasis*, i.e., a complete statement or affirmation. This explains why no verbal form of *kategorein* is used anywhere in the celebrated chapter 4, and is only reintroduced with line 2a 15 of chapter 5, i.e. after Aristotle has announced a theory about affirmations and stated a condition, namely that they may be either true or false.

Although Aristotle does not state it explicitly, the reader begins to sense a lingering problem: what are the proper ways to cast our affirmations so that we may proceed to decide whether they are in fact true or false? Some preliminary work of a logical nature seems to be required at this point. What is needed, then, is to formulate the canons with which any affirmation must comply in order to qualify as correct predication under *kategorein*, before the claim to truth or falsity of the statement can be confirmed. In this regard, *legein*, after it has reached the level of complexity of a *kataphasis*, needs to be further controlled by *kategoreisthai* rules. The difficulty with casual affirmations is that any uncombined expression signifying any one of the *onta* can occupy the place of the subject. Affirmations, as they are being made, are not self-clarifying, i.e. they do not tell what sort of being (whether *ousia* or accident) the subject word as an uncombined *legomenon*, signifies.

The validity of the canons of correct affirmation is derived from the ontology which underlies the referential meaning of the uncombined signifiers. In other words, a *katēgoria* is not only an affirmation or predicative statement, but one that has satisfied the canons of correctness according to the theory of inherence.[8] This, I take it, is the hitherto neglected part of the technical meaning of *katēgoria*.

If *katēgoria* means, as I propose, "an attributive or predicative affirmation made according to canons," it would follow that the interpretation which renders it co-extensive with the predicates that name genera of being is redundant, and at best, an incomplete thesis. "The genera of category," as the expression occurs in the text, is not exclusively designed to cover the types of predicates which name the distinct genera of being. As part of a larger theory, the expression stands for the ultimate modes of predication which satisfy the rules of propositional syntax and the logic of predicates in agreement with the objective structures of the instances of genera of being. A *katēgoria* thus can be understood as definite *kataphasis* done according to canons. The difference between a mere affirmation and a controlled one is this: Whereas a mere affirmation, one which is not made canonically, *may be* true or false, a *katēgoria* type of affirmation is ready to face the test of confirmation. For instance the affirmation "Socrates is Callias" is obviously false, and technically speaking it is not correctly made. It is quite easy to dismiss facile cases of such affirmations as "The shoe is walking," "The plate is dancing," "The boys fly with their five feet," for they are not correctly constructed affirmations although they have the form of a mere affirmation. The issue then is how to decide whether an affirmation has met the canons of predicative correctness to become *katēgoria*, i.e., a statement ready to be tested for its truth or falsity.

On the basis of this wider view of the technical use of *kategoria*, it would seem that when Aristotle wrote his treatise *Categories* he was not concerned to present a detailed account of the part of the theory which dealt with the problem of why the simple signifiers or predicates correspond to and can come under ten ultimate genera of being. Rather, he considered the inventory of *ta onta* as belonging to a different kind of inquiry. What concerned him in his *Categories* was the logic of the canons to refine affirmations for the purpose of rendering them categorical statements in accordance with the correctness of the ultimate genera of being. The search, therefore, which he conducted for the canons of correct attribution makes that treatise ancillary, ie. part of the organon by which statements are prepared for the test of truth and falsity in order to be used as premises in demonstrative syllogisms—and one may add, in refutative and dialectical arguments.

The classification of things is not really a function of the theory of categories: it belongs to the several inquiries, the natural investigations. It is the task of the natural sciences to find out what sorts of things exist and what properties they have. But it is the task of psychology to tell us how we come to know the world as differentiated into distinct things and with what kinds of properties. *Perception* (αἴσθησις) informs us what the facts are but we must still develop the skills of talking and reasoning correctly. Making assertions is a natural function of our elementary use of language. But the art of correct talking and reasoning is a further refinement of the power to talk: it is a development of the logical *entelecheia*. This is a special topic and its treatment lies outside the scope of this paper. However, suffice it to say in conclusion that it is in the *De Anima* that we must look for Aristotle's account of the solution to this problem.

Aristotle's thesis in the *De Anima* is that each act of sense perception is indeed *a judgment* which, when articulated in language, is a statement of attribution. It is not simply the case that each concrete instance of a genus of being is given with each act of sense-experience. That would be pidgeon-holing. We do not experience a case of quality or quantity as such, that is, in isolation from all other kinds of beings. The beings as we perceive them are presented to us in their connectedness, and in some kind of fullness. All that one needs to add here by way of summary is that the physiology of the general faculty of sense perception, according to Aristotle, warrants the claim for a reliable isomorphism between *cosmos* and *logos*, being and predication. Whether we turn to the doctrine of the categories in its wider technical sense or to the account of discriminatory judgments of the *De Anima*, the outcome is the same: the ultimate organic acts of perceiving and talking are not atomic sense-data and words.

We sense, know and talk, on the basis of our native ability to make affirmations which can be recast as correct categorial assertions. These are the real organic ultimates of human language and communication. On this point Aristotle is in full agreement with his teacher, Plato.

NOTES

1. Originally published in *Diotima*, Vol. 3 (1975): 67–81; reprinted with changes.

2. See L.M. De Rijk. *The Place of the Categories of Being in Aristotle's Philosophy*. (Assen: Van Gorcum, 1952), pp. 89–92.

3. E. Kapp. *Greek Foundations of Traditional Logic*. (New York: Columbia University Press, 1942), p. 37.

4. See his "Introduction" to the edition of *Aristotle's Metaphysics*, a revised Text with Introduction and Commentary, 2 vols. (Oxford: Clarendon Press, 1924), p. lxxxiii, note 2.

5. Oxford Translation (E.M. Edgehill), done under the editorship of W.D. Ross. The Greek text reads: Ὑπάρχει δὲ ταῖς οὐσίαις καὶ ταῖς διαφοραῖς τὰ πάντα συνωνύμως ἀπ' αὐτῶν λέγεσθαι· πᾶσαι γὰρ αἱ ἀπὸ τούτων κατηγορίαι ἤτοι κατὰ τῶν ἀτόμων κατηγοροῦνται ἢ κατὰ τῶν εἰδῶν· ἀπὸ μὲν τῆς πρώτης οὐσίας οὐδεμία ἐστι κατηγορία,—κατ' οὐδενὸς γὰρ ὑποκειμένου λέγεται· —τῶν δὲ δευτέρων οὐσιῶν τὸ μὲν εἶδος κατὰ τοῦ ἀτόμου κατηγορεῖται, τὸ δὲ γένος καὶ κατὰ τοῦ εἴδους καὶ κατὰ τοῦ ἀτόμου. *Κατηγορίαι* 3a 33–37.

6. See Ackrill's translation in the Clarendon Aristotle Series, *Aristotle's Categories and De Interpretatione*. (Oxford, 1963): "For all the predicates from them are predicated either of the individuals or of the species." 3a 35ff.

7. The Greek text reads: Περὶ μὲν τοῦ οὖν πρώτου ὄντος καὶ πρὸς ὃ πᾶσαι αἱ ἄλλαι κατηγορίαι τοῦ ὄντος ἀναφέρονται εἴρηται, περὶ τῆς οὐσίας (κατὰ γὰρ τὸν τῆς οὐσίας λόγον λέγεται τἆλλα ὄντα, τό τε ποσὸν καὶ τὸ ποιὸν καὶ τἆλλα τὰ οὕτω λεγόμενα· πάντα γὰρ ἕξει τὸν τῆς οὐσίας λόγον, ὥσπερ εἴπομεν ἐν τοῖς πρώτοις λόγοις.

8. For this see *Met*. Book V. 2, 1109a where inherence in subjects is discussed in the context of "prior" and "posterior": "Some things then are called prior and posterior in this sense, others in respect of nature and substance, i.e. those which can be without other things while others cannot

Aristotle's Theory of Categories

be without them — a distinction which Plato used." As early as the *Apology*, Plato wrote: "Is there anyone who does not believe in horses, but believes in horses' activities? Or who does not believe in musicians, but believes in musical activities? No, there is not, my worthy friend." (27b)

ON THE MEANING OF "KATEGORIA" IN ARISTOTLE'S *CATEGORIES*[1]

I

In a paper, written in 1974 and subsequently published in 1975,[2] I argued that the Aristotelian texts, particularly the one titled *Categories*, allow for a parallel yet distinct interpretation to the traditional and prevalent one that takes the categories to be terms, ultimate classes, types, and concepts. My position there was that the primary use of *katēgoria* refers to well formed statements made according to canons and, to be more precise, to fundamental types of predication conforming to rules sustained by the ways of beings.

In trying to decide how Aristotle uses the term κατηγορία in the treatise that bears the same name, *Categories*,[3] provision must be made for the fact that there is nothing in the text to justify the meanings that ancient commentators, including modern writers, assigned to it and found their way both in translations of Aristotle's works and in the corpus of established philosophical terminology.[4] The present article is written with the hope that it will contribute in some small measure to understanding why certain distinctions in the treatise *Categories* should have prevented interpreters from assigning the traditional meaning of 'genera of being' to the term 'category' and hence giving it the meaning of "highest predicate" rather than fundamental type of predication.

Professor M. Frede published an important article in 1981,[5] defending the same reading of the term *katēgoria* mainly by examining closely the textual evidence in the *Topics*; however, when he addressed the same problem in the case of the treatise *Categories* the conclusions he drew led to a different stand from the one I present in this paper. He defended the view that the text of the

Categories does not contain the elements needed to construct an explicit theory of categories in the form in which Aristotle presented in the *Topics*. Frede's argument as regards the *Topics* is convincing, and I find myself in complete agreement. However, his position contains a strong element that raises a certain difficulty about the thesis of my own paper. In effect, while he has correctly objected to the diverse proposals and their ensuing disagreements concerning the categories as classificatory schemes of all entities, his own formulation of the problem allows the conclusion that it is a mistake, repeated by so many of Aristotle's interpreters, to turn to the treatise *Categories* for an answer to the problem of precise characterization of the categories. This is serious reservation, which may not be entirely defensible. Nevertheless, he has adduced evidence to show that the way in which Aristotle, if he is indeed the author of the treatise, did not actually mean it to occupy the place in the *Organon* so many of his readers thought it did and which in turn has seriously influenced the way the *Categories* has been read over the centuries. He also takes the following strong position:

> We are certainly not in a position to say that the book as a whole was meant to be a treatise on categories. But there is also no reason to think that the text as we have it, or even that at least a part of it, namely the first part, was meant to deal with categories. The treatise as we have it does not say anything to the effect that it is going to deal with categories. In fact it does not even use the word "category" except in two lines (10b 19; 10b 21) toward the very end of the first part. And here the word is used in such an incidental way that nothing of interest can be inferred. Nor does the treatise use any other word for "category." (Frede, 1987, 31)

I will try to argue that the absence of explicit treatment together with that of a doctrine to establish the use of categories, does not necessarily support the inference that the requisite elements to build a categorial theory cannot be found in the treatise. As I hope to show, such elements are present and identifiable, and therefore it is superfluous to insist on too sharp a division between the two treatises, the *Topics* and the *Categories* with regard to the construction of the complete theory. I readily agree with Frede that it is a mistake to read the *Categories* in the traditional order of the *Organon*, and would like to underscore his observation that "to assume that the genera referred to are the categories is just to beg the question." I would like to add here a point I have tried to defend in the past, namely that the interpreters who have conflated the categories and the genera of being were inadvertently perhaps attributing to Aristotle a covert redundancy. Before proceeding with my theme, I would like to make a brief reference to Frede's thesis that the text to turn to is the *Topics*, especially chapter 9, which contains the evidence needed to identify the grounds for saying that Aristotle used the verb *kategorein* for the characterization of the predicative relationship that determines how the predicables genus, definition, proprium and accident stand with reference to a subject (Frede, 1987, 32). He notes correctly, I believe, that whereas the established use of this verb was 'to accuse', "it is clear that Aristotle here is using it in the unprecedented sense of 'to predicate', or one should say, in the sense of 'to predicate truly'." (*ibid.*)

The remark concerning the original use of the verb cannot be disputed though not the claim that its occurrence in the *Topics* is in fact unprecedented. It may be that by accepting Frede's claim we may be passing up pertinent evidence of such a use in the *Categories*, if it can be shown, as I think it can, that this treatise does not support the interpretation of class concepts. I see no difficulty in admitting that the case for the use of *kategorein* may not have been so explicitly formulated in the *Categories* as it is found in the *Topics*, but it is unmistakably there via cognate expressions as well as a weaker sense of *kategorein*. Whatever force the evidence from the *Categories* may be, it detracts nothing from Frede's (1987, 34–5) "three conclusions" about the uses of "category" in the *Topics*: (i) "Aristotle uses the word in the sense of 'predication'." (ii) "Aristotle uses the word in the sense of 'kind of predication'." (iii) "Unfortunately, there is yet another use of the term 'kategoria' [in chapter 9]...that the kinds of predication define classes or kinds of predicates, namely the classes of those predicates which occur in a statement of a given kind of predication." Thus:

> If we accept these conclusions concerning the use of the term "kategoria," we will have to distinguish at least three kinds of things: (i) the categories in the technical sense of the word, (ii) classes of predicates defined by the kinds of predication in question, and (iii) the ultimate genera of what there is as they are distinguished, e.g., in the treatise *Categories*. For the ultimate genera of beings clearly are not kinds of predication. Nor can they be identified with the classes of predicates. (p. 35)

The conclusions Frede draws from the close analysis of the crucial chapter 9 of the *Topics*, about the way Aristotle characterizes the categories in the *Topics*, and the study of the differences that obtain amongst them, lead him to say that "a forteriori that the categories of the *Topics* cannot be identified with the ultimate genera of what there is" (Frede, 1987, 36). I see no particular reason to challenge the cogency of the argument. On the contrary, acceptance of the results of Frede's interpretation agrees with the same doctrinal point I have argued is present in the *Categories*, namely that the ultimate genera of being and the ultimate kinds of predication must not be conflated and that to ignore this stricture is to attribute to Aristotle a careless redundancy. Hence it is reasonable to accept the views as stated in the text of the *Categories* as a preamble to a theory more explicitly developed in the *Topics*. It may be objected that the theory under consideration is not formulated in the *Categories* with comparable fullness, but it is unmistakably there.

Frede has been careful not to dismiss without previous examination of the texts the multiple embedded meanings. It is no

The Meaning of Kategoria 155

surprise to the reader that the term '*katēgoria*' is a special instance of a *pollachōs legomenon*, covering distinct linguistic as well as logical entities, viz. predicates and predication, terms and statements, where even each term, upon closer examination is itself a *pollachōs legomenon*, to be understood as cases of *pros hen*. In preparing this revision of my 1983 paper for publication I thought it useful to go beyond the initial purpose to show why certain distinctions in the treatise *Categories* could have prevented Aristotle's interpreters from accepting and defending the established use of *katēgoria* as official doctrine and to restate my argument in response to Professor Frede's denial of the presence of a theory of categories in the *Categories*.

II

Admittedly, the word *katēgoria* occurs only twice in the text, although the verb *katēgorein* is used more frequently. As for the traditional use of the former term, one should not discard the possibility that the assigning of such meanings as "term," "type," "class," "predicate," was affected by an unconscious borrowing from "interpreted" readings of meanings into *katēgoria*, as it occurs in other Aristotelian texts, then transferred to determine the technical meaning of the word in the treatise. But that is another problem and far too complex to be discussed here without introducing issues related to factors influencing the transmission of interpretations. The main topic before us is the relation and affinity between two terms, *genus* and *category*. Generally speaking our problem is this: What precisely can be said about the meaning of the term *katēgoria* and what clues do we possess, assuming that Aristotle (or whoever wrote the treatise) embedded certain ciphers in the text, which, if fully detected, may help us identify the intended philosophical or technical use. Thus our question becomes: How can we attribute to Aristotle a theory of categories, presumably present in the treatise titled

Categories, when we do not even know for certain whether a technical use was in fact intended to function within that theory?[6] If this treatise, especially part 1 (chapters 1-9), has a dominant theme, let us say to put forth "a theory of categories," how do we establish this claim, as Frede (1987, 15) correctly demands? Admittedly, Aristotle has formulated a detectable doctrine, and while it may be present, at least in bare outline, in the *Categories*, the fuller version can be reconstructed and its unity established only through the collection and collation of all the pertinent passages in the extant works as a special section within what may be called his "general theory of language as logical discourse." As things stand now, it would be advisable to begin with the *Topics* and work from there for a systematic reconstruction of such a theory.

III

The present paper, while basically a discussion on evidence, also supports the thesis I discussed in my 1975 paper, in which I defended a propositional interpretation of the Aristotelian categories.[7] The thesis originally intended to criticize and suggest a way to correct the traditional and still prevalent interpretation of Aristotle's use of *katēgoria*, a view that reaches back to the writings of the early commentators, probably with roots in Aristotle's contemporaries in the Academy. What continues to generate the problem under discussion is mainly the one-sidedness of the established view that takes it for granted that the expressions "genera of being" and "genera of category" (γένη τοῦ ὄντος, γένη τῆς κατηγορίας) can be conflated and hence used interchangeably without the slightest alteration of meaning.[8]

However, the range of the problem does not end here. It should be extended to include not only the problem of the aforementioned conflation but also the discrepancy between the inordinate amount of

The Meaning of Kategoria 157

literature on Aristotle's so-called doctrine of categories, claiming that its attendant interpretation is to be found in the brief treatise *Categories*, on the one hand, and the peculiar absence of a definition of the concept, on the other. To this curious textual lacuna one may add the conspicuous absence of a lexical passage to cover the uses of *katēgoria* in the list of principles in *Metaphysics*, Bk. V.[9]

This being the case, it seems only appropriate to raise the issue of evidence. Since the term *katēgoria* is left undefined in these two key treatises,[10] a close examination of the passages where the words *katēgorein*, *katēgoroumenon*, and *katēgoria* occur in the *Categories*, must be undertaken in order to assess the merits or demerits of the traditional reading of these terms. It may be difficult, but it is not impossible to identify the functions of the concept of *katēgoria* in Aristotle's logical, ontological, and other doctrines. Ancient and later commentators, down to the present, have justifiably devoted lengthy studies to this aspect of his philosophy. In light of the scholarship in this area, it should be pointed out that the history of proposed interpretations exhibits variations of the same fundamental approach, one that is dominated by the quest for ultimate simples, be they genera of beings, of classes, of concepts, or of signifiers. Perhaps the sole exception is a thesis Christian Brandis proposed a century ago that the Aristotelian categories are "the most general forms or species of propositions which are removed and dissociated from sentential contexts."[11] Evidently it found no supporters, and the traditional interpretation continued to prevail intact. One of the curious features its defenders share is the absence of any discussion on the question why *katēgoria* is not defined in the logical treatises or in the *Metaphysics*, despite the fact that every commentator and interpreter has accepted as given Aristotle's "doctrine of categories," a *Kategorienlehre*. Perhaps we will never find a satisfactory answer to that question, but we must not therefore accept the view that a problem does not exist. Briefly stated, it pertains to the range of the functions of the theory, namely coverage of the genera of being, including highest classes of predicates. If so, the problem of range raises the question whether it is proper to extend the range to include a theory of ultimate types of propositions as a basic, although unacknowledged, component of the doctrine.[12] Evidently, the question of a wider range did not find any serious supporters. It had become impertinent.

The history of the commentaries on the doctrine of categories reveals a continuum: the same fundamental approach dominated by the quest for ultimate simples. In order to secure the pursuit, interpreters defended the conflation of Aristotle's distinction between "genera of being" and "genera of category or categories." A tradition was established whereby interpreters persistently argued to identify the categories (a) logically with the κατὰ μηδεμίαν συμπλοκὴν λεγόμενα (things not said in combination), and (b) ontologically with the γένη τοῦ ὄντος (genera of being). The underlying assumption in either case is that the two lists of genera can be conflated conceptually and used interchangeably without serious alteration of the basic meaning of *katēgoria*.

We must therefore re-examine the text of the *Categories* in order to ascertain the correctness of the view that restricts the meaning of the term *katēgoria* to ultimate types of predicates and simple signifiers. The analysis that follows questions whether the prevalent traditional approach to the meaning of *katēgoria* has the textual evidence needed to render its claims definitive. Positively stated, the proposal to extent the meaning of this celebrated term to include the propositional thesis can be supported through a different reading of the related passages. Although Aristotle explicitly refers to ultimate units of signification, the term *kategoria*, as used in the text, does not preclude a reading according to which it stands for propositions as the fundamental carriers of completed attributions whose function is to capture in *logos* the traits of beings.

The position is essentially the same I essayed to present in my several previous publications on the subject, but now with slight modifications. The main thrust of the argument in those papers was to show that instead of assuming that simple conceptual units, however identified, constitute the sole basis for determining the meaning of the categories, we should also consider as suitable candidates the complex units of judgment (κρίσις), which as assertions are cases of "expressions said in combination" (κατὰ συμπλοκὴν λεγόμενα). As such they convey the perceived factual connections of the traits of things (ὄντα). Each confirmable attribution, correctly noticed and reported, is an assertion (κατάφασις).

Since first *ousia* is the ultimate and first subject, the ontic *hypokeimenon*, and is naturally a composite unity, to say what *ousia* is, by capturing its complexity in the activity of speech, *legein*, requires the employment of composite logical unities: attributive statements as signifiers of articulated judgments. There is good reason why the making of attributive statements should be brought under the umbrella of the extended meaning of the *katēgoria*, a word that originally meant "accusation." This abstract noun and the related words that Aristotle added to his terminology derive from the key verb κατηγορεῖν.

I should like to point out certain flaws that attend the conflating of basic expressions. Carried out in the case of the terms "predication" and "predicate" (κατηγορία and κατηγορούμενον), this operation has the obvious advantage of preserving the meaning of categories as simple and ultimate types of signifying predicative units. However, by so doing it also causes confusion and unavoidable interpretive errors. Therefore, it is of the essence that these two terms be kept apart and be discussed separately when obscurities in the text explicitly demand the preserving of distinctions. Comparably, it behooves to exhibit the coordinate function of basic terms without using such alien notions of conceptual subordination of terms as found in the diverse metaphysical or epistemological schemes of categorial deduction. It cannot be denied that our translations from the Greek depend on the use of terminology of conflation and/or unexplained substitutions due to the interchangeable employment of the expressions "predicate" and "predication" for κατηγορούμενον and κατηγορία.[13]

A *katēgoria*, in its functional aspect, stands for the articulated outcome of what speakers do when completing an accusation and, by extension, an attribution. To do what *katēgorein* calls for is to effect by means of verbal signs an attributive statement in order to exhibit a determinate connection between a subject and what belongs to it either essentially or as co-incidental properties, i.e., what the subject *is* and *has*. Given this fuller context, then, a "category" is in function and structure a complex utterance, what Aristotle calls a case of κατὰ συμπλοκὴν λεγόμενον; it employs a subject word and a predicate word, either a noun and a verb or signifiers connected with the copula. One of the key passages that support this position occurs in *Posterior Analytics* I. 22, 82b 37-84a 2, and is reinforced by what is said in *Prior Analytics* I. 46, 52a 15, where *katēgoria* is unambiguously equated to *kataphasis,* "affirmation." Caution is advised at this point, because one must not conclude from uses of *katēgoria* discernable in the *Analytics* that they are also present in the treatise *Categories*. More work needs to be done to show that such is the case. In general, nothing of real value to our understanding of Aristotle is gained by taking the term *katēgoria* to stand for the genera of beings and hence using it to cover the case of highest predicates. What I think is needed is the restoration of the embedded distinction Aristotle introduced between predicate and predication and by so doing preserve the difference between genera of being and genera of categories. The ontic reference of the former must be keep separate from the expressions to which Aristotle refers when he talks about "things said in combination" (κατὰ συμπλοκὴν λεγόμενα), i.e., when he refers to the canonical assertions in accordance with the rules that govern the syntax of attributions to reflect the complex properties of individual *ousiai,* their essential and their accidental

The Meaning of Kategoria

properties. When the distinction is observed, the conditions for the use of language in (a) naming and (b) stating are brought in line with the complexity of things. Truth belongs to the logical-linguistic function of articulating the experience of reality. The categories supply the ultimate propositional forms for announcing and communicating the content of true statements.

IV

In the *Categories* we encounter two expressions, both related to the same root and differing only in the prefix: προσηγορία and κατηγορία. The former is hardly ever discussed as an ingredient in Aristotle's theory of categories, yet there is no doubt that it is part of the broader terminological apparatus to be taken into account when an attempt is made to reconstruct the theory. *prosēgoria* occurs only twice in the *Categories*, in 1a 13 and 3a 14, as part of the following expressions: κατὰ τοὔνομα προσηγορία and σχῆμα τῆς προσηγορίας.[14] We should also note that the second occurrence comes after the two occurrences of κατηγορία in chapter 5, 3a 35 and 37. The verb κατηγορεῖν and the passive form κατηγορεῖσθαι, as well as the passive present participle κατηγορούμενον, occur earlier in the treatise, beginning with chapter 3, 1b 10. Yet the verb προσηγορεῖν is not to be found anywhere either in the *Categories* or in the *De Interpretatione*. The closest expression is προσαγορεύεται, as in 1a 9, in connection with the term *synonyma*, to explain what the latter are: οἷον ζῷον ὅ τε ἄνθρωπος καί ὁ βοῦς· τούτων γὰρ ἑκάτερον κοινῷ ὀνόματι προσαγορεύεται ζῷον. A comparison of uses, as these passages indicate, shows that προσηγορία is limited to "naming" and "appellation" and the related verb "to call by name." This connection to the word "name," ὄνομα, helps us better to understand the technical term *katēgoria*, also whether the operation called "scheme of naming" (σχῆμα τῆς προσηγορίας) is transferrable to the operation to which the expression "mode of predication," σχῆμα τῆς κατηγορίας refers. Since these are two distinct operations, the conflation in question cannot be maintained without an explanation of this difference.

The first occurrence of the verb *katēgorein* makes it clear that what is meant is a complex set of signifiers to state determinate connections between two signified things, between two instances of *onta*, which have presumably been named. We are now beyond the level of *prosēgoria*. One would expect, therefore, that since *katēgoria* signifies the result of articulating a judgment by combining signifiers to form a complete statement, we should expect the disclosure to have articulated a determinate connection between two named things, and, to be more precise, not an unfinished utterance like "the rose and the lady" or "Jane and June." What is expected is an instance of genuine attribution. Chapter 2 makes clear what the term *hypokeimenon* means in two special contexts: (1) to be in a subject and (b) to be said of a subject. The fourfold combination given there provides the parameters needed for the formulation of canons.

As Aristotle proceeds with chapter 3, the ground has been carefully prepared to introduce the verb *katēgorein* in the technical sense. The more general expression *legetai* is left behind.[15] What is said of a subject will now be called *katēgoroumenon*. The preceding chapter has already made clear what it is to be a subject: it is an existent, a being, ὄν, and also the recipient of a *prosēgoria*, a name. The name of the existent is a signifier, a *"legomenon* not said in combination" (λεγόμενον μὴ κατὰ συμπλοκήν). However, qua ὄν it underlies all other types of inhering existents only if it is also a first *ousia*. Being a first *ousia* it cannot be *in* another subject, nor can it be *said* of another subject. We now know what any being must have in order to qualify as *hypokeimenon par excellence*.

Chapter 3 opens with a statement where the verb *katēgorein* occurs for the first time and presupposes (i) the aforesaid clarification

The Meaning of Kategoria 163

of the fundamental meaning of *hypokeimenon* and (ii) the canonical ways of stating the interconnections of beings. With *katēgorein* we move from the names of things, the prosegoric operation, to the complex act of attribution, by means of which predicates are connected to subjects. Given the fundamental position of the subject and the rule that "whatever is said of a predicated thing will also be said of the subject," the pattern of controlled predication of named things, i.e., concrete subjects, and species and genera, including the differentiating properties, is next carefully delineated. We now have become cognizant of the first and crucial type of combined expressions, κατὰ συμπλοκὴν λεγόμενα. The text offers incontrovertible evidence that the verb *katēgorein* is used to cover canonically controlled combined expressions in the making of attributions. The concepts involved in the performance of *katēgorein* are also the ones employed in the classification of individuals and the formation of essential definitions via the use of signifiers of concrete individuals—as ultimate subjects—of species, genera and differentiae.

The next question is straightforward enough. What are the diverse ultimate genera of beings? There are certain things, and we have names for them, which are said of a subject and exist in said subject. This being the case, to give an account of the ways of inherence of such instances is to articulate an existential connection in accordance with the canons of predication. When Aristotle proceeds to present his celebrated inventory of types or genera of beings, he gives us a list of the most comprehensive denotative signifiers; each is a case of κατὰ μηδεμίαν συμπλοκὴν λεγόμενον. Each has its place as an element in the act of *katēgorein*. Together these elements comprise what has been traditionally and, in my opinion, mistakenly labelled "the Aristotelian categories." Yet, the term *katēgoria* is nowhere to be found in chapter 4. Instead, all we have is a carefully drawn and rather uncomplicated set of expressions to cover the following fundamentals: (1) things exist; (2) the ultimate existents are those in which instances of the other genera of beings inhere (a fact that explains why only the former function as the ultimate subjects of canonical predications); (3) shared names of things, i.e., genuine signifiers naming things that came under any one (excluding first *ousia*) of the ten genera of being; (4) how simple signifiers understood as uncombined expressions function denotatively; (5) why, when taken singly, none of these uncombined expressions qualifies to function as an affirmation (*kataphasis*); (6) that affirmations are made by canonically combined simple signifiers;[16] and (7) only canonical affirmations can be said to be either true or false, whereas none of the uncombined signifiers, their denotative power notwithstanding, are either true or false.

The remaining chapters are given to (a) an analysis of the range of denotation of each type of simple signifiers—and with many surprising results, not least of which is the recognition that with the exception of *ousia* all the other general signifiers of types of being are cases of homonymy; and (b) to the itemizing of the subclasses of signified beings that determine which mode of predication which is appropriate to each as the names of denoted entities are assigned their place in well-formed statements with referential claims.

Now we may turn our attention to chapter 4. There is no technical term in this brief Chapter to justify the traditional view adopted by the earlier commentators and continued ever since, that identifies the "ten categories" with the ten most general types of signifiers or ten uncombined signifying expressions: *ousia, quantity, quality, relative, where, when, position, having, doing, undergoing.*

Neither the verb *katēgorein* nor the noun *katēgoria* occurs in this chapter. The expression that provides a clue to explain its absence is *kataphasis*. However, the rule of forming proper affirmations, of stringing signifiers to produce referential combinations with truth claims, is not disclosed either. The four examples of uncombined expressions that Aristotle gives at the end of the chapter, i.e. (a) 'human being' (b) 'white', (c) 'runs' (d) 'wins', if randomly combined,

The Meaning of Kategoria 165

do not necessarily produce affirmations. Obviously, certain combinations must be ruled out at the outset, e.g. 'white wins', 'runs wins', 'runs white', 'wins man', etc. Acceptable candidates are 'man wins', 'man runs', and cases where a copula is supplied, in the combination 'man... white'. The point is anything but trivial, as the next chapter makes clear.

Chapter 5 deals with *ousia* on two levels: ontologically, it is recognized that *ousia* is the most fundamental signifier, and logically, it hold the key that discloses the conditions for canonical combinations of signifiers of beings. After introducing the distinction between the primary and secondary meanings of *ousia*, Aristotle suddenly changes his 'saying' verbs, and shifts from *legetai* to the more technical verb *katēgorein*, "to predicate" (and its passive form *katēgoreisthai*), i.e. to attribute what one signifier denotes to what another signifier names according to the ontological order of essence and inherence of things. The ontic settings of things determine the correct modes for effecting proper combinations of signifiers. The verb *katēgorein* as used, legislates requisite restrictions for the weaving of signifiers in reporting the objective complexity of being as first *ousia*, and as species and differentia and as genus. Since no first *ousia* can be predicated of another first *ousia*, the remaining substantive signifiers fall into place in accordance with essence and inherence.

The only two occurrences of the word *katēgoria* in this chapter are related to the formulation of the two rules that govern substantive predication, one positive and one prohibitive.[17] (a) *Positive*: In all canonical predications involving secondary *ousiai* and *differentiae*, the assertions are about either individuals or species (3a 34-5). Thus the rule is that in substantive statements of attribution the subject position is occupied either by a first *ousia* signifier or a species signifier. (b) *Prohibitive*: No predication using first *ousiai* as attributive signifiers is legitimate or even comprehensible. The rule is that no first *ousia* functions as *katēgoroumenon* in a well-formed predication.

Before proceeding with the discussion of *katēgorein* and *katēgoreisthai*, and the third occurrence of *katēgoria*, it is important to note that neither the verb nor the noun is employed in the special analysis of the range of denotation of each general type of signifiers, i.e., what the traditional view calls "categories." The verb Aristotle uses almost invariably in this long portion of the treatise is *legetai*. Each genus comes in for an analysis (though not exhaustive) and enumeration of the subordinate subclasses of signifiers of things that are collected together under the umbrella of an inclusive and ultimate class. Whether this is an analysis of "categories," an unpackaging of inclusive types of names, is highly debatable, to say the least. Whatever it is that Aristotle is doing there leaves little room for speculation. What needs to be re-iterated is that nowhere in these analyses of ultimate classes of signifiers does he use the term *katēgoria* to refer to the classifiable things these denote.

V

All commentators who have suppressed the terminological difference between predicate and predication (κατηγορούμενον and κατηγορία) conclude that *katēgoria* means "predicate," thus lending their authority to a misreading of the passages in which Aristotle uses the word κατηγορία *to mean* "attributive proposition." The position I have taken in this paper is presented as an argument to support a different reading and with the hope that the established interpretation can be corrected through a fresh examination of the textual testimonies to accommodate the suppressed part of Aristotle's theory of categories as ultimate types of canonical propositions. The thesis I have sought to advance is, in technical language, that the categories stand for fundamental types of attribution that conform to rules formulated in accordance with the ontology of first substance (πρώτη οὐσία).

In order to make the argument stand I think it necessary to propose that this reading, since it draws attention to the logical and grammatical syntax of predicative statements, requires in the context of the treatise *Categories* a shifting of emphasis from simple expressions or, what Alexander of Aphrodisias called "the most general parts of *logos* whose purpose is to signify simple things and simple concepts about simple things,"[18] to *things said in combination par excellence*. The objective now becomes one of showing how the fundamental modes of predication (τὰ σχήματα τῆς κατηγορίας), in accordance with the ontic range of the ten genera of being, can be determined through a careful scrutiny of canonical attributive statements. In these statements it is always the case that the signifying exemplars in each distinct genus of being are introduced and assigned to occupy the subject and predicate positions by conforming to the logic of rules in accordance with essence and inherence.

The critical review of evidence must begin reasonably enough with the brief treatise *Categories*. Most authorities agree that this treatise contains a number of fundamentals to be found in Aristotle's theory on the subject. Yet the claim seems somewhat paradoxical when we stop to think that nowhere in this treatise does Aristotle elaborate on the use of this term. To this peculiarity we must add the conspicuous absence of a special chapter in *Metaphysics* V to explain the concept of category as a principle, although there are separate chapters on such genera of being as *ousia*, quantity, quality, and the other genera of being mistakenly identified with what tradition calls "categories." As for the term *kategoria*, in the *Categories*, much to our surprise, it occurs only in two passages, in chapter 5 and in chapter 8, twice in each chapter, for a total of four occurrences,[19] and all come *after* the presentation of the listing of uncombined expressions, i.e., the signifiers of genera of being, ones that comprise the celebrated list of traditional categories.

Of greater weight is the frequent occurrence of the verb κατηγορεῖν-κατηγορεῖσθαι and the passive present participle κατηγορούμενον. The first occurrence of κατηγορεῖν in chapter 3, 1b 10, makes clear that it refers to the activity of connecting two signified things in the manner of attribution. The logical and ontological grounds have already been made clear in what is said in chapter 2 with reference to what it means to be "in a subject" and to be "said of a subject." The fourfold combination they produce yields the parameters for the formulation of the canons of correct attribution, which in turn determine the type of predication (κατηγορία) under which any well formed affirmation (κατάφασις) falls. The technical sense of κατηγορεῖν is undeniably present; by implication as well as use, the same holds for κατηγορία. Neither of the two, nor the term κατηγορούμενον, is employed in the analyses of the denotative scope of the genera of being that follow the discussion on *ousia*. Instead, we see a systematic use of the verb λέγεται for the unraveling of their uses and denotations. The word *katēgoria* makes its last brief appearance in chapter 8, where it can mean either "predicate" or "predication," the latter being the more suitable reading. In view of these facts, one cannot help but wonder how so many interpreters came to accept the *Categories* as the unquestioned source of a non-Aristotelian doctrine of categories.

The Meaning of Kategoria

NOTES

1. This paper was presented at the December 28, 1983 meeting of the Society for Ancient Greek Philosophy, Boston, MA. Published in A. Preus and J. P. Anton, eds. *Essays in Ancient Greek Philosophy*, Vol 5: *Aristotle's Ontology*. Albany, N. Y.: State University of New York Press, 1992, pp. 3–18; reprinted with minor changes.

2. Anton (1975), 67-81.

3. The title of the treatise was a subject of considerable dispute in antiquity. For a recent survey on this problem see M. Frede 1987b, 11-28. According to Frede "the question of authenticity is crucially linked to the question of unity" (12). The problem of the unity covers the relation of the early part of the treatise to the part that discusses the post-predicamenta.

4. There are many surveys of interpretations concerning the categories. I do not plan to offer another survey, for my main interest lies in the investigation into what we can learn about the theory of categories in the *Categories*. Nor am I concerned with reproducing and commenting on the table of enumeration of the "categories" in Aristotle's works. The list can be readily found in Apelt 1891, conveniently reproduced in Elders 1961, 194–6. One can still raise the question about the intent of the list or lists. If a defense of objections can be made to the reading that makes the list of "categories" refer to classes of being, then we have an alternative before us, which has not been adequately explored, namely whether the list refers not classes of being or classes of predicates but to the types of statements that pertain to the attribution of genuine features present in the entity named in the subject position. It is the existence of the concrete individual qua subject that sets the context for the selective lists of relevant types of attribution.

5. Reprinted in Frede 1987, 29–48; originally in O'Meara 1981. Much to my regret Frede's article became available to me after I presented my paper in December 1983, and therefore had no opportunity to address his thesis at that time.

6. It is debatable whether it is correct to speak of a fully formed and theoretically developed "categorial theory," in the modern sense of such a theory, embedded somehow in Aristotle's logical works. It certainly cannot be found in the manner in which Kant (1952), A81/B107 for instance, developed such a theory. Aristotle never defines the term *category*, yet he uses it in ways that he must have believed that his students and readers understood him. He used it in a technical sense, but not in the sense that his Neoplatonist commentators, medieval and modern, attributed to him. His theory, if it can be fully reconstructed, seems to belong to his theory of language, his philosophy of *logos*, of rational discourse as the capacity to articulate the structures and processes of the world, including those of the human existence.

7. See also Anton 1981, 214–220 and 1982, 60–77.

8. The expression τὰ γένη τῶν κατηγοριῶν does not occur in the *Categories*; it is found in *Topics* I. 9, 103b 20, 29, 39; also in *Soph. El.* 178a 5. In *Topics* I. 15, 107a 2-3 the text reads: τὰ γένη τῶν κατὰ τὸ ὄνομα κατηγοριῶν. Here the expression is used to identify *homonyma*, cases where the same genus is illicitly predicated of all things having the same name but not sharing in the definition.

9. *Met.* V, devotes separate chapters to the following fundamental concepts, traditionally called "categories"; ὄν: 7, 1017a 7-b 9; οὐσία: 8, 1017b 10-25; ποσόν: 13, 1020a 7-32; ποιόν: 14, 1020a 33-b 25; πρός τι: 16 1020b 26-1021b 11; πάθος: 21, 1022b 15-21; ἔχειν: 23, 1023a 8-25.

10. A stipulative definition is also absent in the *De Interpretatione*, a work in which this term occurs only once. This is rather strange, especially in view of the fact that Aristotle assigns technical meanings to 'name' or 'noun', and 'verb', 'affirmation', 'negation', 'proposition' or 'statement', and 'sentence' (*logos*).

11. Quoted in Brentano 1975, 177 n. 141. See Brandis 1862, 394, citing three passages in support of this view, *Top.* I. 9, 103b 20, *Met.* VII. 2, 1028a 26, and XIV. 2, 1089a 26; also Brandis 1862a, 430–1.

The Meaning of Kategoria

12. The prevailing view on the subject in the long history of philosophy has not changed since the time of the early commentators. For instance, Iamblichus, summarizing the venerable tradition of the Neoplatonists, declares that the categories are "expressions signifying things by means of concepts." Simplicius, *ACG*. VIII, 2. 30–3. 17, where he lists the names of the interpreters who in his opinion came closest to Aristotle: Alexander of Aphrodisias, Alexander of Aegae, Porphyry (who borrowed from the views of Theophrastus and Boethus), Herminus, Iamblichus, and Syrianus; also at 67. 26ff. he gives his and Iamblichus' views on what the division into ten genera means and what it contains. Kant's views are too well known to call for comment. In more recent times Bonitz declared the categories "the highest genera of being," while W. D. Ross 1924 (lxxxii–lxxxiii, and lxxxiii, n. 2) called them "the predicates *par excellence*." On the whole, the views on the subject have varied but slightly, all of them favoring the thesis that the categories stand for ultimate simple predicates or concepts, either in the sense of the highest genera of things or the highest concepts of the mind.

13. Consider the difficulty a translator must face when asked to revert to the original language and identify equivalent terms for the ones he has selected from his own language to render texts. In English, the expressions used to translate the categorial passages in Aristotle are "to predicate," "predicable," and "predication." Now, if *kategoria*, in its technical sense, can only mean "predicate," the translator would be at a loss to come up with a separate term to cover the case of predication as the equivalent of "proposition." By avoiding the conflation, this puzzling problem disappears. I bring up this issue mainly because it shows how interpretations seriously affect the manner of translating complex texts as well as of discussing substantive issues.

14. LSG list several meaning of προσηγορία; Aristotle's use in *Cat.* 1a 13 is translated to mean "addressing" and in 3b 14 to mean "appellation," "name."

15. Guthrie 1981, 142 n. 4 differs on this point, as he remarks in a note meant to correct what I intimated in my 1975 article. His comment to the effect that *katēgoreisthai* and *legetai* are used indifferently is not convincing, as we shall see.

16. Subsequent to this, Aristotle states in chapter 10, 12b 9-10 that τῶν ὑπὸ τὴν κατάφασιν καὶ τὴν ἀπόφασιν οὐδέν ἐστι λόγος: the component elements of affirmations and negations, being uncombined signifiers, are not statements and hence are neither true nor false.

17. The positive in *Cat.* 5, 3a 33-37: Ὑπάρχει δὲ ταῖς οὐσίαις καὶ ταῖς διαφοραῖς τὰ πάντα συνωνύμως ἀπ᾽ αὐτῶν λέγεσθαι· πᾶσαι γὰρ αἱ ἀπὸ τούτων κατηγορίαι ἤτοι κατὰ τῶν ἀτόμων κατηγοροῦνται ἢ κατὰ τῶν εἰδῶν. ἀπὸ μὲν γὰρ τῆς πρώτης οὐσίας οὐδεμία ἐστὶ κατηγορία,— κατ᾽ οὐδενὸς γὰρ ὑποκειμένου λέγεται—. The prohibitive passage is in 8, 10b 12-25: Ὑπάρχει δὲ καὶ ἐναντιότης κατὰ τὸ ποιόν, οἷον δικαιοσύνη ἀδικίᾳ ἐναντίον καὶ λευκότης μελανίᾳ καὶ τἆλλα ὡσαύτως, καὶ τὰ κατ᾽ αὐτὰς δὲ ποιὰ λεγόμενα...ἔτι ἐὰν τῶν ἐναντίων θάτερον ᾖ ποιόν, καὶ τὸ λοιπὸν ἔσται ποιόν. τοῦτο δὲ δῆλον προχειριζομένῳ τὰς ἄλλας κατηγορίας, οἷον εἰ ἔστι ἡ δικαιοσύνη τῇ ἀδικίᾳ ἐναντίον, ποιὸν δὲ ἡ δικαιοσύνη, ποιὸν ἄρα καὶ ἡ ἀδικία· οὐδεμία γὰρ τῶν ἄλλων κατηγοριῶν ἐφαρμόζει τῇ ἀδικίᾳ, ποσὸν οὔτε πρός τι οὔτε πού, οὐδ᾽ ὅλως τι τῶν τοιούτων οὐδὲν ἀλλ᾽ ἢ ποιόν· ὡσαύτως δὲ καὶ ἐπὶ τῶν ἄλλων κατὰ τὸ ποιὸν ἐναντίων.

18. Ammonius, *CAG.* IV, 13. Philoponus quotes Ammonius and concurs with Alexander of Aphrodisias, according to Simplicius, *CAG.* VIII, 10, 10-19; also Brandis 1836, 31a 6.

19. Frede (1987, 16) claims that κατηγορία occurs only once in this treatise: 10b 19-20, but corrects this later to say that it occurs twice in a passage "in two lines" (10b 19; 10b 21): "The treatise as we have it does not say anything to the effect that it is going to deal with categories. In fact, it does not even use the word 'category' except in two lines (10b 19; 10b 21) toward the very end of the first part. and here the word is used in such an incidental way that nothing of interest can be inferred. Nor does the treatise use any other word for 'category'" (Frede, 1987, 31). Two

The Meaning of Kategoria

reservations are in order: (a) *kategoria* in the singular occurs in chapter 5, 3a 35 and 3a 37, and in the plural in chapter 8, 10b 19 and 10b 21. (b) To say that nothing of interest can be inferred from *all* four occurrences seems to be a rather rigid position to take, even if all the ingredients that comprise a complete theory of categories are not identifiable in the text as we have it.

ARISTOTLE'S THEORY OF CATEGORIES AND POST-CLASSICAL ONTOLOGIES[1]

This paper consists of two parts: (a) a thesis concerning Aristotle's categorical theory and (b) a critique of the established tradition that has lasted to the present day.

I. Thesis

A close examination of the philosophical theory that undergirds Aristotle's conception of the categories allows for an alternative interpretation that goes against the traditional approach. I intend to show that his conception rests firmly on his ontology and that it is a theory of discourse dealing) with statements and propositions rather than such things as terms, simple notions or concepts. My view is that Aristotle's categories are better understood when identified with complex expressions *ta kata symplokēn legomena* and thus distinguishable from the genera of being *ta genē tou ontos* i.e. contrary to what the traditional interpretations have invariably done. What matters in either case is the fact that the texts do not allow us to conclude with certainty that Aristotle intended the term 'category' to mean simple rather than complex expressions.

In a paper, "Some Observations on Aristotle's Theory of Categories", which I published some years ago, I discussed in considerable detail and defended the thesis that the expressions 'genera of being' and 'genera of predication' *genē tou ontos, genē tēs katēgorias* are not interchangeable. Taken as technical expressions, the two sets of concepts do not cover the same grounds. By attending to their difference Aristotle not only meant to exhibit the functional interrelationship between his theory of being and that of discourse about being, but also to formulate the canon or canons that govern the basic and irreducible types of correct attribution. My related thesis was that the modes of predication, *schēmata tēs katēgorias* as in accord with the genera of being, ten at the most, can be arrived at by means of a careful scrutiny of assertive couplings when signifying examples of each distinct genus are introduced to occupy the subject and predicate positions.

I am fully aware that these two theses lead to conclusions radically different from the ones the established tradition has supported. Thus, in the first part of this paper I will try to indicate why it is that the established tradition, from Porphyry to Ryle, which views the Aristotelian categories as ultimate predicates, is systematically misleading. There is an explanation for the persistence of this lopsided Aristotelianism, as I hope to show in the second part of my discussion. Generally speaking, the traditional approach is the result of the illicit placing of Aristotle's categorical doctrine within ontological frameworks signally different from his own; furthermore, it was made to solve philosophical problems Aristotle had not regarded crucial to his own investigations. The post-Aristotelian ontologies of Stoicism, Neopythagoreanism and Neoplatonism, and also the ones worked out in the philosophical theologies of Scholasticism, each in its own way, reiterated the tradition of viewing the categories as elemental units and conceptual simples rather than canonical assertions. Briefly put, Hellenistic and Medieval philosophies filtered Aristotle's ontology and categorical theory through their own frameworks and interpreted them accordingly to serve their own objectives: the quest for absolute simples, whether things or ideas, and the discernment of the units of ultimate reality. The later goals were carried out under the aegis of the Infinite.

The fact remains that for Aristotle *ousia* is the fundamental and primary being; it is composite and yet individual, a complete unit, a formally and functionally integrated whole, the *focus* of activities and the *locus* of all *symbebēkota*. Admittedly, the texts allow for two uses of the term 'category': (i) ultimate predicates and (ii) ultimate types of predication. However, it is only through considerable straining that this term can be made to refer only to types of simple and ultimate predicates referring in turn to ultimate simples. A *categoria*, being the expression of a judgmental act, favors the second alternative. *Katēgoria* is the *par excellence* case of the *kata symplokēn legomena mē kata symplokēn legomena genē tou ontos* the fundamental unit of intelligent discourse: judgment become articulate. The referential force of *katēgoria* is directed to the *ousiai* and their features, i.e., to the unified composite things and their interactions, the beings that constitute the domain of nature.

II. Critique

The traditional interpretations of the Aristotelian categories have invariably chosen to identify the categories (a) logically, with the *mē kata symplokēn legomena* and (b) ontologically with the *genē tou ontos*; thus they either neglected or suppressed the alternative view, namely that category also means a well-formed assertion according to canons derived from the nature of things and the responsive functions of human judgment. Aristotle's non-reductive ontology, which carefully avoided the polarization of the 'one-many' distinction while acknowledging the complexity of beings, was gradually abandoned or subsumed under different theoretical principles in the postclassical ontologies. In this section I will (a) examine certain crucial cases that depart from, but alter significantly, Aristotle's own position, and (b) indicate the transformation in ontological thinking that necessitated the deviations which in turn provided the basis for misinterpreting Aristotle's ontological theory, particularly with respect to the categories.

With the advent of Hellenistic thought we witness a revival of interest in theological cosmology. It brought with it the reversal of the place Aristotle had assigned to the inquiry into being, mainly by appending ontology to genetic views of reality. As a result, the meaning of *ousia* underwent new transformations.

Stoic materialism made *ousia* the primary and quality-less ultimate matter of all beings. This primordial *ousia* is at once the agent of action and its passive receiver. The Stoic technical expression *ousia tō n ontōn*, *ousia* of beings, is as un-Aristotelian as that of *apoios ousia*. Given this basic difference, it is patently unsound to suggest that the Stoics improved upon Aristotle's ontology by reducing the ten genera of being to their own four: *ousia*, quality, disposition and relative disposition.[2] The Stoics proved ingenious in developing a logic suited to their 'process' universe and its continuous qualifications. However, their four types of being are not categories, and to call them so is nothing but a terminological misnomer. It is debatable whether the Stoics ever used the term *katēgoria*. My own view on this subject is that the search for an analogue may strike better luck by turning to the Stoic theory of *lekta*.

The ontology of Plotinus marks a turning point in the development of Western categorical theory. Given his conception of the One, all predication becomes necessarily restricted to derivative kinds of reality. Yet the ultimate objects of prediction are not the sensible entities but the intelligible ones: *nous* and its ideas. By reviving and extending Plato's treatment of the sensible *ousiai* Plotinus not only assigned in his own conception of reality a low place to Aristotle's genera of being, but also carried out a devastating criticism of Aristotle's categorical theory. Plotinus' acceptance and revision of Plato's five *megista genē* provided the conceptual apparatus he needed to show that Aristotle's genera of being are not applicable to the realm of the intelligible; even worse, they prove inadequate for apprehending correctly the nature of the sensible objects. After Plotinus' attack and Porphyry's accommodating interpretation,

Aristotle's categorical theory became the subject of continuous distortion and misunderstanding from which it never fully recovered.

For Porphyry, Aristotle's categories are taken to be incomplex modes of signification. Simplicius' writings leave no mistake about this. Porphyry's view was faithfully adopted and followed by all the ancient commentators. He did more than just provide the impetus for this tradition: he also presented an Aristotle 'in reverse' by advocating the study of the predicables as the proper way to understanding the *Categories*. The roots of medieval realism go back to the writing of Porphyry.

As late as the fourteenth century even the staunch critic of Porphyry and the Neoplatonist Aristotelians, William of Ockham, found it impossible to free himself from the established tradition that had conflated the genera of being and the categories. *Kategoria* and *kategorēma* had become indistinguishable. As a critic of logical realism, Ockham rejected Porphyry's priorities only to replace them with some of his own, including that which places acts of signification over the modes of Porphyrian predication. For Ockham, the categories as names are of second intention, and, in another sense, every category is a simple term of first intention. Affirmations and negations are composed of just such simple categorical terms. This, he holds, is "the view of the ancients." Ockham, the nominalist, never seems to have questioned what all realists maintained, namely, that Aristotle's categories must belong to the *mē kata symplokēn legomena*.

Antoine Arnauld's *Port-Royal Logic* (1662) added nothing new to the tradition. If anything, it created new middles. Arnauld's ambivalent comments on Aristotle *Organum* need not concern us here. There are three important references to the doctrine of the categories that carry special weight, particularly in view of the influence this handbook had on subsequent philosophical developments. (i) The Aristotelian categories are identified as "the different classes into which Aristotle divided objects of thought."

Arnauld's discussion of the case of substance as either corporal or incorporeal is manifestly indebted to the "Tree of Porphyry." (ii) After dispelling the "mystery" about these famous categories, Arnauld assures his reader that they are of little use, and they help but slightly the formation of judgment and often even hinder it considerably; they are "arbitrarily founded on the imagination of a man who has no authority to prescribe a law to others." (iii) Finally, he finds the doctrine dangerous in that it "accustoms man to be satisfied with mere words." Arnauld's disparaging remarks are as interesting as is his misunderstanding of the doctrine, inexcusable, given the master of logical skills that he was. Be that as it may, his work had much to do with the manner in which the categories were discussed in the seventeenth and eighteenth centuries.

In his *Critique of Pure Reason*, Kant admits readily, though probably somewhat hastily, that in agreement with Aristotle he will call his concepts of pure understanding "categories," stating also that while his primary purpose is the same, his own position diverges widely in manner of execution (A 80). Kant's reservations regarding the number and origin of Aristotle's categories is another matter. What is relevant here is his characterization of the doctrine. Kant's rationalist thesis, one which identifies the categories as concepts, reaches back to the tradition that started with the early Neoplatonist commentators. In this regard, Kant is in line with all his predecessors who opted for the view that the categories are *mē kata symplokēn legomena.*

What in the terminology of the *Port-Royal Logic* was called "ideas" became in Kant's language "pure concepts of the understanding." Two other points need mentioning here. First, Kant believes that Aristotle arrived at his theory empirically, a view that can easily be defended on the basis of what Aristotle says in the last chapters of the *Posterior Analytics* and elsewhere. However, as an interpretation it will not hold since it rests on the assumption that the categories, insofar as they are concepts must stand for the genera of being. So far, Kant's remarks, as stated in the first *Critique* contain nothing that he could not have derived from his *Inaugural Dissertation* of 1770, when he was still making ontology logically prior to epistemology. Given the early rationalist metaphysics of Kant, Aristotle cannot be other than an empiricist, for the fact is that their respective ontologies face in opposite directions. The second point is that in his first *Critique*, Kant carries Arnauld's dissatisfaction a step further, and although he is careful to distinguish between predicaments (= *categories*) and the predicables, he sees himself as being unlike those who used induction and who gathered their categorical concepts rhapsodically and as the result "of a haphazard search after pure concepts" (A 81). Even Kant could not extricate himself from the powerful influence of the traditional approach to Aristotle's thought.

III. A Concluding Remark

What I explored in this paper was the ways in which the shifts in post-Aristotelian ontologies led not only to the formulation of different categorical doctrines, but also to the building of different frameworks for the interpretation of Aristotle's own, as in the case of Plotinus and his followers. While the late Hellenistic conceptions bear a certain terminological resemblance to Aristotle's views, the similarities cease at this point. I then tried to explain why it is that the post-Aristotelian interpretations of the categories which claimed to be superior must be regarded as significant deviations from of attacks on Aristotle. The explanation I offered rests on the fact that these later theories employ radically different theories of being and are guided by a different ideal of knowledge. My goal was to treat this topic in connection with (a) the possible influence Aristotle's doctrine had on the development of the two major Hellenistic movements, Stoicism and Neoplatonism, and (b) the challenge that Aristotle's philosophy of *ousia* and its attendant logic presented to the scholastic ontologies as they proceeded to build their interpretations of Aristotle on the heritage of Porphyry. I also tried to show that neither the nominalism of Ockham, nor the logical work of Arnauld was able to cut loose from the established tradition. The same holds for Kant's view, despite the fact that his own systematic approach to categorical concepts may be regarded for all practical purposes as having laid the foundations for radically new explorations in this philosophical area. Kant's revival of theoretical interest in categorical concepts and his answer to the problem of the nature and scope of the categories, constitute the beginnings of a totally new framework. He shifted decidedly the angle of inquiry into the theory of categories from ontology to epistemology.

The new directions in which post-Kantian philosophy developed rendered the problem of reconstructing the original framework of Aristotle's doctrine of categories twice as difficult than it had been when the Neoplatonist interpretations and the related scholastic tradition were carrying the day. Whether this paper has contributed something toward a fresh exploration of this age-old problem, is open to judgement. I have only endeavored to raise the curtain once again and propose a tentative solution in hope that it is not without some merit.

NOTES

1. Proceedings of the World Congress on ARISTOTLE, Thessaloniki August 7–14, 1978. Publication of the Ministry of Culture and Sciences, 1981. Reprinted with minor changes and corrections.

2. *Ousia, poion, pōs echon, pros ti pōs echon.*

THE UNITY OF SCIENTIFIC INQUIRY AND CATEGORIAL THEORY IN ARISTOTLE [1]

I. Introduction

The concept of the unity of the sciences as interrelated domains of inquiry, aside from its recent setting, had also an Aristotelian setting in antiquity. Its usefulness in the latter period was not to serve as the logical basis to build a system of systems. Although there is much to recommend it as a solution to the communication of "public" knowledge, it also seems to have functioned as the basis for the continuity between being and the perception of being, between fact and value. There is more to the concept of the unity of the scientific inquiries than the sharing of methodological principles, for instance, the pervasive axioms and the requirement for special theses and hypotheses, as Aristotelian terminology would have it in the concluding chapters of the *Posterior Analytics*, Book II. There is also the model of the ordered facts, i.e., the conceptual determination of the ultimate facts within a type of subject-matter: the Aristotelian model of *wholes* qua *ousiai*, which constitute the ontological counterparts of the proper subjects of statements. These ontic wholes are the ultimate *loci* of the fundamental properties of typical facts, they are the irreducible wholes of parts. Thus the articulation of the mode of attribution of properties of facts to the facts as wholes, i.e., the connecting the *symbebēkota* (co-incidentals) to their *ousiai*, is the function of scientific predication. Language, when it is canonical discourse covering the full span of all subject-matters, serves us well, both in announcing encountered facts and attributing properties to facts. Given that universal and near-universal statements can be made in each of the sciences, the explanation of phenomena, the securing of a conclusion in any demonstrative syllogism, is tied to the quest for middle terms, itself in line with the model of wholes and the rules of categorial theory.

Aristotle argues in *Physics* VIII. 1, 251a8–252a4 that the world has no beginning and no end. It is a thesis that covers only part of a broader view, for he is equally convinced through both observation and argument that the world is one of logical stability in the sense that it is a system of interrelated processes. At the heart of the system is the factuality of the structural regularity of the types of entities in the world. Finding, identifying, and articulating these regularities and exhibiting the modes of their interrelations is the fundamental quest of *episteme*, which in its final form is conformable to the demonstrative model. However it must not be concluded from these two theses, i.e., the eternality of the world and the logical stability of its contents that change does not occur or when it occurs as a matter of fact that it can be dismissed as a secondary consideration in the quest for knowledge. The changing aspects of things, including the radical changes of things demarcated by the contrariety of generation and destruction (*genesis-phthora*), are highly significant events, but knowledge of them can be pursued and established only and primarily in conjunction with the search for regularities.

In consequence, inquiry must answer a number of questions related to the nature and source of regularities, particularly in connection with the claim that they are ultimately traceable to wholes. Thus we need to know how things qua wholes behave and whether the behavior of wholes is a phenomenon explicable with reference to the subsistent regularities that may govern the behavior of the constituent parts of ultimate wholes. The latter deserves special consideration insofar as it is an issue that ancient philosophy and science raised and answers were provided however limited in depth and scope their explanatory efficacy proved to be. Discussions on wholes and parts abound in Aristotle's writings,[2] and it would be obvious to anyone familiar with the ancient texts that he was neither the first nor the only thinker to raise and explore the issue. Be that as it may, he argued consistently in favor of a philosophical explanation that assigned to wholes both priority over parts and irreducibility of the regularities determinative of the former to the collected pattern of regularities, whatever they may be, characteristic of the latter. That such a position in physical theory, more often than not, became subject to continuous criticism and final attack and rejection by modern scientists, is a different matter. What is of primary concern for the purposes of this paper is the philosophical significance of Aristotle's theory of wholes and the merits of the attendant principle of irreducibility together with the mode of explanation that are steadily and uniformly worked out in the treatises in accord with the basic tenets of his categorial theory.

II. The Inquiry into Principles and Its Affinity into the Investigation of Subject-Matters

The diversity of distinct types of wholes provides the subject-matter for scientific inquiry necessitating therefore a diversity of sciences. We encounter these subject-matters, the facts of nature, empirically, not through the principles that guide and control the investigation of what is encountered. The inquiry into the principles, how we become aware of them in consciousness and articulate them, and how we establish their connections and continuities with the facts of nature, constitutes a distinct set of problems, a special subject-matter for a separate inquiry or series of inquiries. It is no accident that these problems come up for discussion as logical problems in the *Posterior Analytics,* as psychological in the *De Anima* and as ontological in the *Metaphysics,* although no single treatise seems to have by itself completed the task of the inquiry into principles. Given the diversity of the sciences, based on the gamut of empirical subject-matters and the ensuing abstractions thereof, a different question may be raised about the principles that enable the inquiring mind to ground the continuity of scientific work and the interrelatedness of the sciences, regardless of how these may be organized into branches and fields. The issue here is not one of establishing a hierarchical scheme of the diverse sciences through the use of a teleology of values assigning to each subject-matter a level of importance in the order of cosmic ends. Aristotle was not a Neoplatonist. His teleological analyses were not appended to sequences in a *scala naturae* but to the understanding of processes within the specifiable contexts of individuals and their formal and functional determinations. As his doctrine of the four determinant factors or causes makes clear, the search for an ultimate source of value to serve as the final ground of a theory of explanation is irrelevant to scientific performance. Instead, he made use of principles that render intelligible the basis for interscientific understanding through the communal use of language and the coordination of findings as they become crystallized in the results of the diverse modes of investigating the available subject-matters. This is *logos* reflectively emancipated from the intrusions of subjective feeling and the passions.

Yet there is more to the quest for interscientific understanding than what ensues from a theory of scientific discovery and the arrangement of empirical regularities stated in language suitable to function as premises in accordance with the model of apodeictic syllogisms. For Aristotle, the quest had to be expanded to a systematic investigation meant to cover the domain of *logical* regularities. Considerable work had already been done by Plato himself, as a number of dialogues of the middle and later periods testify. Aristotle, however, once he became convinced of the theoretical superfluity of the transcendent theory of forms, he accepted the legitimacy of the quest for interscientific understanding but also saw clearly that it had to be brought in line with the contextualism of methods appropriate to the special sciences. Thus an investigation of the domain of logical regularities not only had to exhibit definite affinities with any and all of the special inquiries into natural subject-matters but also with the necessities that govern canonically the correct use of language, in the technical sense of *logos,* both as the structure of intelligence and as the tool, the *organon,* which effectively articulates the structures of the investigable subject-matters.

There is a special feature characteristic of the extended investigation into *logos* that calls for mention. The fruitfulness and the consistency of the work Aristotle carried out in his logical investigations as well as in those treatises that are either incidentally or systematically connected to the logical writings (for instance, the *De Anima),* were made secure through the same conception of wholes qua unities we see employed in the study of nature in general. It comes therefore as no surprise to the informed reader that the theory of regularities concerning natural wholes and the concept of wholes as individuals, *protai ousiai,* in the formulation of his categorial theory, work in complementary ways and stand in parallel formation. Given this relationship, the principle of continuity holds between the natural sciences, in the inclusive sense of the term as Aristotle would have it, and the logical investigations. Consequently, approaches such as have been proposed in recent times to make logic totally separate from ontology would have to be counter-Aristotelian, as for instance is the case with E. Nagel's well-known thesis in his 1944 article "Logic Without Ontology."[3] To arrive at such a non-Aristotelian view on the relationship between the logical and natural subject-matters, it would be mandatory to challenge and subsequently reject the concept of whole in scientific explanations, which would also entail the rejection of Aristotle's categorial theory. It matters little whether one states the rejection at the logical or natural side of Aristotelianism. Since the two sides are mutually supportive of the broader view and constitute integral components of the same theoretical framework, the outcome leads to denial of their unity.

I think it can be maintained that it is not possible to dismiss the Aristotelian approach to science without extending the refutative undertaking over to the field of logical theory and to categorial theory, in particular. For Aristotle, natural facts and logical entities are not totally different and separate domains. Successful rejection of this thesis would in effect refute and terminate any claim to the existential continuity of subject-matters.

III. The Pervasive Relevance of Wholes

Equally pertinent is the question whether it is possible to salvage Aristotle's conception of the pervasive relevance of wholes to the natural sciences and to logic from the attacks of recent criticism. Such attacks on the whole stem from the logical accounts of scientific investigations into ultimate particles and their behavior to propound in turn explanations of the behavior of ostensible wholes. I think "field" concepts in physics also make claims which seem to render the Aristotelian concept of wholes irrelevant. In the long run, since the advent of modern science, such investigations were conducted independently of the debated issue whether wholes were Aristotelian substances or not. Be that as it may, the vast literature on the subject notwithstanding, the substitution did in fact take place, but along with the new conception of wholes came as a gradual realization the admission that no principle ensuring continuity, comparable to the one Aristotle had established, was forthcoming. The implications of discontinuity are still being felt in many quarters that have identified the persistence of discrepancies in the fabric of our culture which in turn are being held responsible for some type of malaise or other. For some, the operative discrepancies are more conspicuous in the field of communication since they obstruct the meaningful exchange of

The Unity of Scientific Inquiry 191

information between "two cultures," as C. P. Snow expressed the issue some decades ago; for others, they are reflected in the division between fact and value running through all cases where deep gaps are suspected rendering thereby the sciences and the humanities two distinct worlds; in other quarters still, the problem was perceived as an unbridgeable chasm between the theoretical entities of mathematical physics, on the one hand, and the valued objects of gross experience, on the other. In this latter conceptualization of the problem of discontinuity we can begin to appreciate, by way of contrast, the cultural and theoretical usefulness, if not truthfulness, of the Aristotelian approach or rather solution.

It may not be impossible to salvage the principle of continuity and perhaps make it immune to the attacks that recent criticism has marshalled against the explanatory efficacy of the Aristotelian conception of wholes. To begin with, the terminological device of atomicity should be preserved as applicable for macrocosmic uses, necessitated in the wake of major discoveries in physics. The modifications in nomenclature were made to meet the conceptual demands of "existents" at levels of ultimacy beyond the physical atoms of modern chemistry. But in essence the problem extends its scope beyond issues in terminology. As is known, the critical attacks that led to the rejection of the Aristotelian model of wholes stemmed in the main from the need to make fundamental revisions in accordance with the theoretical direction modern scientific investigations were taking in the quest for ultimate particles. The cumulative result was that the propounded new explanations of the behavior of wholes were constructed through a coordination of quantifiable relational regularities of constituent parts. The modern type of explanation became sharply distinct from the traditional one, resting as the latter was, on an ontology of substantial form, associated with the philosophy of Aristotle. The spectacular attainments of the modern science of mechanics and the adoption of its model of explanation by the other disciplines, especially biology and psychology, were soon to take effect but what was not immediately fully apprehended was the serious compromise of the principle of continuity. The development of modern philosophical systems and their preoccupation with epistemological problems form the long record of intellectual labor to resolve the endemic paradox resulting from universalizing the powerful model of explanation in the science of mechanics.

On the assumption that the discrepancy in the model of explanation was yet to be removed before we are able to restore harmony in our arts and sciences, in the domain of fact and of value, a revised and extended formulation of the Aristotelian theory of wholes may still serve as a key to the solution of the problem. Fundamentally such an amplified scheme would require the systematic treatment of the parts of wholes, which in modern physical theory acquired an independent status of their own, to be defined not as ultimate particles, however provisional their ultimacy may be, but as entities not reducible to the relational pattern of their constituents. To use traditional language, this approach would call for treating both wholes and parts contextually and assigning to both a status that would allow the investigator to view them as Aristotelian *ousiai*. Whether such a practice is theoretically feasible is another issue, yet its potential fruitfulness cannot be easily dismissed. Despite the prevailing tendency to avoid the revival of Aristotelian models of the ultimacy of wholes with attendant modifications in the logic of explanations, the recent discoveries in the physical and biological sciences have provided ample and irrefutable evidence against the postulated existence of ultimate simples. Actually we have witnessed the re-confirming of the ontological principle of the presence of unity as wholeness at all levels of natural complexities. The advancements in recent science have rendered meaningful the confluence of the Anaxagorean view of complexes and the Aristotelian conception of wholes as contextual *ousiai*. It would seem as though basic

The Unity of Scientific Inquiry 193

speculative insights in antiquity, whatever their basis in empirical observation, are nowadays receiving experimental confirmation.

The purpose of the aforementioned remarks was to sketch in bare outline the significance of the Aristotelian model of the interconnectedness of the special scientific enterprises and of the theoretical bonds that tie together ontology and categorial theory through the consistent use of the concept of wholes. Whatever the limitations of this model to accommodate the methodology and the findings of modern science, it cannot be denied that it succeeded where the modern view has not, namely in preserving the principle of continuity. It has been mentioned in passing that the proper signification of the concept of the whole is a function of the meaning of *ousia,* and in two fundamental contexts: (a) *ousia* as the ultimate subject (*hypokeimenon*), which in its collective sense denotes naturally ordered facts, i.e., types of subject-matters available for systematic ordering in a series of logically interconnected statements to form the body of truths in a given science; (b) *ousia* as the fundamental categorial concept denoting any and all particular existents, which as wholes, as well as unities, are the primary beings in which all types of properties must inhere in order to exist. *Ousia* is thereby both the context for the signification of all types of co-incidental properties (*symbebēkota*) as well as the agency through which all processes occur when they do.

The study of wholes in their natural setting is prerequisite to explaining them through science, i.e., the kind of knowledge that terminates in the form of a demonstrative syllogism. Thus to claim to know that "X is the case" requires not only declaring that X is a fact and that the statement expressing it is true, but also another set of statements which together make evident the logical grounds, the reasons why "X is the case," being a statement of fact, is true.

Collecting in piece-meal fashion facts and stating the conditions for their occurrence, how and by what means the facts are correctly perceived, is a matter of research. It is a necessary phase but not sufficient to terminate inquiry and complete the scientific task. The first phase must be followed by a process of systematization of the collected facts through strict principles emerging from the nature of the facts, ending with a structured set of interrelated statements, tying major premises to minor ones through the bond of an explicit middle term. Once demonstration is made secure and the requisite conclusions, answering the *why* are drawn, the order of knowledge has itself become a fact, a determinate accomplishment of the inquiring mind.

The study of wholes in their natural setting, leading as it does to the systematic organization of facts in special sciences, requires the complementary study of wholes in the linguistic setting. To be more precise, it requires a set of fundamental distinctions to formulate canons of signification of designated wholes properly identifiable to function as categorial subjects (*hypokeimena*). The doctrines concerning the referential use of expressions, be they names, verbs or other linguistic units having signifying force, have been discussed in the treatises titled *Categories* and *De Interpretatione*, and the syntax of statements controlling the background and foreground of the logic of demonstration received systematic exposition in the two *Analytics*. If by 'categorial' *hypokeimenon* we mean the signifier that occupies the subject position in any well-formed statement, be it an affirmation or negation, the object which the signifier names belongs to the realm of observable entities, the things for which Aristotle reserved the inclusive and fundamental term "*ousiai*".

To know the world is to render it intelligible as a system of true statements covering not only the great diversity of types of *ousiai* and their inherent properties, but also a theoretical system of principles conformable to inter-objective universal and necessary traits of things to which the name '*ousia*' pertains. But rendering the world of *ousiai* intelligible is itself a fact of the world, although it occurs qua fact as an activity and an actualization of a special kind of conduct exhibited under certain civilized conditions by a certain type of *ousia,* human beings. Though the sciences of diverse types of *ousiai* and the science of the principles of the sciences and the arts are confined to human beings, knowability is still a fact of the world, itself not an *ousia* but a generic trait of all existents, be they *ousiai* or their *symbebēkota*. Fundamentally, then, the presence of intelligence in a world of *ousiai* is irrefutable testimony to the referential and explanatory power of the sciences as well as to the genuine utility of the arts that apply the findings of the sciences to the making of things and the improvement of conduct. Even if we grant, as Aristotle does, that the knowability of the world is an on-going process of a real actualization, effected through the sciences, still in principle the universe has no dark secrets and no unfathomable mysteries. Furthermore, in principle the rule of knowability extends itself equally in the other direction: the human domain. Humanity is no mystery unto itself. The abuse of knowledge is a matter of passion and misguided judgment, not a failure of science.

Constructing the system of sciences and a theory of principles, which is precisely what the actualization of the knowability of reality means, is properly done, according to Aristotle, when the signifying use of the naming of entities in coordination with the syntax of true statements places unexceptionably in the subject position wholes that stand for *ousiai* or events analyzable into *ousiai*. Another way of saying the same thing is that, for Aristotle, the correct reflection of the intelligible structures of things to be worked out in human *logos* cannot be constructed as a system of physical, biological and human sciences when the starting point in each science is a set of statements, even if true, where the co-incidental properties rather than their *ousiai* are turned into ultimate subjects. This is not to deny the knowability of *symbebēkota;* rather, it means to draw attention to a rule of systematic correctness in bringing about the ends of science. Insofar as any complete set of parts and their relational regularities are not equivalent to the *ousia,* as the whole in which the set of parts inheres, no science of co-incidental properties can ever succeed in actualizing the fullness of nature's intelligibility.

The assignation of *ousia* qua whole as the ultimate categorial subject throws light on Aristotle's insistence in proposing that the proper subject-matters of the particular sciences cannot consist of sets of accidental properties or of the changes they exhibit, however variegated the latter may be. But denying them the status of priority qua subject-matter does not imply that they are exempted from inquiry. What it means is that such inquiry must in due course relate its findings to the designated sciences of the *ousiai* that provide the contexts for the understanding of the regularities of co-incidental properties qua parts. The same holds for disparate events which involve *ousiai* of diverse types. Insofar as events have no generative principle of their own, they lack formal stability. Not being "complete and distinct individuals" they have the status of effects of the co-incidental properties of *ousiai*. Again to make them the object of scientific investigation does not thereby grant them the status of *bona fide* ultimate subject-matters.

The point of the above is that the confluences of the *symbebēkota* of diverse *ousiai*, the concurrences, are not themselves *ousiai*. This may provide a way of understanding even the concurrences of diverse *symbebēkota* as events related to members of a species, e.g., human beings. From this perspective the special sciences that select as their subject-matter this or that activity or property of human beings, i.e. the "human" sciences, from history and economics to law and poetics, all presuppose a more fundamental science of humankind, a science of life in its human setting, where subject-matter consists of *ousiai* qua wholes. Such a science is what Aristotle seems to have worked out in the *De Anima*, itself a chapter, as it were, of the science of living beings. The special sciences that select aspects of human beings qua *ousiai* but do not claim to be investigating them as wholes, are limited in what they can disclose in the explanations they offer concerning the selected facts. Valuable as their findings and

The Unity of Scientific Inquiry 197

projections may be, no special human science, by being an inquiry into a part or parts, is entitled to proclaiming the set of regularities it establishes adequate to the fullness of the human *ousia*. The social sciences in our times, individually and collectively have persistently ignored this point.

What an *ousia* is cannot be defined by concatenating even a complete set, if that is possible, of predicative statements referring to co-incidental properties. The result of such a procedure would be description, not explanation. The difference between description and definition takes us back to the distinction of wholes and their parts. Complete sets of statements regarding the regularities of parts do not exhaust the essential being of *ousiai*. Parts of *ousiai* exist, and we do make statements about them that are both true and useful. However, only *ousiai* have the existential status requisite to ensure the inherence of properties. The latter, being parts, may be assigned explanatory and definitional roles but, in Aristotelian science, they remain logically deficient and derivative in the sense that their significatory function can be fully understood only on the condition that an appropriate substantive context, that of a whole, is invoked and explicitly stated. Answering questions about "whatness" (*ti esti*) pertains mainly to *ousia* (*Met.* 1028a16–b2), and in this regard, the identification of the "whatness" of an *ousia*, stated in precise language, gives us the definition. Further down in the same work (*Met.* 1030a18–20), Aristotle also says that *ti esti* is not confined to cases of *ousia*. *Symbebēkota*, such as quality, quantity and place also have their own *ti esti*, yet we are acquainted with them better when we come to know the *ti esti* of each of them. Passages such as these leads us to say that we can have universals in the case of co-incidental properties.

Aristotle's theory of the genera of being (*genē tou ontos*) makes clear that the genera, other than the genus of *ousia*, refer to types of coincidental properties, each type being a family of properties exhibiting a classificatory order different from the one typical of the biological species and genera characteristic of *ousiai* qua wholes, i.e., within the context of inherence, their study must ultimately identify the *ousia* as both individual and *eidos*. But what about a general science of *symbebēkota*, and can there be such a science? The answer would have to be in the affirmative but conditional.

The investigation of the *symbebēkota* and the ordering of findings as a system of statements in Aristotelian science, is well known as part of the record of the history of ancient science. What is of special interest at this point is whether the whole-part or *ousia* and its *symbebēkota* relationship as a model can be reconstructed and sufficiently modified to serve present needs. More to the point, the issue is whether it is workable to extend the Aristotelian conception of whole qua *ousia* and the attendant one of co-incidentals qua integral parts, to the ontic levels of the microscopic and macroscopic realities. Carrying out this task would no doubt require collective competency and ingenuity to effect adequate recasting of terminology. Essentially we are faced with the concept of complexity and of variations in degrees or regularities in the behavior of *symbebēkota* as constitutive parts and properties of wholes. Systems and sub-systems of living things, as recent discoveries have shown, present us with hitherto unsuspected patterns of complexity without necessarily demanding the rejection of wholes for their understanding. As inquiry moves to non-living phenomena, rigidity in regulated continuities takes on different forms and accords with different structural principles. For the detection of their forms and principles we find it necessary to depart significantly, if not entirely, from other models of wholes. In theoretical physics we end up with particles "constructed" with aid of statistical wholes and law-like generalities, as the case may be.

Although the Aristotelian theory of explanation is tied to the fundamentals of the concept of the genera of being and thereby to the concept of whole, the latter is by no means referentially functional exclusively to Aristotle's approach to subject-matters. By the same token, nor is the Aristotelian categorial theory rendered inapplicable to the canonical formations of statements in modern scientific systems. The language of the logic of relations, which proved to be of immense value to the systematization of modern scientific findings, may well be a highly technical modification and extension of Aristotelian categorial theory to suit the demands of alternative ways in deciding issues for the selection and treatment of "facts." Explaining and expounding on this claim is too vast a topic to be treated in this paper, but suffice it to say that there is no definitive argument advocating the need to surrender the concept of "whole-*ousia*" and regard it superfluous by reducing it to nothing more than the sum of its parts in the sense that a whole is but the cumulative product of interlocking regularities of constituents. In Aristotelian language such a reductive thesis implies the primacy of *symbebēkota* over *ousia*. Small wonder therefore that the world of the Greeks and the world of our times, as the sciences correspondingly construct them in theory, speak two different languages and project two different visions. Even less surprising would be the fact that the attitudes toward the world in each case conceal uncomfortable disparities. From a practical point of view alone, it would be sheer folly to dismiss either world and ignore its advantages. Continuing to do so only exacerbates the consequences of a serious flaw in the fabric of contemporary culture.

IV. The Price of Discontinuity

When the unity of science movement picked up strength during the first half of the century, it heralded trends promising the general adoption of standards for accepting theories as well as the promotion of policies making the scientific attitude indispensable for the improvement of personal and social life. The movement gained momentum with the refinements of research methods in the diverse scientific fields, from observation and experimentation to measurement techniques and the analysis of the logical structure of theories. But the movement also issued serious warning against indulging speculative tendencies favoring the creation of a general system of science in the form of a super-science. Instead, it sought to promote the cooperation of the particular sciences to effect operative solutions to complex problems that resisted the efficacious methods of unilateral approaches. That scientists in the fields of physics, chemistry, biology and mathematics pioneered a spirit of interdisciplinary research and cooperative teamwork, was only a normal outcome of the novel extensions of the experimental methods.

A comparable development took place in the social sciences, but the task in this area has yet to match the progress made in the natural sciences, if only because the logic of the exact disciplines did not succeed, for whatever reasons, in yielding a high level of reasonableness in the attitudes requisite to understanding and solving social and political problems, be they international conflicts or organized interruptions in the balance of ecosystems. Even the humanities in many respects and to the extent that they transfer uncritically to their domains the quantification techniques, in hope of gaining new mastery of issues related to value, have side-stepped from their primary objectives. We have now come to realize that the humanities and the arts cannot profit from the scientific conception of unity beyond a certain point. The problem was not one of attitude; it had its roots in the limited design of the model of "whole-parts." The scientific models for conceptualizing subject-matters did not include the requisite parameters for *ousia,* so central to the humanities and in obvious ways to social inquiry.

Not everyone would accept this way of stating the problem of discontinuity. Assuming for a moment that there is a grain of truth in the formulation of the problem as stated, a number of obstacles need to be removed before reasonableness can prevail in the understanding and treatment of human problems. Probably, we will see no evidence of steady progress toward a culture free from institutional discrepancies before technology is finally brought in line with economic policies to serve a broader and unified spectrum of human concerns, i.e., closer to the whole that human *ousia* is. In the meantime, our institutionalized ways of knowing and acting will suffer from the effects of discontinuities, and nationalistic fanaticism will continue to operate at the expense of international cooperation.

Understanding the function of the concept of continuity for the integration of the ways of knowing has been divorced from a corresponding demand to do the same in the ways of acting. It is a bifurcation that has allowed driving a wedge between what Aristotle saw as a continuum with a distinction between the theoretical and the practical virtues. The resultant compartmentalization of human activity is but a short step from turning human conduct into a "many-splendored thing." When the ways of knowing and the ways of acting move in separate directions political reforms become necessary to control the growing dissonance of ends. The issue can be readily cast in Aristotelian language as the problem of social *akrasia,* i.e., collectively knowing the political good but, on account of a certain weakness, being unable to do it. Once again we are led back to the compromise of the concept of whole qua *ousia* or, to use a more blunt expression, to its dismissal.

The persistence of social *akrasia* in the modern world has been repeatedly discussed by specialists in a variety of disciplines. Yet the discrepancies and discontinuities that cause it remain operative. It would be a truism to say that what is needed is a thorough diagnosis and treatment requiring changes in conduct and improvements in method. Whether either or both can be brought about will fundamentally depend on the conceptualization of the model that can secure the principle of continuity in knowing, doing and making, as it did in antiquity. Aristotle's way of keeping together the unity of scientific inquiry and categorial theory for the understanding of being and the investigation of political being, may not, as a set of recommendations, be adequate to solve the complex problems in their contemporary setting. However, the Aristotelian conception of whole qua model, being free of dissonances and discontinuities in the body of culture, remains, so it would seem, both pertinent and useful; it kept *theoria* and *praxis* together in the pursuit of the common good. The practical value of scientific research, aside from serving theoretical needs, lies in providing the basis to act from a position of knowledge, not from the motive to impose through power or passion. The fruits of knowing can be used to enhance power, but the exercise of power contributes nothing essential to the pursuit of truth. When power makes its inroads into the bloodstream of a culture, the loss of wholeness is certain to follow.

NOTES

1. Published in *Greek Studies in the Philosophy and History of Science*, eds. R. Cohen and P. Nikolakopoulos. Boston Studies in the Philosophy of Science Series. 1990, pp. 29–43.

2. See on "One-Many" *Met.* V. 6, 1015b16–1017a6; on "Part" *Met.* V. 25, 1023b12–25; on "Whole" *Met.* V. 26, 1023b26–1024a10; *Met.* XII. 1, 1069a18–b2; *Phys.* IV. 2, 185b11–186a3; *Phys.* IV. 3, 210a14–b21.

3. Appeared in *Naturalism and the Human Spirit,* Y. H. Krikorian, editor, Columbia University Press (New York, 1944); repr. in E. Nagel, *Logic Without Metaphysics,* The Free Press (Glencoe, Illinois, 1956), pp. 55–92.

REVOLUTIONS, REFORMS AND EDUCATIONAL PHILOSOPHY IN ARISTOTLE'S THEORY OF CONSTITUTIONAL LAW[1]

Aristotle states in *Politics* VIII. 1, 1337a 10-14: "No one will doubt that the legislator should direct attention above all to the education of youth; for when his neglect happens in the governing of a city, harm comes to the constitution."

The complement to the idea expressed in this quotation is Aristotle's argument that human beings need the external authority of law, and more precisely the right law, to guide them in their efforts to fulfill their *entelecheia*. In the case of education, then, legislation functions not to prescribe punishment for crimes or evasion of duty and responsibility, but to regulate the process and secure the appropriate means for the upbringing and maturing of youth. The goal is to prepare the young to become citizens and function as responsible agents in the pursuit of the good life and the common good. Aristotle's analysis of the complex relationship between law and society led him to the position that education is so fundamental to the shared good of human communities that its office must belong to the *polis*. On the strength of the thesis that the final cause of human communities and the fulfillment of human nature coincide (1277b 30), Aristotle concludes that private education falls short of meeting the interest of the community as a whole.

The problem is not whether public and private education conflict or work at cross purposes, but how education takes place in the diverse types of constitutions, and if there are certain types that compromise the idea of justice or tolerate the abuse of power by individuals or groups at the expense of the rest of the people, what is the role of education under such circumstances?

It is an empirical fact that all constitutions, good or bad, just or unjust, normal and deviant, aim at self-preservation. This objective calls for determining how education must function in each case to assist in maintaining constitutional stability and avoid disruptions in the established ways of public life. There are two basic concepts that enter into Aristotle's argument in support of his philosophy of education as a public institution in the service of constitutional stability: (a) Different constitutions formulate special educational policies to ensure stability. (b) Since some constitutions deviate from the norm of justice, in the sense that they fail to promote the common good, a criterion is needed to guide reforms through legislation either to correct abuses or to prevent sedition.

The purpose of this paper is to examine the place of legislation in the institutionalization of education in types of constitutions that invite or discourage political activity for constructive reforms. It may appear to some readers of Aristotle that he has formulated his theory of education in *Politics*, Books VII and VIII mainly to design a curriculum for a utopian ideal, and that this is the weakest part in his *Politics*. My paper will argue against that interpretation. I will try to show that Aristotle takes the position that there is a difference between education to maintain the momentum that may bring about the government of the ideal *polis*, which is a Platonic theme, and education that seeks to construct the model of an appropriate curriculum for the normal forms of government. The latter is what Aristotle develops in the last two books of the *Politics*. What the model recommends is a curriculum ready to be adapted to the needs of the normal constitutions when reforms are in order; it provides the requisite program for youth to reach political maturity and for rulers to secure the future of the *polis*. As for the deviant constitutions, as we shall see, since their stability depends on the suppression of change and resistance to reforms, Aristotle's program of education

Theory of Constitutional Law 207

will appear unacceptable. The reason for rejecting it, if made available, is due to deviancy from the norm as given in *Politics* VII. 1, 1323b 33-36: "The fortitude of a state, and the justice and wisdom of a state have the same energy, and the same character, as the qualities which cause individuals who have them to be called brave, just and wise" (tr. E. Barker). Since constitutions operate to preserve the status quo, it is incumbent upon the leadership, be it of one, few, or many, to initiate and promulgate legislation on all facets of life that contribute to the conservation of the character of the system. This function of the art of statesmanship must be distinguished from the question of the correctness of the constitution. Stability advocates resistance to change either because the constitution is already good or because the abuse of power requires continuation of same. The former presents no problem except that of preventing down-sliding, in which case legislative measures will be needed to discourage unjust practices through corrective reforms. Thus, the rule is that good forms of government, kingship, aristocracy, politeia, secure stability through deliberation and planned reforms. Such however, is not the case in deviant constitutions, where stability is a critical issue. It would be a misreading of Aristotle's *Politics* to say, as some have, that he defends the preservation of the civil order that constitutions provide no matter what their quality. A recent writer has taken the view that Aristotle is inconsistent when he recommends political stability in a general way, while in the case of extreme constitutions, which are inherently unsafe, he is reluctant "to support means of making them stable which do not also involve altering their character."[2]

There is no inconsistency or ambivalence in Aristotle's position. His task, as I see it, is basically one of undertaking a critical evaluation of available types of constitutions in order to identify the ones that promote the conditions that serve the common good and the good life for its citizens. Extreme constitutions are "deviant" forms of government precisely because leadership perverts these conditions, causing thereby a compromise of the common good, or even worse, substituting for it, under whatever guise, personal gains, power, wealth and other private ends. The general thrust of the argument shows that (a) the deviant types generate dissatisfactions and unrest, and although they may succeed in averting revolutions, they do so by causing further social damage and rupture in the fabric of institutions; (b) securing preservation is not an inviolable political principle to grant its authority to deviant constitutions for the sake of maintaining unjust civic order; and (c) reforms prove effective only when either of the following conditions prevail: (i) legislation is used to assist normal constitutions to prevent deterioration from within, and (ii) extraordinary opportunities to alter deviant forms present themselves and are seized to introduce laws that secure peaceful transition to normalcy. On the whole then, Aristotle's intention in using the concept of stability is subordinate to the ultimate end of political life: to effect and maintain the stability of institutions in those forms of government, and those forms only, that promote the common good.

Instead of looking for inconsistencies in Aristotle it would be more to the point to investigate the tension between two strong objectives in the art and science of statesmanship: the quest for the good life through the offices of normal constitutions, especially that of education, on the one hand, and the avoidance of destruction of human life and property, on the other, especially when people resort to revolution when injustice becomes intolerable. The idea of stability in normal types of constitution requires no defense. But prolonging stability in deviant types only fosters injustice. The choice then is one between revolution and reforms. Aristotle's position is against the use of revolutionary means. The gist of his argument is that revolutions, besides being destructive, hardly ever succeed in attaining their goals. But to acquiesce in the injustice perpetrated in deviant constitutions is hardly a solution. This realization led Aristotle to make his diagnostic analysis of causes and cures for revolutions and deviant constitutions. The source lies in the persistence of problems in distributive justice and this in turn calls for identifying the motives for dissidence: they range from profit, honor, threat to one's status, indignation, abuse of office, acts of violence, insolent rule, to other causes such as changes in the size of community through the emergence of new classes demanding rights and power. Aristotle's purpose is to provide practical advice to statesmen on how to prevent revolutions, and make intelligent reforms.

There is still the problem of converting a deviant constitution into a normal one through rational means and legislative acts. Since this rarely happens, sedition is often inevitable. Deviant forms of government cannot in fact be preserved because of their inability to control the steady increase of dissatisfactions. The obvious answer is internal reforms but if the reforms are meant to support the common good, the deviant government will be engaging in self-destruction. Hence the resistance to reforms that improve the lot of the injured citizens. As a result, the persistence of injustice forces the injured to resort to revolutions. This leaves the political scientist powerless to provide a cure for deviant governments, except when there is a radical and sudden change in the attitudes of the ruling class. The more pertinent question then should be: How is any constitution preserved? Aristotle believes that the answer lies in insuring the loyalty of the subjects, by keeping loyal citizens in positions of power and the disloyal ones outside the executive, legislative and administrative leadership. Loyalty is a function of satisfactory treatment of citizens to ensure trust. The difference between normal and deviant constitutions is reflected in the methods used to sustain loyalty.

Aristotle identifies three things to which rulers need to pay attention to secure the confidence of the people: (i) the material conditions of all classes, (ii) the values and attitudes of the subjects, and (iii) the system of education.

It is useless to have the most beneficial rules of society fully agreed upon by all members of the constitution, if individuals are not going to be trained and have their habits formed for that constitution, that is to live democratically if the laws of society are democratic, oligarchically if they are oligarchic. (V. 9. 1308b 20-24)

The detached tone of this passage makes it clear that Aristotle is fully aware of Plato's critique: education is consciously manipulated, even when neglected by the government. Rulers in deviant constitutions intentionally discourage their subjects from espousing the aspirations and values of the upper class. Superior values are taught to the heirs of power, a practice which makes for two types of educational programs, one for the rulers and another for the ruled. There is good reason why Aristotle did not prepare separate educational programs for each type of constitution, particularly the deviant ones. The latter, to be sure, are hardly amenable to constructive recommendations since their aims of education are bluntly doctrinaire or doctored to resemble those that genuinely serve the common good. Normal constitutions, on the other hand, are obligated to serve the cause of justice and continue to introduce legislation to improve existing educational policies when social problems pose novel demands.

Since deviant constitutions make their special values and pursuits the main purpose of political life, educational policy becomes inescapably part of the perversion. Therefore no improvements can be officially approved, for that would be self-destructive, and hence no progress is encouraged. The paradox here lies in the fact that deviant rulers, e.g., tyrants and oligarchs in particular, while determined to preserve their rule at all costs, are unable to understand why they should prevent their offspring from adopting a life of luxury and abuse of wealth. The fate of the despot is a foreclosed issue. In due course the deviant rulers become soft and weak, arrogant and blind to the spread of dissatisfactions. The other paradox is that these rulers cause the instability they seek to prevent. Aristotle, who never

Theory of Constitutional Law 211

withholds advice, even if destined to go unheeded, recommends moderation. Tyranny is a more difficult case, for it prefers to leave its subjects without benefit of leisure or education proper. Teaching, within approved limits, is usually restricted to elementary skills for useful production and for dispositions to be trained to induce willful obedience. Deviant monarchy, by its nature, is incapable of legislating procedures that promote either practical or theoretical excellence.

By way of summary, the main cause of sedition is injustice, once it reaches intolerable limits. The main cure of political disturbances that end in sedition is the timely adoption of laws that punish acts of injustice. The immediate cures issue from appropriate legislative action to correct inequities in distributive justice. The long-term cures come mainly through education in citizenship, i.e., in dispositions to accord with the social ethos of justice. The reason why legislation is called upon to regulate educational practices within the structure of a permanent institution is because human beings cannot depend for successful social interaction on the lessons of experience derived from dissatisfactions and the painfulness of past abuses. All future citizens stand in need of training to understand and observe the principles of justice, which is basic to acquiring the practical virtues. The statesman who acts in the capacity of educator is thereby expected to possess accurate knowledge of the nature, range and functions of human dispositions in order to conceptualize and legislate the requisite means for individual and social improvement.

The spirit of the constitution, normal or deviant, is actually a way of life. Education, therefore, is the institutionalized method and content appropriate to training in citizenship, i.e., habituation for public conduct. In pursuing this end, legislators must act on two principles: (a) constructively, by promoting the development of human potential for the common good, and (b) preventively, by cautioning prospective citizens to avoid works and attitudes that may lead to downsliding of character and loss of the required sense of responsibility to serve the common good. In either case, educational policy and constitutional structure are treated as being inseparable and harmonious.

Aristotle was an empirical observer as well as a political theorist. He readily recognized that "The Athenians every-where brought low the oligarchies, the Spartans the popular governments" (V. 7, 1307b 19-24). He identified normal constitutions but did not discover an ideal cities. There is little, if any, practical sense in expecting a normal form of government to become the embodiment of an ideal vision of the perfect *polis*. Rather, what his times, and all times, needed was a model of education whose purpose was to be adaptable to the special circumstances of normal constitutions in order that each may continue to improve and preserve the gains it had made. Legislation, therefore, has the responsibility of assisting in the work that consolidates in action the aims of education. The function of law-giving remains the same for all good constitutions, even when the problems and circumstances differ. The common good is the same, for it coincides with the universal good. Aristotle is a pluralist and a universalist.

The program of education as outlined in the *Politics* is of no help to deviant states. They cannot even envisage what it means to do justice to the three stages of human development that determine the phases of education: *physis* as natural disposition, *ethos* as habituation in the practical virtues, and *logos* as rational deliberation and self-determination. Whether intentionally or inadvertently, it makes no difference, deviant constitutions abuse and distort *ab initio* all three. What is most damaging to their own cause, is that they come to view human reason exclusively as an instrumentality while *ethos* is allowed to become an appendix to over-grown and unpruned dispositions. When this is encouraged under the guise of a social value, power passes for nobility and mind falls into servitude to unbridled passions. In such cultural climates as tyrannies and oligarchies maintain, corrective legislation become impotent, for the thinking that is required for reforms is already part of the deformity. The greatest paradox of all is the ease with which the force of passions gain supremacy in political life compared to how difficult it is to govern through law and reason for the common good. If Aristotle is right, there is no cumulative record to be found in the history of politics, only a few landmarks in political wisdom, often missed by the hurrying crowds.

NOTES

1. Presented at the Twelfth World Congress on Philosophy of Law in the History of Human Thought (Athens 1986), and published with a different title, "Revolutions, Reforms and Educational Philosophy in Aristotle's Theory of Constitutions," in the *Proceedings, Supplementa*, Vol II. Steiner, Stuttgart, 1988, pp. 58-62. Reprinted with minor changes.

2. R.G. Mulgan, *Aristotle's Political Theory* (Oxford, 1977), p. 136.

POLITEIA AND *PAIDEIA*: CONSTITUTIONAL DEVIANCIES AND EDUCATIONAL NORMS IN ARISTOTLE

I. Introduction

Perhaps the most challenging problem in understanding the *Politics* is how to deal with his distinction between the good citizens and the good man. We should note the peculiar mean of "good citizen" in *Politics* when it is used in the context of deviant constitutions. Furthermore, we have the related problem of how to understand what it means to be a good citizen under a tyrant or in the case of revolutions.

Whereas Plato is radical, Aristotle is basically interested in how to understand deviations from normal states and how to correct deviant states rather than how to bring about the "Ideal State." Again, Plato worked out in detail the curriculum of higher education as the instrumentality for effecting the ideal state; Aristotle, in contract, does not have this sort of section in his *Politics*.

In his *Politics*, Aristotle discussed the ends of education (*paideia*) and outlined a curriculum appropriate to meet them. When we consider his educational theory in the light of the central books of the *Nicomachean Ethics,* we understand more clearly not only the mediating role of education for the attainment of *eudaimonia* but also the political conditions that a viable constitution is expected to secure for its citizenry.

There are critics who have taken issue with the normative aspects of Aristotle's theory of education, but that is not a problem I wish to examine here. Rather than debate the foundations on which his theory of educational norms rests, I think that a significant problem of wider ramifications needs to be studied: the relationship between political action and educational reforms. The question I wish to propose is one that is highly relevant to our own situation, one that is as serious for us as it was for the period in which Aristotle's theories were worked out.

Let us suppose that Aristotle's normative proposals constitute a viable set Or educational ideals and that there may be other such proposals of comparable worth, and also that there have been other counter-proposals in Western society that are not only objectionable but simply damnable and perversely manipulative. Thus, if we admit Aristotle's conception as one of the positive views that deserves serious consideration, if not adoption, the question I raise is this: How is it possible to pursue an educational policy like the one he recommends unless we can also secure the requisite political conditions that permit its effective implementation? In other words, it appears that Aristotle's normative philosophy of education and the ethical conduct it seeks to sustain cannot function properly apart from the stipulated political conditions he outlines in his discussion of the "healthy" forms of government. Certain critics of Aristotle see a serious gap between the normative and descriptive books of the *Politics*. However, the problem is not as serious as his critics mike it once the normative aspects of his politics are read in the context of his philosophical analysis of human nature and the functions of education.

The aim of education in the broadest sense, is to assist the people to become citizens. In line with Plato and the other Greek thinkers, Aristotle viewed the *polis* as the matrix of civilized life. However, as Plato's critique had shown and Aristotle's own empirical studies of the various constitutions of Greek city-states disclosed, not types of government are genuinely conducive to keeping the aims of education in line with the norms and ideals of the ethical and political life. Aristotle's classification of the types of states has a direct bearing on our subject. Given that he finds three healthy types and three corrupt deviant or extreme forms, and since cities are governed by constitutions that often fall within these types or some mixed form in between, the real issue is one of how the educational process is used—and abused—by the ruling forces behind any given constitution to keep themselves in power.

Throughout the *Politics*, Aristotle, tries to impress upon the reader the question why it is that the connection between the functions and offices of the state, on the one hand, and the pursuit of normal educational objectives on the other, must display coherence in practice. A philosophical theory of education cannot treat the one without reference to the other. This interdependence is more evident in his discussion of the distinction between the ruler and the ruled. All rulers, especially those of the correct or healthy types of constitution become good through education and training in practical wisdom. In the last analysis, a ruler is himself a citizen and an educator whose activities include that of ruling educators as trainers of future citizens, always with the common good in view. Therefore the responsibility of the ruler or rulers for deciding the future of the state is of the highest order. There is one more component in the upbringing of a ruler: he has been trained in the art of being ruled! Hence, *qua* citizen he knows how to rule and be ruled.

Given these considerations it should be obvious that the ruler disqualifies himself from holding office if by his own acts he either distorts or compromises the common good and thereby perverts the concomitant aims of education. Similarly, in any constitution that fails to promote and sustain the common good, education, in Aristotle's sense of political *paideia*, does not really take place. Given the different types of constitution, the policies of ruler-educators can be anything, from those of an enlightened leader to what ruthless users of power often impose. When the latter happens, the rulers exclude the ruled from the processes of social deliberations and legislating for what is presumably the common good. When this happens, we have a case of a deviant constitution. We are thus left with the problem whether it is possible at all for education to stay on a course of normality under conditions of politically deviant constitutions, and conversely, we have the problem of how to explain the presence of just citizens in corrupt types of state. The crucial issue is what happens to the educational norms under perverse political conditions. Aristotle intimated his answers in those parts of the *Politics* where he dealt with the processes of political reforms, the nature of revolutions and legislative measures for social *therapeia*. Suffice it to say at this point that deviant constitutions and the perversion of education are cases of social pathology.

II. Basic Concepts

The state, what the ancient Greeks called "politeia," provided through its *thesmoi*, the *ethos*, the pattern or norms, the conceptions of the ends of life, that is, the good life.

The most intelligent citizen would be the one best adapted toward these ends. He will be most prudent and the one to whom others will look for guidance, especially the ones who do not have enough intelligence.

Aristotle accepted and promoted the classical ethos. The concept of a norm or philosophically defensible ethos is not very popular today. We are more interested in changing adaptable norms to changing conditions. Our inquiries are concerned with finding out how a given ethos changes rather than how it can be perfected.

For Aristotle, the good man cannot exist in isolation. All his activities take place in the city, in a social context. The city, for Aristotle, is a telic association of communities. It came into existence so that men might live and live well. Furthermore, the state is instrumental, and its function is cultural and educational; it exists in order that it may provide the means and the conditions for the development of good and happy human beings. Yet, in another context, the *polis* as the collective good is an entity that possesses greater value than individual happiness.

The properties of good men consist of habits, trained dispositions, which perform in certain ways to respond effectively and appropriately to certain situations. When the good man performs he does so excellently, for his habits are excellent. The perfect response can be such only in relation to a stimulus, an environment, yet guided by the *summum bonum*: eudaimonia. The good city-state and the conduct of the good man are interdependent. In *Nic. Eth.* Bk. IV, we find a list of the excellences of the good man: Wisdom, Prudence, and Art.

The key question this paper raises for discussion is: "To what end must the state educate the citizens?" The most significant issue involved in the question is that of how to establish a proper norm which will serve as the end of education. This end must be one that can be philosophically defended and hence reasons given for its priority over competing ends. A further issue of related importance is whether the philosophically defended end, as pursued through educational policies in normal constitutions, becomes distorted in the case of deviant types of constitutions. Hence it is important to ask: "What happens to the normal ends and functions of education when a deviant constitution replaces a normal type?" Furthermore, an equally tantalizing question is the following: "Given that a state has not had the benefit of a good or normal constitution or type of government, how is it possible for it to introduce and sustain educational ends pursued by non-deviant states?" In order to answer this and other related questions, Aristotle found it necessary to define the proper end of what he regarded to be a healthy constitution and establish the appropriate educational norm that would be in line with the state's end. Without this part of political theory, worked out in normative terms, the critique of educational practices in deviant forms of constitutions becomes not only difficult but also arbitrary—"ideological," we would be tempted to say today.

He state in *Politics* 1277 b 30: "The excellence of the good citizen requires an experience of ruling and being ruled." If so, we need to know how does a citizen gain this experience of ruling and being ruled in the case of good and also bad or deviant constitutions. Actually, Aristotle provides something like a rule in *Politics* 1288 a 33: "the goodness of the good man and that of the good citizen in the best state must be one and the same." Evidently, in bad constitutions the good man and the good citizen are not the same. Further down, at the end of Book III (1288 b 1) he states:

> It clearly follows that just the same method and just the same means, by which a man achieves goodness, should also be used to achieve the creation of a state on the pattern of aristocracy of kingship [n.b., i.e., the pattern which makes the goodness of the good citizen coincide with that of a good man]; and thus the training and habits of action which make a good man will be generally the same as the training (*paideia*) and habits of action which make a good statesman or a good king. (H. Rackham, tr. Loeb)

III. The Theory

Aristotle's *Politics* VIII, vii, i.e. last book, last chapter ends rather abruptly on the following note:

> Therefore some musical experts also rightly criticize Socrates because he disapproved of the relaxed harmonies for amusement, taking them to have the character of intoxication, not in the sense of the effect of strong drink, for that clearly has more the result of making men frenzied revellers, but as failing in power. Hence, even with a view to the period of life that is to follow, that of the comparatively old, it is proper to engage in the harmonies and melodies of this kind too, and also any kind of harmony that is suited to the age of boyhood because it is capable of being at once

decorous and educative, which seems to be the nature of the Lydian mode most of all the harmonies. It is clear therefore that we should lay down these three canons to guide education, moderation, possibility and suitability (1392 b 33-35).[1]

Here is where Aristotle's treatment of educational curriculum ends. Though it stopped with music, it did not fail to give us his three canons or conditions of educational policy: moderation, possibility, and suitability. The reader, so it seems to me, has the right to expect from Aristotle, had he not stopped at this point, to have applied these canons to his treatment of higher education as well. It is unfortunate that he did not write the part that dealt with the college and graduate curricula, i.e., the higher intellectual and theoretical studies. Probably his higher level of studies would have coincided with the courses at the Lyceum. Somehow, this reminds one of Plato's reluctance to write his definitive lectures on the Higher Dialectic, or what he planned to do in the dialogue he never wrote, the *Philosophos*, which was supposed to cap the trilogy, whose other two members are the *Sophistes* and the *Politikos*.

Without the needed information about the content of higher education, we are in a difficult position to judge the viability of his recommendations as being appropriate to the needs of our own age or those of some other port-classical period. Probably we could solve the problem of reconstructing the general outline of what Aristotle would have prescribed for higher education by going to the central books of the *Nicomachean Ethics* and supplementing the needed content by borrowing from the *Metaphysics* and his other works as taught at the Lyceum. I say this because the task of developing the practical and intellectual excellences is on which can be carried out only during the post-adolescence period. In a way, Aristotle has given us enough information to work out the theory and content of higher education. However, we still have a problem and it amounts to this: How is it possible to adopt and implement an educational program, such as the one Aristotle recommends and defends, unless there are definite guarantees that the political context permits its promotion by virtue of agreement with its presumed usefulness. In other words, the normative philosophy of education Aristotle proposes can never be fully implemented apart from a modicum of political conditions and practices present, to say the least, in the normal types of constitutions. Without them, the three canons make no sense.

I will not belabor the obvious point that some education is always taking place no matter what political conditions prevail in any given society. Hence, our question must be raised at a different and higher level: i.e., What are the most desirable political conditions for a qualitative program of education, such as the one Aristotle has developed? How do programs become accepted and, in turn, define the type of public life subsequent generations of citizens may regard suitable to the human condition? In view of this pressing question, I must return to the hidden issues in the closing sentence of the *Politics*: "It is clear therefore that we should lay down these three canons to guide education: (1) moderation, (2) possibility and (3) suitability." Of course, the context of the paragraph in which this sentence occurs gives no special hints to the reader. Yet, it does not preclude a wider reading; i.e., one which takes us beyond the mere psychological and moral sense of *meson, dynaton* and *prepon*. I think it would be in line with the general spirit of Aristotle's *Politics* to try to delineate the broader context, namely the political. Only after we have done so, will it be possible to decide the issue of the significance of the canons as well as the ideal they purport to sustain.

IV. Norms and Deviations

Since my analysis depends mainly on some previous understanding of Aristotle's views on political norms as reflected in healthy and deviant types of constitutions, and also on Aristotle's conceptions of the political aims of education, a word is needed at this point with regard to his indebtedness to Plato's views. When Aristotle went to Athens to study at the Academy in 361 B.C., he was about 18 and Plato 62 years old. He was there when Plato wrote his mature works, especially the *Statesman* and the *Laws*. When Plato died in 347 B.C., at the ripe age of 81 or 82, Aristotle was in his midthirties. In the years that followed he extended and built upon the doctrines of his teachers, especially the later doctrines of Plato. Two items must be mentioned as related to my theme:

(a) Aristotle adopts the sixfold classification of the states already used in the *Statesman* of Plato: three law-abiding states and three corresponding lawless corruptions. (In the *Republic* we have: (i) the ideal state of pure monarchy replaced by the corrupt form of timocracy or military state; (ii) oligarchy or government by the rich is a corruption of timocracy; (iii) democracy is a corruption of oligarchy and tyranny is a corruption of democracy.) It is in the *Statesman* that we find the classification Aristotle will follow:[2]

1) Rule of one yields monarchy and tyranny
2) Rule of few yields aristocracy and oligarchy
3) Rule of the many yields democracy in a moderate and extreme form.

Clearly, education is in a city, and cities are governed by constitutions that fall within these types or some mixed form in between. In order to avoid confusion we need to make a distinction between what is educationally viable with respect to basic goals of constitutions as related to the Greek *polis*, and what we may want to extract from the educational experience of the ancients as conceivably valuable to our own ways of life. Thus, we can talk about the "viability" of an ancient educational ideal within certain limits. It must not be forgotten that the polis, which for Aristotle was the matrix of civilized life, is radically different from the modern state, a difference which is not merely one of size. Hence, the educational needs and objectives do not necessarily run in parallel grooves. I hope to make these points clearer as I develop my thesis.

(b) In the *Laws*, where Plato discusses the permanent institutions of the state, he proposes that the twelve divisions of the council must act, each in its term, in conjunction with the executive magistrates, who are the guardians of the law. These thirty-seven magistrates are selected in the general assembly, and each holds office for twenty years, provided that each magistrate has reached his fiftieth year at the time of the election and must retire at the age of seventy. Anyway, their main function is to ensure observance of the law; they are the *nomophylakes*. Their presiding officer, their chairman, is the member who is charged with the care of education; i.e., the minister of education. This *epimelētēs tēs paideias*, is elected from the ranks of *nomophylakes*, on a secret vote by a joint assembly of all the magistrates of the state, and is expected to hold this office for a term of five years. He must be the best of all the citizens in all respects (766A); his office is by far the greatest even among the highest offices of the state (765E). The intent is clear: to have the Minister of Education serve as the Prime Minister. The sort of person Plato wants to serve as the educational leader must match the lofty nature of the office he is to hold.

When we turn to Aristotle we do not find as clear-cut a statement as this one by Plato, but we are given to understand throughout the *Politics* that he intends to impress upon the reader why it is that the ties between the diverse aspects, functions, and offices of the state on the one hand, and the aims of education on the other, must remain unbroken in a way that the one cannot be treated without reference to the other.

It should be remembered that for Aristotle it is a major premise that the aim of education, considered in the broadest sense, should be that of assisting the youth to become citizens. And, as he tells us in *Politics* (1277 b 25–29):

Politeia and Paideia

Practical wisdom alone of the virtues is a virtue peculiar to the ruler; for the other virtues seem to be necessary alike for both subjects and rulers to possess, but wisdom assuredly is not a subject's virtue, but only right opinion.

The message is clear; a citizen who is ruled today but aspires to rule tomorrow, must demonstrate that he has practical wisdom.

The flavor of the passage is unmistakably Platonic. He also tells us that the excellence of the good citizen requires experience "in ruling and being ruled." As we saw in *Politics* 1288 a 36, ideally speaking, the rule is that "the excellence of a man and that of a citizen in the best state must by necessity be one and the same." And he concludes Bk. III as follows:

The being the case it is evident that a man becomes good in the same way and by the same means as one might establish an aristocratically or monarchically governed state, so that it will be almost the same education and habits that make a man good and that make him capable as a citizen or a king. [...ὥστ' ἔσται καὶ παιδεία καὶ ἔθη ταὐτὰ σχεδὸν τὰ ποιοῦντα σπουδαῖον ἄνδρα καὶ τὰ ποιοῦντα πολιτικὸν καὶ βασιλικόν.]

The meaning is clear. All rulers, especially those of the correct forms of government become good through education and training in the requisite habit, then ensure practical wisdom. Human nature, in order to be fitted for proper participation in the affairs of civilized society must be fashioned for these tasks by education and practice. This may well be regarded as commonplace; what matters here is the distinction between ruler and ruled with respect to education.[3] We may view the person who is a ruler in two ways; (a) as an educator and as a citizen, and (b) [by extending (a)] we may view the ruler as an educator who rules educators in their capacity as citizens and as trainers of future citizens. These two aspects combine to make the responsibility of the ruler extremely sensitive and decisive as far as the future of the state is concerned.

Given this connection, it should be obvious that a ruler becomes disqualified from holding high office when by his very acts he comes to compromise the common good or perverts his fundamental commitment to the educational policy of the state. More concretely he is disqualified if he (a) fails to promote the common good and/or (b) through acts of commission or errors of omission, he fails to assist the citizens in their effort to attain the needed virtues to be properly ruled or share in the ruling as the case may be.

Of course, Aristotle does not develop a technical vocabulary suitable to cover all the functions citizens perform in their roles qua educators, but his analysis of the work which is normally done in the city-state allows us to extract the general line of his argument. Our problem has nothing to do with the fact that minimal educational processes are inevitably carried out even in the simplest types of human associations. The issue is a different one. Unless a constitution supports and sustains some significant aspect of what may be regarded as an irreducible common good, education, *paideia*, in Aristotle's sense of the term, does not really happen. Instruction in skills for purposes of survival or securing external goods and related means, is one thing, but instruction in moral and intellectual education, quite another. Without the latter, Aristotle maintains, we fail to promote the common good just as we miss having a theory of education.

Let us consider now the citizens as "ruled." Among these are also the ones who "educate" either by way of assisting in adding to the expertise of the ruler, the wise educator, or by carrying out the dictates or policies formulated by the ruler. Given the different constitutions, the ruler-educator may be an enlightened leader or a dogmatic user of power; and when the latter, the ruled are essentially excluded from the βουλευτικόν, the decision-making process, and the ways of administering justice, the νομοθετικόν, legislating for the common good. In other words, we are dealing with a deviant constitution.

However, before we proceed to take a closer look into the problems one can raise in connection with the meaning and functions of education in the case of deviant constitutions, we must conclude our remarks on Aristotle's indebtedness to Plato's *Laws*. *Politics* VIII, quite likely an early essay, opens on the following:

> That the education of the young requires the special attention of the lawgiver, nobody would now dispute that. Indeed the neglect of this in state is injurious to their constitutions; for education ought to be adapted to the particular form of constitution, since the particular character belonging to each constitution both guards the constitution generally and originally establishes it—for instance the democratic spirit promotes democracy and the oligarchic spirit oligarchy; and the best spirit always causes a better constitution. Moreover, in regard to all the faculties an crafts certain forms of preliminary education and training in their various operations are necessary, so that manifestly this is also requisite in regard to the actions of virtue. An inasmuch as the end of the whole state is one, it is manifest that education also must necessarily be one and the same for all and that the superintendence of this must be public, and not on private lines, in the way in which at present each man superintends the education of his own children, teaching them privately, and whatever special branch of knowledge he thinks fit...all citizens belong to the state. (Loeb tr.)[4]

Earlier in Book VIII (chapter iii), he states: "It is therefore clear that there is an education which is for the training of the youth, not because it is useful or necessary but because it is liberal and good" [῞Οτι μὲν τοίνυν ἔστι παιδεία τις ἣν οὐχ ὡς χρησίμην παιδευτέον τοὺς υἱεῖς οὐδ' ὡς ἀναγκαίαν ἀλλ' ὡς ἐλευθέριον καὶ καλήν, φανερόν ἐστιν. 1338a 30–32].

In the very next sentence he promises to investigate at some later point whether there is one such type of "liberal and good education" or more. However, the promise is not fulfilled. One can take a guess here. Aristotle restricted himself to developing a curriculum which could be adopted by any of the correct constitutions, and he worked out a program of studies or subjects of education with respect to reading and writing, gymnastics, music and also drawing. What we miss in this last book of the *Politics* is what must follow the type he calls "education by habit." He states (1338b 5): "Education by habit must come before education by reason (*dianoian*)."

Although we do not find the curriculum for the "education of reason" developed in *Politics* VIII, the omission is not a serious one. What really counts is another question, a political one. Given that useful or necessary education does in fact occur in all constitutions, is it possible to ensure under the conditions of a deviant constitution an education suitable to bringing up the youth to become free and excellent (which is what education "by reason" requires)? We may ask the same question in a different way, and somewhat platonic: can an unjust constitution—illiberal and based on the perversion of the common good—produce a just citizen? Even if we grant that this is not the goal of the ruler of such a constitution, is it possible for someone to be educated as a just citizen in an unjust constitution? Furthermore, can there be just educators in unjust constitutions?

The real issue, however, is not whether it is possible for a person to attain a state of personal justice in an unjust constitution but rather what happens to education as a process under perverse political conditions. The crucial problem about the political context of education is not how to implement a program of liberal education in a healthy constitution but what to do in the case of a deviant constitution, if anything can in fact be done at all. This is a question that Aristotle did not really try to answer in a systematic way in the normative books of his *Politics*, where he dealt with the philosophical foundations of a normal curriculum.

V. Standards of Correctness for Education

In *Politics* III. 1 we have an initial, tentative definition of citizen (1275a 22–34), followed by remarks on the relationship of citizen to constitution: (a) the notion of citizen depends upon that of constitution; (b) constitutions differ in kind; (c) correct constitutions are "prior" to deviant or mistaken constitutions, παρέκβασις vs. ὀρθότης; and (d) priority-posteriority of constitutions must not be construed temporally.[5]

It follows that there is no single, common notion of citizen (1275a 35–b 5). Aristotle's analysis makes evident the goal of political associations and also "provides a clear explanation of why democracies, oligarchies and tyrannies are called constitutions. They are essentially deviations from polity, aristocracy, and kingship..." (Fortenbaugh, 133). Only the latter are correct and primary forms.

Correct constitutions are prior in (a) a conceptual sense and (b) an evaluative sense. A note on the grading of constitutions is called for at this point. Aristotle talks about "better" and "less bad" constitutions. Anyway, he does give us an ordering of correct constitutions. In 1289a 30–33, he recognizes the superior value of kingship and aristocracy. In 1289a 38–b 5, also *E. N.* 1160a 35–b 22, he offers a single series running from best to worst political arrangement.

The standard of correctness is one that has to do with correctness of goal. Thus (a) correct constitutions consider as their aim the common good; (b) deviant constitutions consider the rulers' "good" (1279a 17–20). The grade of correct institutions is decided on the basis of an additional criterion. That correct constitution is best which is managed by the best of men. (1288a 32–34, end of *Politics* III).

This standard of grade is important because it introduces the notion of excellence.

1. Kingship is deemed best (*E. N.* 1160a 35), for the monarch is a man of quasi-divine qualities. (1284a 10; 1289a 40).

2. Kingship and aristocracy (ideal) may be grouped together and rated best (1289a 30–33 and 1310a 34-1311a 8), or possibly aristocracy is to be preferred (1289b 3–7).

3. Polity comes 3rd because a large number of citizens cannot possess virtue fully (1279a 40).

Given this background, we may regroup the questions we raised in the previous section: *What is the proper function of education in the correct and deviant constitutional types?* More specifically:

I. Since we have three correct constitutions, is the educational process the same for all?

II. Since we have three deviant forms, what is the function of education *de facto* and *de jure*? If we grant that these deviant forms have already compromised the common advantage, i.e., the criterion of correctness, what becomes of the function of education? In other words, can education function properly once the standard of correctness has been altered and "excellence" can be neither pursued nor seriously invoked to test the grade of incorrectness or its lack thereof?

IIa. Given Aristotle's grading, such as "better" and "less bad," what functions does education perform under certain fluid and transitional political conditions when we pass from one constitution to its opposite?

Our investigation of these problems is likely to stumble on some very difficult issues, mainly because it is not quite clear to us today who in Aristotle's time were the counterpart of our many sorts of educators. We have developed a "professional class" that collectively combined a great number of functions, and only rarely extends to the legislative one. However, we do influence the legislative branch of government through unions and their pressure groups. Now, in a very fundamental sense, the ancient citizen qua legislature is an educator as well. Here we must distinguish between the hired "teacher" who could be a *metoikos* or even a slave. Hence when we raise the question of the παιδαγωγός, "What is the role of education in deviant constitutions?" we are asking a very complex question. We need to specify not only what the function of education is in general as a norm, but also (a) what happens to this norm in deviant constitutions and (b) who is the educator in each constitution.

There is one sense in which we can speak of the philosopher as being a superior educator, i.e., he is one who knows how to teach political science, political theory. Since political science is fundamental to the ends of education, we can say that the philosopher is the teacher *par excellence* of what all teaching is about, and hence the one who can guide legislation regarding the aims of education and the means for their implementation. In a passage where Aristotle follows Plato closely we read:

> Now since earlier generations have left the subject of legislation unexamined, it is perhaps best that we should ourselves study this, and the problems of political life and constitution in general, in order to complete, to the best of our ability, the philosophy of human affairs. (*N. E.* 1181b 13–16).

The real problem begins when leadership falls into unphilosophical hands or when philosophers fail to impart their knowledge to those who will assume legislative duties. In either case, the results are deplorable. Let us suppose we are philosophers-educators and we find ourselves living in a deviant constitution. We are faced with the following possibilities.

1. If the deviant state has been in operation for an extended period of time, especially prior to our own birth, the chances that we will be able to become philosophers, i.e., knowers of the correct goals of education are rather dim. Hence we can do very little, if any, profound social criticism.

2. If the deviant form came into force during our own lifetime, but after we had some philosophical training, we will be unhappy, for we

will know that we have been deprived of the conditions to pursue the good life; thus we run the risk of losing what little wisdom we have come to possess. The obvious solution would be to go into self-exile, i.e., a selfish act.

3. If the deviant form seems destined to outlast our generation, there is little we can do as educators and philosophers, except restrict our teaching to the transmission of tools and skills, i.e., the lower curriculum which stresses utility and comforts. We thus will adjust to deviancy.

In all three cases just outlined, we are left with a peculiar feeling of futility. It amounts to a sense of powerlessness to do any reforming, to turn things around so that a deviant constitution may become a correct one. This is precisely the issue I want to press here: what, according to Aristotle, are the limits of correct education to act in deviant constitutions?

To begin with, since education is founded on political theory, and since the normative aspects of politics are binding on educational practice, it is evident that the aims of education and the preservation of deviant constitutions are incompatible objectives. An educator who lives in a deviant state is destined to be not-happy, not only because the common good has been perverted, but also because the deviant state distorts wisdom and thwarts individual fulfillment. It simply prevents the exercise and sharing of the social excellences. We need to remember Aristotle's stipulation:

> If all communities aim at some good, the state or political community, which is the highest of all, and which embraces all the rest, aims at a good in a greater degree than any other, and at the highest good. (*Politics* 1252a 4–6).

Of course, political philosophy is not only about the best state, for the "ideal"state is not the only or even the main subject of political philosophy. It is also about rules, laws, regulations, and institutions.

Since we have many types of correct institutions, we want to know what are the most suitable means to preserve them.

We know that one of the emphases in *Politics* is on how to secure the stability of a constitution or a government. Of course, a government is an organization not likely or easily overthrown by a rebellious or revolutionary movement from within. The concern here is how to make the condition of governmental stability work to the advantage of the community. On the issue of stability Aristotle is opposed to violent political changes more so than Plato. He is confident that political theory can be of educational value providing guidance to practical statesmen. He is also concerned to show why it is necessary to consider an "ideal state theory" logically "prior" and also practically important as a disclosure of the "end-in-view."

There can be no dispute about the role of education as an agent concerned with the selection and transmission of certain desirable dispositions, skills or excellences. In the present context, we take it for granted that excellences are "transmitted by being taught," and "transmitted and acquired by practice."[6] The theme of my paper is not so much about such factors as native endowment, favorable physical conditions or a sufficient span of life, as it is about the problem of adverse conditions due to political causes.

According to Frankena,[7] there are three questions for any normative philosophy of education:

(1) What dispositions are to be cultivated? Which dis-positions are excellences?

(2) Why are these dispositions to be regarded as excellences and cultivated? What are the aims or principles of education that require their cultivation?

(3) How or by what methods or processes are they to be cultivated?

My theme is more closely related to the third question but mainly in the context of deviant types of constitution. It should be evident that the selection of dispositions to be cultivated and their justification through a set of principles of education, constitute issues that usually come under close scrutiny in the case of deviant forms of government either because such dispositions do not suit the power-oriented aims of the ruler(s) or because the methods required for the cultivation of excellences, as required by the correct constitutions, are directly opposed to the methods used in deviant ways of treating public affairs. Hence, it is impossible for a deviant constitution to promote its aims without subverting the goals of education through a distortion of the idea of excellence.

For the purposes of our argument let us assume that Aristotle has reasonably satisfied the demands that questions 1 and 2 pose for his normative philosophy of education. Since it is a fact of history that bad states can become good and good states backslide into decadent forms of government, what we need to know is how to meet the demands which question #3 poses, especially when the methods and aims of education conflict with those employed by deviant constitutions.

IV. Conclusion

1. Most accounts of Aristotle's philosophy of education explore the aims, principles, and methods of education as delineated in the *Nicomachean Ethics* and *Politics*, but mainly in the light of the ideal state, i.e., a correct constitution. There is no doubt about Aristotle's contextual and applied approach to problems of education and what he recommends. Obviously, the curriculum he proposes for the ideal state is also a working model for all actual and correct constitutions. Given this normative political context, there is no way in which the educators and the statesmen may entertain conflicting theories especially with respect to what desirable dispositions are to be developed into moral and intellectual excellences; nor will there be any serious disregard for the common good of the community.

Disagreements, if any, would be limited to differences of opinion over means, not ends; the correct constitutions remain constant in their acceptance of the principles of excellence. However, since (a) deviant constitutions are not inevitable, (b) they occur with unpredictable frequency either because of ambition, greed, etc., from within, or aggression and conquest from without, the problem of education in deviant constitutions presents a special moral and political anomaly we do not encounter in the correct ones.

In view of the fact that modern constitutional history and contemporary political practices have become the subject of much discussion from a non-normative point of view, the Aristotelian distinctions and correlations between political theory and normative philosophy of education take on special significance if used as theoretical platforms to raise questions about educational responsibility, the meaning of excellence, educational policies and their administration in the present scene.

But aside from the relevance of Aristotle's views, we may say that on the whole it is his theory of the constitution he calls *politeia* that holds the key to a viable political environment for education. *Politeia*, because of its moderate outlook, makes it amenable to rationality. Hence, it is to the citizens' best interests to want to promote only the educational goals, curriculum and knowledge that cultivate and sustain the excellences appropriate to the good man. In *politeia*, the common good cannot be easily subverted. In other words, *politeia* works best when its citizens are well educated; and conversely, when education is available by way of equal opportunities to all citizens, *politeia* maintains its balance, the mean, and in effect prevents sliding toward either extreme. Consider now how distorted the function of education becomes in the case of a polis which sinks to some lower form of community by not pursuing the good life for its members. Such a "lower" form of polis degenerates into a mere alliance in which members stay at a distance from one another, i.e., they feel alone yet they remain physically together (1280b 22 ff).

Lower type communities substitute the relation of utility for the "common pursuant of the good" (consider here the analogy to the three types of friendship in its gradation: utility → pleasure → common pursuit of the good).

When both oligarchy and democracy, because of their emphasis on property as the end of the association, reverse the gradation of ends, and hence human beings cannot "live alone together," evidently oligarchy and democracy inherently tend to distort and degrade the normative functions of education.

Thus the question arises: How does a citizen behave as an agent of education in these "lower types" of government, i.e., deviant constitution? What are the limits of action, practice, legislation and what are the chances for attaining the theoretical life? Given the compromise of the educational norm, what paths remain to correct the conditions of deviancy?

2. The contemporary mass state has moved in the direction of new extremes: In our own case of a United States, we still have a "mixed constitution", in some respects like and in others unlike what Aristotle recommended. *Quantitatively*, even the larger cities are way out of line from the community of 100,000 he suggested. *Qualitatively*, the federal government is too remote to exercise practical involvement with the citizenry and assist in directing the dispositional qualities, passions and activities, in all their various patterns of personal development and conduct. *Substantively*, it is based on the principle of the equality of citizens and the trinity of ends—life, liberty, and the pursuit of happiness, which, with some straining the imagination and good will, brings it closer to what the Greeks called the "common good." But the fact remains that the material condition for the pursuit of any of the three ends is property or rather the possession and increase of wealth, individual and corporate.

It is against this background that we have to understand the role, functions and foundations of education in our modern massive state.

What then is the political context of education in our case? Is it possible for ourselves to think seriously about bringing together the political theorist and the statesman, and both with the philosopher? Is there a common good for these three types, whether we view them as citizens of the same community or as specialists with only overlapping areas of expertise? I can only say that I feel more confused now than when I began.

I still have a problem to face in this paper: In what sense is Aristotle offering a viable alternative to what we are doing? How are his views relevant to our own pursuits?

To answer these questions, I need to address myself to the major issue "What is the character of our times?" The problem here is that we cannot speak of a contemporary mind but rather only of variants of value frameworks available today, some demanding stronger allegiance than others. The Aristotelian alternative may be regarded viable to some and irrelevant to others. Anyway, I would risk some suggestions here about the relevance of the Aristotelian model and the values it involves.

(1) It calls for a clear relationship of politics and education. (2) It stands for a closer and stronger role of reason in political thinking and educational planning. (3) It aims at promoting an outlook of eudaemonistic ethics.

APPENDIX

A. A Note on Aristotle's School

This brief account of the curriculum in Aristotle's own school is based on what information we have on the subjects taught at the Lyceum. As such, the curriculum must not be regarded as one that fulfills the educational norm as discussed in the *Politics*, although there is no opposition between the two.

1. While admission to Plato's school called for meeting the famous entrance requirement μηδεὶς ἀγεωμέτρητος εἰσίτω, "Only geometers may enter," Aristotle used another qualification for lecturing to students, according to the testimony of Aulus Gellius (a Roman of the 2nd century A.D. who lived in Athens and attended philosophy there, under a Platonist Calvisius Taurus)

> In the Lyceum he devoted the morning to the *acroatic* subjects (i.e. lecture courses) and did not allow anyone to attend without assuring himself of their ability, educational grounding, keenness to learn, and willingness to work. (*Noct. Att.* 20.5; Düring, p. 431).

2. Curriculum consisted of two sections: (a) Morning lectures and (b) Evening courses. Pupils prepared basic collections of material, (natural, cultural, political); these materials were used to practice the inductive method and to encourage the students to pursue the empirical sciences as well as sharpen their powers of observation. Aristotle and his assistants made their notebooks available when a particular project by a student got under way. Aristotle assigned particular subjects to other assistants: Botany to Theophrastus;

Politeia and Paideia   239

Medicine to Medon; History of the Exact Sciences, e.g. arithmetic, geometry, and astronomy to Eudemus of Rhodes.

Basically the curriculum was divided into two classes: (a) *esoteric* or special advanced work on theory, scientific method, dialectic, and logic, etc., and (b) *exoteric*. Aulus Gellius describes them as follows:

> The exoteric lectures and speech classes (rhetoric) he held in the same place in the evening and opened them to any young men without restriction. This he called his "evening walk," the other the early one, for at both times he walked as he talked. His books also, treatises on all these same subjects, he divided similarly, calling some *exoteric* and others *acroatic*.

B. A Note on Burnet's Interpretation

J. Burnet in his *Aristotle on Education*, p. 131, makes the following remark:

> It is by no means an accident that the theory of education is treated by Plato and Aristotle as a part of politics and Aristotle has told us why. It is true he says, that the good of a single individual is the same as the good of a whole state; but it is no less true that it is only in the state that we can realize this good in all its completeness.

Concerning "the Value of the Greek view for us," Burnet believes that (a) all education must have reference to some community or other, and (b) all education has still the mission to fit the young to become members of a community. What we must do in order to make the Greek view relevant to our circumstances is to examine what different elements have been introduced into the modern idea of a community. (i) Family is the simplest form of community. On this entity our views differ greatly from those of the Greeks. Plato would abolish the family, at least for the guardians. "Even Aristotle does not lay much stress as we should on the family as an educative influence. He seems to be more alive to the dangers of home influences than to their value" (132). (ii) We have a very large number of associations and communities (some overlapping, some including others, etc.) than the Greeks. The Greeks had mainly two: family and *polis*: "...while Plato's treatment of education in the *Republic* is complete, Aristotle's in *Politics* is, for some reason or other, a fragment."

Burnet points out that Aristotle intended to discuss, firstly, the education of the body (gymnastics), secondly the education of character — the instrument for doing this is music — and thirdly the education of the mind, which is supposed to crown the whole process. Yet, there is nothing in *Politics* about the last one.

Burnet states that "We have no record of Aristotle's views as to scientific education at all... What the scientific training recommended by Aristotle was, we can only guess" (pp. 134–5). After stating what in his view were the special subject fields, Burnet notes:

> We may also be sure that the shoe was intended to lead up to what we call Metaphysics and he called Theology and First Philosophy. We know from the *Ethics* that happiness at its highest is to be found in that form of activity which displays itself in the contemplation of the divinest things in the universe. Aristotle is quite as emphatic about that as Plato ever was. (136)

And further down he states: "...Plato and Aristotle are quite at one with regard to the true function of education" (136). The training of character comes first and with the practical requirements of the community in view. Yet "the highest function of education goes beyond the practical life" (136).

Here, Burnet concludes, we hit the paradoxical situation of human attainment in the ethical and political spheres: the more an individual approaches the end of developing "the divine" in human nature, the less he is dependent on association with other human beings.[8] If this interpretation is accepted at its face value, it would leads to a conception of self-sufficiency that would allow the conclusion that the complete theoretical life is also the least concerned with the political conditions of εὖ ζῆν.

Aristotle has anticipated the problem of the "paradoxical situation" and stated its consequences in *Pol.* I. 3, 1253a 27-29: "He who is unable to live in associations, or because of self-sufficiency does not need any part of the *polis*, is hence either beast or god." Such is the case of the *apolis* individual. Whether the attainment of the theoretical life also opens the possibility of the *apolis* life is hardly what Aristotle had in mind when he formulated the ideal of human fulfillment.

NOTES

1. ...δῆλον οὖν ὅτι τούτους ὅρους τρεῖς ποητέον εἰς τὴν παιδείαν, τό τε μέσον καὶ τὸ δυνατὸν καὶ τὸ πρέπον.

2. According to G. Sabine: "The only difference between Plato's treatment and Aristotle's — and it appears to be important — is that the former describes his true states as law-abiding, while the latter describes them as governed for the general good. In view of his analysis of what constitutional government means, Aristotle must have thought that the two descriptions came nearly to the same thing." (*History of Political Thought*, 106). Aristotle broke away from Plato but not completely, since he tried to combine descriptive methods, through the study of 158 constitutions, with speculative work. Sabine remarks: "Moral ideals — the sovereignty of law, the freedom and equality of citizens constitutional government, the perfecting of men in a civilized life — are always for Aristotle the ends for which the state ought to exist." (Ibid. 109).

3. On this see *Pol.* VII, xiii, 1332b 12 ff. "But since every political community is composed of rulers and ruled, we must therefore consider whether the rulers and the ruled ought to change, or to remain the same through life; for it is clear that their education will also have to be made to correspond with this distribution of functions." Επεὶ δὲ πᾶσα πολιτικὴ κοινωνία συνέστηκεν ἐξ ἀρχόντων καὶ ἀρχομένων, τοῦτο δὴ σκεπτέον, εἰ ἑτέρους εἶναι δεῖ τοὺς ἄρχοντας καὶ τοὺς ἀρχομένους ἢ τοὺς αὐτοὺς διὰ βίου· δῆλον γὰρ ὡς ἀκολουθεῖν δεήσει καὶ τὴν παιδείαν κατὰ τὴν διαίρεσιν ταύτην.

4. Ὅτι μὲν οὖν τῷ νομοθέτῃ μάλιστα πραγματεύειν περὶ τὴν τῶν νέων παιδείαν, οὐδεὶς ἂν ἀμφισβητήσειεν. καὶ γὰρ ἐν ταῖς πόλεσι οὐ γιγνόμενον τοῦτο βλάπτει τὰς πολιτείας· δεῖ γὰρ πρὸς ἑκάστην παιδεύεσθαι, τὸ γὰρ ἦθος τῆς πολιτείας ἑκάστης τὸ οἰκεῖον φυλάττειν εἴωθε τὴν πολιτείαν καὶ καθίστησιν ἐξ ἀρχῆς, οἷον τὸ δημοκρατικὸν δημοκρατίαν, τὸ δὲ ὀλιγαρχικὸν ὀλιγαρχίαν· ἀεὶ δὲ τὸ βέλτιστον ἦθος βελτίονος αἴτιον πολιτείας. ἔτι δε πρὸς πάσας δυνάμεις καὶ τέχνας ἔστιν ἃ δεῖ προπαιδεύεσθαι καὶ προεθίζεσθαι πρὸς τὰς ἑκάστων ἐργασίας, ὥστε δῆλον ὅτι καὶ πρὸς τὰς τῆς τέχνης ἀρετῆς πράξεις. ἐπεὶ δ' ἓν τὸ τέλος τῇ πόλει πάσῃ, φανερὸν ὅτι καὶ τὴν παιδείαν μίαν καὶ τὴν αὐτὴν ἀναγκαῖον

Politeia and Paideia 243

εἶναι πάντων καὶ ταύτης τὴν ἐπιμέλειαν εἶναι κοινὴν καὶ μὴ κατ' ἰδίαν, ὃν τρόπον νῦν ἕκαστος ἐπιμελεῖται τῶν αὑτοῦ τέκνων ἰδίᾳ τε καὶ μάθησιν ἰδίαν ἥν ἂν δόξῃ διδάσκων. δεῖ δὲ τῶν κοινῶν κοινὴν ποιεῖσθαι καὶ τὴν ἄσκησιν. 1337α 10–27. For Aristotle it is assumed that the legislator is obligated to direct his attention above all to the education of youth, for, as he says, "the neglect of education does harm to the constitution."

5. W. Fortenbaugh *TAPA* 1976 (125) has argued against the "temporal" construction. He suggests that we must not adopt chronological interpretations just because Aristotle refers to a temporal use of "prior" (*Cat.* 14a 26–28) or speaks of a city in chronologically prior ways (1252a 24–1253a 39, 1278b 15–30). For Aristotle it is common advantage that brings human beings together (1278b 21–22); this common advantage is the declared goal of correct constitutions 1279a 17–20. Fortenbaugh also argues that we must not conclude that "correct constitutions are temporally prior, being due to some sort of natural, primitive instinct for association and common advantage" (126). E. Barker, in his *The Political Thought of Plato and Aristotle*, 310–11, points out that Aristotle does not want to say that deviant constitutions arise only when the motive of common advantage has been lost, for there may be other reasons. Von Fritz and Kapp, in the Introduction to *The Constitution of Athens*, state: "The construction of such an ideal state may then still serve a useful purpose, inasmuch as it helps clarify the general direction in which the true good of a political community is to be found. But, for all practical purposes, it will be much more important to find an answer to the question of what specific form this ideal will assume under particular geographic, social, economic, and generally historical circumstances. There will also be the question of what means can or may be used to bring a state, even if it were by only a little, nearer to this specific goal. For it is now acknowledged that, with the exception of absolute tyranny, which according to Aristotle and Plato, is no government and no real political community at all, a violent overthrow of the existing form of government produces more harm than good. (56)

6. W. Frankena, *Three Historical Philosophies of Education*, p. 5.

7. Ibid. p. 8.

8. See K. von Fritz and E. Kapp, "Introduction," in *Aristotle Constitution of Athens*, p. 47.

ARISTOTLE ON JUSTICE AS EQUITY[1]

The treatment of Justice in Aristotle's *Nicomachean Ethics* has been universally recognized as a major contribution to the understanding and practice of equity. In essence, modern practice is built on the Aristotelian conception of equity in a threefold connection: (a) common law corresponds to the results of legislation (*nomothesia*), (b) equity presupposes justice and rights, and (c) courts of equity aim at serving justice in remedial ways.[2]

The main objective of this paper is to examine the framework that Aristotle uses to define the equitable person as a judge. The text shows that the portrait, so to speak, of one who qualifies to serve as judge is drawn on the basis of the relationship that ties equity to justice. The issue is imbedded in the question "Who is the just judge?" We read in *Nic. Eth.* 1132a 20-25 the following:

> ...people have recourse to a judge when they are engaged in a dispute. To go to a judge means to go to the just, for the judge wishes (βούλεται), as it were, to be the em-bodiment of what is just.... The judge restores [unjust situations] to equality. (M. Ostwald tr.)

In developing this theme I have tried to bring together the following interrelated topics: (a) the judge (δικαστής) qua just (δίκαιος) and equitable (ἐπιεικής): and (b) justice and equity (δικαιοσύνη, ἐπιείκεια). The central thesis, as Aristotle states it, is that the equitable is a rectification, a restoring of legal justice (ἐπανόρθωμα νομίμου δικαίου).

It is axiomatic with Aristotle that for the administration of justice we proceed on the principle that in all cases of injury and transgression, all parties be regarded as equal and treated as such before the courts of law. Apart from this principal consideration of human conduct, discussion about equity is bound to be empty of meaning. The ground is laid in *Nicomachean Ethics* V. 1132a 2-7, where the equitable person is contrasted with the bad (ἐπιεικής vs. φαῦλος), yet both are regarded equal before the law where injury is concerned.

> It makes no difference whether a decent man has defrauded a bad man or vice versa, or whether it was a decent or a bad man who committed adultery. The only difference the law considers is that brought about by the damage; it treats the parties as equals and asks only whether one has done and the other has suffered damage. As the unjust in this sense is inequality, the judge tries to restore the equilibrium. (M. Ostwald tr.)

The context for the analysis of the concept of equity as a case of justice is established, as we saw, in *Nicomachean Ethics*, Bk. 5, where equity is treated as a habit or character within the family of virtues and vices. It is sufficient for the purpose of this paper to proceed without discussing the issues that pertain to the sources of rules. Acceptance and obedience for the promotion of justice presuppose conformity to the laws of the state as well as the possibility of their violation.

Aristotle distinguishes between universal justice and particular justice. The former is tantamount to conformity to law. Particular justice as fairness is of two kinds: (a) distributive and (b) rectificatory. The latter, whether remedial, corrective or compensatory, aims at redressing harm done to a plaintiff due to a transaction in which the injured party was involuntarily involved from the outset. I deal here only with the process of rendering rectificatory justice, and more specifically with the role of reasoning in deciding cases calling for equity on the part of the judge as the equitable man.[3]

The person who possesses the quality of ἐπιείκεια is thereby fair, decent, equitable. As such this person is also in a definite way good,

Justice as Equity

although the term *epieikēs* does not enjoy the same precision as the term 'good'. The reason is that the person who is *epieikes* exhibits this quality because of the flexible attitude he is able to take toward a variety of indeterminate situations, i.e., situations that cannot be determined and resolved by strict conformity to the legal formula. Hence the need to resort to fair judgment.

In *Nicomachean Ethics* V. 10. 1137a 31ff., Aristotle discusses the virtue of equity to explain how it relates to what is fair and what is just (τὸ ἐπιεικὲς καὶ τὸ δίκαιον). Following a brief exploration of usage and logic of terms, Aristotle comes to say that the difficulty in grasping the difference between the two lies in the following:

> This means that just and equitable are in fact identical (in genus), and, although both are morally good, the equitable is the better of the two. What causes the problem is that the equitable is not just in the legal sense of "just" but as a corrective of what is legally just [δικαίου]. (1137b 9-13, tr. M. Ostwald). αἴτιον δ᾽ ὅτι ὁ μὲν νόμος καθόλου πᾶς, περὶ ἐνίων δ᾽ οὐχ οἷον τε ὀρθῶς εἰπεῖν καθόλου...

The analysis of the *epieikes* is this chapter is simply brilliant. It establishes the conclusion that what we always want is for justice to prevail. Insofar as justice is according to law (legal justice), and since law (*nomos*) has always the form of a universal statement, the fact that cases occur that are not covered by the law, demands that we must resort to justice as equity. The resulting action takes the form of rectification of law but without an attendant demand to challenge its universality.

However, it does not follow that laws are necessarily defective. Aristotle's position is that generality must be pursued (a) when all cases are covered or (b) when the majority of cases are clearly covered. Since either or both are not always possible to obtain, we must identify the source of the difficulty. For, he states:

The flaw is not in the law nor is it in the legislator but in the nature of the situation. (1137b 16-17). Τὸ γὰρ ἁμάρτημα οὐκ ἐν τῷ νομοθέτῃ ἀλλ᾽ ἐν τῇ φύσει τοῦ πράγματος ἐστίν.

Two questions arise at this point: What is this *pragma*? and What is its nature? In the next sentence he tells us that the *hamartēma*, namely the flaw that affects the attainment of complete universality in law-making and which as a result compromises absoluteness, lies in the fact that *the material of human actions is essentially irregular.*

Legislators have no choice but to seek to regulate with the aid of *nomos* that which is by its nature irregular. This being the case we should not be surprised when we see that a *nomos*, although formulated as a universal statement, is actually an elliptical generality and therefore unable to cover deviations. The practical question that arises from the theoretical investigation is this: How should we decide when we discover that what the lawgivers have formulated, namely general rules, are wanting in precision and completeness? It is at this point that *epieikeia* enters. The judge rectifies the rule of the lawgiver as he himself would presumably have done if he could be present to decide the case before us. This leads Aristotle to say that "...the equitable is both just and also better than the just in one sense; not better than the just in general, but better than the mistake due to generality of the law" (1137b 23-25). This I take to mean that (a) the *epieikēs* is just, but only of a certain kind, and if so it is not superior to a general law; (b) it is superior to one kind of the just, presumably a law with a defective aspect to it, but still not superior to the concept of the absolute just; (c) the superiority of the *epieikēs*, however limited, is due to the unavoidable defects of *nomos* and its attendant claim to generality. As Aristotle puts it, this generality conforms to the regulative intent of the legislator but not to the totality of the facts of human actions and their irregularities.

Although Aristotle does not go into the issue, it is clear that he thinks that the *nomos* of the legislator is neither a discovery not an explanation with predictive efficacy over the facts that come under its

Justice as Equity 249

purview. He could have argued as follows: When a scientific law, cast in the form of a general statement, is challenged by new findings, the scientist withdraws the claim and seeks a viable replacement. But the scientist is not an *epieikēs*, for his conduct is not virtuous in respect of justice, although it is so in respect of truth. But when a person exhibits *epieikeia*, he rectifies rather than replaces a law. This means that to be equitable, one must remain within the rule of laws instituted for the regulation of human practices. If I am not mistaken, the same thesis lies at the basis of his analysis of revolutions and their reformative efficacy.

The acts of rectification to be just must take the form of decisions to extend, interpret, and work within the framework of existing rules of law to cover whatever exceptions are at hand or may arise in the future. Exceptions, in turn, are not to be viewed as "new facts" calling for the replacement of certain laws, as though they have now been falsified. Rather they must be treated as unanticipated cases to be addressed in a way that allows the judge to preserve the general legal statement to be enforced. Accordingly, he corrects what is defective in the law on account of the difference between the intent of the legal generality, its regulatory function, and the nature of the situation to be regulated.

A close reading of chapter 10 shows that for Aristotle the person who is *epieikēs* is not a necessarily a lawgiver, a *nomothetēs*, but primarily a man of virtue who complies with rather than works against the law. The kind of superior justice he effects is not superior to the law, within whose jurisdiction the equitable person acts, but superior only to the shortcomings due to the unexceptional application of generality. Since it is expected that at least some general laws will not be free of defects, it is required of the judge to understand the facts of human practices, that is, their irregular nature, which is the reason why all acts are not conforming to the law (1137b 27-28): αἴτιον τοῦ μὴ πάντα κατὰ νόμον εἶναι. The wise judge is one who perceives the human situation such as it is in each case. He knows that there are cases to which it is impossible to apply the law unconditionally, and is therefore prepared to advocate in favor of special ordinances to cope with the problem at hand: περὶ ἐνίων ἀδύνατον θέσθαι νόμον, ὥστε ψηφίσματος δεῖ.

Thus Aristotle's position is that it is necessary to distinguish between laws and ordinances. The latter are as expedient and useful as the former are necessary and more fundamental. However, he excludes two distinct theses — I call them "theses" because they have been formulated as such and defended by other theorists and philosophers of jurisprudence. (a) Given the irregular character of human conduct, law and justice need to be formulated and expressed as universal statements serving thus as guides to regulate human affairs. (b) Since the irregular character of conduct does not extend over all human nature, for there is no irregularity or anomaly in the case of the essential properties concerning the nature of human reason (*entelecheia*), it should be clear that such truths as are contained in the definition of human nature as well as the facts they cover, are free of the defects of the regulative laws. There is a complement to these two theses, namely that since *eudaimonia* and the common good, the good in its personal and political settings, are constant, laws come to occupy an intermediary position between *episteme*, the universal truths of science, and the corrective role of ordinances, the ψηφίσματα. The latter are introduced as complements to the rule of law. To conclude, according to Aristotle, law is neither reducible to ordinance not derivable from the collecting and interconnecting of converging sets of ordinances.

Since the equitable person is not a scientist in the strict sense nor a lawgiver, it is fair to ask questions about the kinds of functions he must perform. His corrective tasks, as Aristotle sees them, require that he be deliberative and practical (προαιρετικὸς καὶ πρακτικός). Yet in order to perform well acts of equity he should not stick to the letter of the law, for to do so could in certain cases make things worse. Therefore, he should be satisfied with exacting less than what

Justice as Equity

the law, although on his side, literally demands. He is fair and decent: ἐλλατωτικὸς καίπερ ἔχων τὸν νόμον βοηθόν, ἐπιεικής ἐστι. The continuous performance of equitable acts is evidence of possessing this virtue. Thus we can speak of *epieikeia* as a virtuous habit, and since the equitable person is at once deliberative and practical it is obvious that he possesses the cardinal ethical principle Aristotle calls *hexis prohairetikē*. He acts in the domain of the practical virtues rather than that of the theoretical ones. More specifically, this *aretē* is a special case of the more inclusive virtue of justice.

Chapter 10 leaves the reader with the impression that Aristotle is addressing his remarks to the application of the law by magistrates and judges. The assessments judges make are decisions that bring the law to bear on particular acts; they terminate in pronouncements of rewards and punishments to settle issues of guilt and innocence. The citizens serving in the capacity of judge, whether elected, appointed or self-appointed, are expected to fulfill the obligation to equity. Whether a judge *qua* private person, or any private person for that matter with a sense of equanimity, will in fact discharge the obligation of equity where his own interests are involved, for instance where he has caused or suffered injury, is another issue. A just society can only be one whose members demonstrate their respect for and possession of the virtue of equity as well as that of justice.

What Aristotle evidently recommends is that all judges, including persons who are placed in one way or another in the position of judge, possess the excellence of *epieikeia*. These must be persons with the habit of finding reasonable solutions, knowing how to act in accordance with decency when the generality of the law calls for rectifying its inadvertent defects. The important question in this case is"How does one come to possess this deliberative habit?" or, if one prefers, "How do we become proficient in *epieikeia*?" The correct response is essential from those who are entrusted with the law, its application, correction, as well as the prevention of its abuse.

It would seem that the answer, at least in part, lies in providing the citizens with the requisite education to acquire mastery of syllogistic thinking, particularly of the principles that distinguish practical syllogistic from demonstrative thinking. Equity in this logical context is the habit of decision-making of a special kind. Συλλογισμοὶ τῶν πρακτῶν is Aristotle's expression for the English translation "practical syllogism," and means literally deductive thinking about what must be done. (*Nic. Eth.* VI. 7. 1144a 31-32.) This requirement leads one to view the person of equity as one who is also to an appreciable extent "prudent" (φρόνιμος). This is a person with the proper thinking habits, which according to Aristotle sustain the power to deliberate in the manner of syllogisms that establish conclusions recommending reasonable solutions.

The relevance of *phronēsis* to the art of politics is too obvious to require special comment at this point. Suffice it to say that wisdom in its highest form within this art is exhibited as legislative activity (*nomothetikē*) whose chief objective is to plan policies for the attainment of the common good. In a related way the practical syllogism guides the performance of the judge in the effort to display equity and prudence in the rectificatory function of the office.

Although there are more technical matters that need to examined in connection with the office of the judge, I will limit my remarks to a few observations that summarize and extend what has been already said.

1. The judge is primarily a person of equity, and when viewed in the context of the art of legislation, is not a lawgiver but a rectifier. As such, then, the judge is supplied with the major premise in each practical syllogism he makes, although he is free to ascertain independently the truth of the premise. As a citizen he has this right, but the point is that he must work within the bounds of statements of law as universal premises.

Justice as Equity 253

2. The judge does not introduce the minor premise. The structure of the practical syllogism is such that it requires that the minor premise be a particular statement. The factual contents of the minor premise the judge uses report the particular act that has now come under judgment. Presumably, this is a violation of the law.

3. The judge connects the major and minor terms of the supplied premises to deduce the conclusion that will serve as the basis for the assessment of the action. At this point, the judge has entered the phase of decision-making.

4. The test of the judge's equity is a function of his ability to detect the deficiency of a law once the claim is made that the particular comes unqualifiedly under the universal. The conclusion he will arrive at is determined not merely by the availability of the major and minor premises, i.e., the general law and the particular act, but the series of deliberations he himself will introduce to establish the quality of the connection that has allegedly been obtained between law and act. The principle that generates *epieikeia* lies therefore in the judge's *wisdom of interpretation*, which in this context may be seen as a special instance of *phronēsis*.

5. In pronouncing judgment, the judge acts by moving ἐπὶ τὸ εἰκός, i.e. toward a decision that reasonably seems to be nearest to what a perfect and complete law, promulgated with the intent to cover all similar cases, would provide. However, in the absence of such a perfect law, one must act reasonably and opt for that which is a second best: the closest possible resemblance to a general rule. To do so calls for the antecedent preparation and training that establish firmly the deliberate habit of *epieikeia*.

6. Acts of equity are therefore considered to be decisions that maximize justice by redressing injustice brought about by the

generality of a law. Diverging from what is ethically correct in practical choice and deciding whether it is blameworthy because of erring in the direction of the more or the less (*Nic. Eth.* 1109b 18-23), must be distinguished from diverging from what is a rule of law. The latter is the case of the judge who diverges from the universal law in order to attain equity. Diverging from virtue and the universal in ethics is not the same as diverging from an established rule of law. The former is *erring*; the latter is correcting what might otherwise be injustice due to the indiscriminate application of the rule of law.

7. It would be difficult to disagree with Aristotle in his insistence that the exercise of equity, its extent and frequency, basically depends on the adequacy of the existing laws and the state of the art and science of legislating, (*nomothetikē*), in a given society. Given this insistence, one can readily understand why Aristotle placed politics at the pinnacle of the architectonic of the arts. As he says in *Nicomachean Ethics*, I. 9. 1099b 29-31, "the end of politics is the best of ends; and the main concern of politics is to engender a certain character in the citizens and to make them good and disposed to perform noble actions" (tr. M. Ostwald).

8. As a final comment I wish to say that insofar as equity is required as a complement to justice, it should also be seen as the best means we have as political beings to correct the flaws of legal rigidity as well as avail ourselves of a model to cultivate the virtues needed for the critique of existing laws. The practice of equity remains one of the best guides to understanding the art of legislating and logic it employs.

Perception plays an important role in diverging from rule of virtue, as when one errs, and in diverging from rule of law, as in correcting a flaw in the law, in order to secure equity and serve justice. Perception in either case is grasping the precise quality of the

Justice as Equity

particulars.[4] Now, there is a difference between *ethical acts* as diverging from universal concepts that pertain to the particular problem at hand and the *judicial decisions* that aim at equity. What this means is that the moral agent works differently from the judge. The former performs an act; the latter interprets a rule of law to apply to an act already performed. Since the judge is not responsible for the act, he is neither praiseworthy nor blameworthy for the act he judges. His decision as well as his thinking must therefore be evaluated in a different light. Yet, in another sense the process may be regarded as ethical. Consider, for instance, the case of the judge who is promoting a kind of justice or is hindering it, and if the latter, he becomes blameworthy for blocking equity. Insofar as a judge's decision can have consequences of an ethical nature, these are usually with respect to (a) character, (b) condoning injury already done, and (c) validating an otherwise flaw in a given rule of law.

On the basis of Aristotle's distinction between absolute just and political just (ἁπλῶς δίκαιον, πολιτικὸν δίκαιον), how is the judge to succeed in being just? What shall he use as the criterion of success, the absolute just or the political just? Perhaps both? However, when a conflict arises between the two, as it frequently does, how is the judge to decide between the two concepts of the just without himself becoming unjust, jeopardizing thereby the principle of equity? These are not easy questions to answer. Evidently they call for more wisdom than the ordinary citizen has. Presumably, they are questions for the philosophical statesman, and we may leave them at that.

NOTES

1. Published in the *Proceedings of the Second International Symposium on Greek Philosophy*. K. Boudouris, ed. Athens, 1989, pp. 1–8.

2. See Black's *Dictionary of Law*, under "Equity." A recent statement on the subject underscores this judgment about the historical significance of the *Nicomachean Ethics*, Bk. V: "Chapter 7 on Natural and Legal Justice...is a classical source for the long and still vital tradition of natural law, and the theory of Equity in chapter 10 has had a direct effect on the development of legal institutions that is still felt." In Feinberg, J. and H. Gross, *Philosophy of Law*, (Wadsworth: Belmont, CA, 1980, second edition), p.286.

3. Equity in relationship to judges (δικασταί) is also discussed in *Rhetoric* 1354a 31-b12, esp. Bk. I. 13. 1374a 25ff. Plato refers to the excellence of the judge (δικαστοῦ ἀρετή) at *Apol.* 18A, where Socrates says that he he expects the judges to demonstrate their excellence by showing that they are capable of assessing what he is about to state and whether what he says is just or not. On the other hand, the excellence of the speaker or orator lies in his speaking the truth. See also *Gorgias* 485Ef. for equity as an attitude.

4. See also M. Nussbaum's analysis of the role of perception in corrective reasoning, "The Discernment of Perception: An Aristotelian Conception of Private and Public Rationality," *Proceedings of the Boston Area Colloquium in Ancient Philosophy*, Vol. I, 1985, edited by J. J. Cleary (University Press of America, 1986), 151-201.

IDEAL VALUES AND CULTURAL ACTION IN ARISTOTLE

I

We are told in one of the opening statements in the *Nicomachean Ethics* 1094a 1-5 that "the good has been well defined as that at which all things aim." Probably it was Eudoxus who first came up with this formulation. Aristotle accepts it, as is evident from 1094a 1-5 and also from *Rhet.* I. 6, 1362a 23. To the preceding quotation we add now a couple more statements from *E. N.* I. ch. 2: "The end of politics is the good for man." [τέλος πολιτικῆς]: τοῦτ᾽ ἂν εἴη τ᾽ ἀνθρώπινον ἀγαθόν. Again: "The attainment of the good for one man alone is, to be sure, a source of satisfaction; yet to secure it for a nation and for states is nobler and more divine." Text: εἰ γὰρ καὶ ταὐτόν ἐστι ἑνὶ καὶ πόλει, μεῖζόν γε καὶ τελειότερον τὸ τῆς πόλεως φαίνεται καὶ λαβεῖν καὶ σῴζειν ἀγαπητὸν μὲν γὰρ καὶ ἑνὶ καὶ μόνῳ, κάλλιον δὲ καὶ θειότερον ἔθνει καὶ πόλεσιν. (1094b 9-11).

A few lines before this passage, Aristotle had posed the question of there being a highest good, and he answered it in the affirmative. Then he added the following: "Will not the knowledge of this good, consequently, be very important to our lives? Would it not better equip us, like archers who have a target to aim at, to hit the proper mark? If so, we may try to comprehend in outline at least what this good is and to which branch of knowledge or to which capacity it belongs." Text: ἆρ᾽ οὖν καὶ πρὸς τὸν βίον ἡ γνῶσις αὐτοῦ μεγάλην ἔχει ῥοπήν, καθάπερ τοξόται σκοπὸν ἔχοντες, μᾶλλον τυγχάνομεν τοῦ δέοντος; εἰ δ᾽ οὕτω, πειρατέον τύπῳ γὲ περιλαβεῖν αὐτὸ τί ποτ᾽ ἐστι καὶ τίνος τῶν ἐπιστημῶν ἢ δυνάμεων. δόξειε δ᾽ ἂν τῆς κυριωτάτης καὶ μάλιστα ἀρχιτεκτονικῆς.

Next, Aristotle tells us some important things about the conditions the inquirer must meet in order to get on with the study to find the highest good and profit from this study. Thus:
1. "The end of this kind of study is not knowledge but action."
2. For those persons who "follow their emotions," their studies will be pointless and unprofitable.
3. However, "those who regulate their desires and actions by a rational principle, *logos*, will greatly benefit from a knowledge of the subject." Text: τοῖς δὲ κατὰ λόγον τὰς ὀρέξεις ποιουμένοις καὶ πράττουσι πολυωφελὲς ἂν εἴη τὸ περὶ τούτων εἰδέναι. (1095a 10f).

So far the qualified hearer—and we may safely assume that present company is included in this privileged class—does not yet know what is meant by the ἀνθρώπινον ἀγαθόν, the human good. And if not, then the hearer is not sufficiently equipped to pursue it or act accordingly, despite the fact that every human being is an agent who possesses potentially the human good in the form of the human entelechy. Thus, the ἀγαθόν while exclusively *anthrōpinon*, human, will not fully surface until we acquire knowledge about it by actively pursuing it. Prior to this work we are not in a position to say under what genus of being it is to be brought for proper classification, whether under *ousia*, quantity, quality or one of the others. So much about the ontic character of the human good, for the time being.

There seems to be another problem here. Despite the announcement already made that the inquiry is about the human good, that "every *praxis* and deliberate undertaking," like every art and inquiry, is directed toward some good, the present investigation, although about *the most important good*, is done in the presence of few, i.e., those attending Aristotle's lectures.

Are we to infer from this accident that a great many human beings are either disqualified to participate in the inquiry or to profit from it after they have heard it? Is Aristotle subscribing to the reservations Heraclitus expressed about human beings in his famous Fragment 1?

Ideal Values and Cultural Action 259

"...the rest of men fail to notice what they do after they wake up just as they forget what they do when asleep."

One suspects here that the intention is to say that many human individuals are somehow excluded from understanding what is being said and profiting, some inadvertently, others inevitably, even if only temporarily and while certain unfavorable conditions prevail. Excluded are (i) those governed by their emotions, (ii) the young, as unfit to study political science, (iii) people not present at the time of the lecture to partake in the inquiry, even if qualified by way of talent, and (iv) that broad category of people, the multitudes of humanity in the streets, the market place, the harbors and the mountainsides, and alas, all those already dead or ignorant of Greek. Yet it is about theirs and everyone's good that Aristotle is conducting his investigation. How then can we insist, with Aristotle, that the inquiry can in fact affect beneficently all human beings. And if we suppose that these excluded masses will remain unaffected how can we seriously say that Aristotle is on safe grounds when he seeks to determine the human good and also conclude that once this is clarified and properly defined, it is realizable in a pervasive way as a community value and ideal?

Are the potentially *aristoi* and *phronemoi* and *eudaimones* to be found only among the members of the Peripatetic School, and perchance among the brighter Atheneans? Do we have a paradox here, whereby the common good is rarely realized and hence quite uncommon in actuality? To put it differently, and also more bluntly, are most human beings to live non-happy lives for lack of exposure to the inquiry into the conditions for grasping the concept of the good?

Most human beings are not likely to gain real knowledge of the human good and even if they are fortunate enough to become sufficiently informed, they may not be able to act on this knowledge and thereby attain what the good stands for. However, the opening statement of the *Metaphysics* remains true in that it reports a fact:

"All human beings by nature desire to know" (980a 21). The statement reports a fact of nature, not a *praxis* in ethics. And something else: Aristotle does not use any expression referring to "the moral nature of man" when he makes this statement. Elsewhere he reports another fact of nature: "Man is by nature a political animal." We have a problem here. To put it in the language of the *De Anima*, the good is common as first entelechy but shockingly uncommon as second entelechy.

II

This brings me back to the image of the archer-τοξότης. It is related to the problem of the method of induction and rational intuition in ethics. How does the archer ever come to know the principles that pertain to ethics and the concept of the highest good, especially the definition of *eudaimonia*? To be sure, the image of the archer is rather puzzling. Who is the archer and who is the non-archer? Evidently, the archer is *prima facie* the proper candidate who qualifies to enter the process that leads to the final intuition of the highest good and thus set himself on the road to attain happiness. Be that as it may, and we shall return to this issue, what can be said about the non-archer, especially in view of the denotation of the term, covering as it does the major part of humanity? Who is the non-archer and how does he get started, not so much in the process of *ethismos*, of habit formation, since it is inevitable that we all are subject to this process, but to qualilfy for the art of archery, as Aristotle means it as a metaphor for candidacy to apprehending the ethical principles. What happens if one never gets started on this art? Are the consequences as disastrous as one suspects at this point?

That there are archers must be taken as given. They will do their work and at the same time serve as examples for *mimesis*, regardless of what the imitators can do or will do. Since archery is an art, not all artists are destined to become masters of this art. It is to be expected that some archers will hit a bull's eye and some will fail to aim so perfectly as to direct the arrow straight to the center of the target. The latter, for some reason, are not yet to be included in the *aristoi* and perhaps may never become *aristoi*. On this basis then one can well imagine what sort of fate awaits those who do not come near having a talent for archery.

A society that holds genuine promise for its citizens makes certain that every citizen has a chance to learn the art of archery, that is presented with the opportunity to embark on the process of intuiting the concept of the highest good. This will satisfy the principle of equality of opportunity. But there are some problems here. What if Aristoboulos has bad vision, or Aristoxenos has unsteady hands, or Aristophemos has only one hand and Aristodemos no forefingers. And what about Aristomenes who started hitting the bars in his mid-teens, or this or that? In short, what if Aristoboulos, a citizen with good intentions, and coming from a nice family, really wanted to become a good archer but did not get the proper training at the proper age, if there is such a thing? And what chances does one have, knowing that the right target is there, if one of the necessary conditions for success is missing? What if one does not succeed at all? How does one go wrong? First, there is the failure to intuit the concept of the good and give the definition of happiness, and secondly, alas!, never attain the highest good: Happiness. Are we to infer from all this that we now have the perfect explanation why most human beings never reach happiness, and what they really get out of life is but a phantom of *eudaimonia*? Does this mean that only the best of archers, so few to be sure, can possibly attain eudaimonia? If so, it would seem that Aristotle has cast his ethical theory with the aid of a strange paradox. On the one hand, he declares the ubiquity of the condition for happiness by assuring us that the desire to attain it is universally distributed, and on the other, he raises such road blocks to the final goal that stations at all points between unfortunate beings chasing phantoms and living on crumbs of pleasure.

But, maybe the situation is not as desparate as all that. Archery may well be analogous to an educational curriculum. If so, we would have to understand politics as the art and science that, among other things, calls for instituting and legislating for the proper form and content of education. The function of education then is to take all citizens by the hand and lead them to the level of correct and competent performance of archery. Let us assume that such is the *ergon* of education. Can we prove to our satisfaction the following statement: If someone knows the good he is expected to be able to assist others to reach *eudaimonia*. The consequent, however, may or may not follow from the antecedent. Knowledge of the good is a necessary condition; but is it also a sufficient one? We may exclude the opposite, namely that it is not possible for one who does not know the good to help others reach *eudaimonia*. We are still left with the problem whether knowledge of the good is sufficient. The issue is whether knowers of the good are also in a state of *eudaimonia* and necessarily so. If we can point to knowers of the good who fail to transmute this knowledge into *praxis* the transition from *knowing the good* to *doing the good* is only tenuous. In other words, the activity of the archer does not reach beyond the trajectory of the arrow although the arrow has succesfully found its theoretical target.

So far all we can say is that the archer has received excellent training, but we cannot point to any facts to show that he also has *phronesis*, by which term Aristotle means the wisdom to act or practical wisdom. *Phronesis* is needed in ethics and in politics. If there are knowers of the good who cannot enter into *praxis*, the implications for politics are serious. Let us assume that the archer can be so successful as to attain theoretical wisdom. Aristotle tells us that *phronesis* is not the same as theoretical wisdom. Would it be correct to say that both are needed for the attainment of *eudaimonia*? We are not ready for the answer yet.

Ideal Values and Cultural Action

Lest I mislead the reader to think that Aristotle's concept of the archer was restricted to students of ethical theory, I can prevent giving that impression with the aid of a brief quotation from the *Eudemian Ethics* (A 2, 1214b 6-14):

> Everyone who has the power to live according to his own choice (προαίρεσις) should dwell on these points and set up for himslef some object (σκοπός) for the good life to aim at, whether honour or reputation or wealth or culture, by reference to which he will do all he does, since not to have one's life organized in view of some end is a sign of great folly. Now above all we must define to ourselves without hurry or carelessness in which of our possessions the good life (τὸ εὖ ζῆν) consists, and what for men are the conditions of its attainment. (Tr. J. Solomon, Oxford [with changes])

When Aristotle wrote the *Nicomachean Ethics* he introduced another and more skillful order of archers. This new group is the one to be entrusted with the task of systematic inquiry into the common good, which is also the human good, which is also the highest good. In other words, the archers now are the students of ethics who know that this inquiry comes under the architectonic art and science of politics, whose prime theoretical objective is to grasp the *archai* and formulate correctly the definition of the ideal of happiness.

It is not clear from the text that Aristotle meant the archers to become statesmen, but he did expect that they should contribute to the knowledge of statesmanship. And statesmanship, he tells us, "ordains which of the sciences should be studied in a state, and which each class of citizens should learn and up to what point they should learn them." (1094a 28-b2). That the statesman's end in view is the happiness of the citizens is clearly stated in X.7, 1177b 14, a passage in which Aristotle makes eloquent use of his technical definition of happiness as it pertains to the statesman's life as well as to that of the citizens. He has already told us in VI. 13, 1145a 6-9 that the function of statesmanship is to promote the conditions for the study of mathematics, physics, and philosophy by those citizens capable of pursuing such studies. In other words, it is assumed that the best archers will blossom in cities whose constitutions secure these conditions. Athens for a while did, although not in so lofty a degree as Aristotle envisaged in the aforementioned passage.

No doubt the archer's life is a complex one. From the *Eudemian Ethics* we learn that he is performing ethical acts, whatever their value, which means he is *in ethics and in politics*, though not necessarily in the inquiry into ethics and politics. The latter emerges with full force in the *Nicomachean Ethics*. This opus gives us a complete disclosure of the work expected of the student of ethics. In a way he resembles the guardians in Plato's *Republic* who are qualified to enter a new cycle of studies into the higher dialectic. Aristotle's archer-student is able to grasp the *archai*, is capable of the superior level of induction in the process that leads to the rational intuition of the principles and concepts of ethics and politics. Presumably this superior student has mastered the second book of the *Posterior Analytics*. He knows that his inquiry aims at identifying and marking a special kind of arche: the highest good which is also the human good which is also a universal good. He may or may not know how principles are grasped but he certainly has the native ability of grasping principles. He has this capability by virtue of his *nous*. The lesson on how principles are grasped comes in *E. N.* I. 7.[1]

Aristotle tells us that the subject matter of ethics, being variable, refers to facts capable of being otherwise (I. 3, 1094b 14). Now we have reached the point where we must exercise caution. Aristotle does not mean that variability applies to the *end*, i.e., the human good, although he concedes the obvious point that people do in fact conceive of the end in a great variety of ways. The competent archer comes to understand that the human good is a constant, an *arche*, as such invariable; it is embedded in the nature of all human beings. When he speaks of variable subject matter he refers primarily to the part where complete precision is not to be expected: the material that

Ideal Values and Cultural Action

enters in one of the premises of the practical syllogism. The complete lack of agreement, not suprisingly, come in the case of rules, means, etc., where practical rules always admit of exceptions. The good archer must understand this and must also not fail to grasp the important distinction between arguments on their way to principles and arguments on their way from principles.

Being an archer is one thing. In a sense everyone is an archer more or less. Being a good archer, quite another. Aristotle, the theorist, is training good archers. He is at once a theorist of ethics and of politics. He is guiding those who aspire to becoming the latter, not so much to enter politics, for they may already be doing that, but for the sake of rising to true statesmanship. There is also the problem of living the good life. Both pursuits are in the last analysis inseparable.

Given all the goods, the *telos* is the best, and it is action. All human activity aims at some end, and this end can be either the activity itself or something produced by it. Now we come to three kinds of good: goods as means only, as means and as ends, and as ends only. Assuming that this is an exhaustive classification, the crucial question is: What sort of good is the human good? Aristotle proceeds to give his answer in 1095a 17-22:

> Verbally there is very general agreement: for both the general run of men and people of superior refinement say that it is happiness (εὐδαιμονία), and identify living well and doing well (εὖ πράττειν) with being happy, but with regard to what happiness is they, and the many, do not give the same account as the wise. (Tr. W. D. Ross, Oxford)

According to the account of the many the most prevalent view of happiness is identified with pleasure, wealth and honor. The account of the wise Aristotle mentions and discusses is mainly that of Plato. With both out of the way, Aristotle proceeds to give us his own view, presumably a wise account. Thus: "the good for man turns out to be activity of the soul in accordance with virtue, and if there is more than one virtue, in accordance with the best and more complete; but we must add 'in a complete life'" (1098a 16-18). This is the target every competent archer must find, and he had better not miss it. But how will they know they have not missed it? This is exactly why they need training in induction and intuition, on the logical side, and great familiarity with the study of physics and psychology, on the factual side. Given such training, the archers will know what they must define and how to define it. Aristotle himself offers it in two ways: (a) with reference to its features, and (b) with reference to its funtions. This is what makes chapter 7 of Book I so basic to our inquiry. We learn there the following central doctrines:

1. The good, 'achievable in action,' must be (i) final, τέλειον, (ii) self-sufficent-αὔταρκες, as such making life desirable and lacking in nothing, (iii) preferable above all other goods, and (iv) attainable-ἐφικτόν, something that Plato stubbornly omitted.

2. The good is identifiable via the function-ἔργον of man. Here Aristotle makes use of the doctrines in *De Anima* II, his general theory of life and the proper *ergon* of the human soul which is found in the distinctive character of human life. This *ergon* is conveyed through the differentia.[2]

Aristotle is clear on the purpose of ethics; it is practical. As Hardie puts it, "practical, in the sense that, starting from concepts of ends to be achieved, it concludes, or should conclude, with the formulation of rules for achieving ends, e.g. with an account of the ideal political constitution."[3] Perhaps it would be more to the point to say not the "ideal" but the "best" political constitution. The expression "ideal" still has the Platonic ring of non-attainability to it.

III

The good society is not an ideal-utopian society. What I aim at stating in the concluding part of this paper is that the philosophy of education and the curriculum constructed in the final book of the *Politics* is neither ideal nor utopian educational policy. I think it is unfortunate that most interpreters of Aristotle took it as such. The *praxis* of the competent archers who have by now crossed the line and assumed the responsibilities of statesmanship is fundamentally educational. In this regard, the program developed in Book X is a culmination of practical ethics and politics rather than an exercise in a utopian experiment, as so many of his critics have said. It is offered as the proper program for all non-deviant types of goverment. It is the kind of educational program that secures the initial movement to start the actualization of the human entelechy, and hence it belongs to the proper means for the attainment of the highest human end.

The archer is now beyond the problem of finding the target. He has entered the domain of political *praxis*. He is no longer an archer; he is now accountable to the citizens and to the knowledge he has acquired. He is on his way to the second entelechy, which qualifies him to serve as the object of ethical mimesis, a bearer of ideals, a critic of constitutions and one of those men of wisdom who know the good by living the good life. They become good not just by talking and inquiring into virtue and *eudaimonia*, but by means of conduct that testifies to the exercise of excellence, fulfilling thus Plato dictum: ἀσκεῖν τὴν ἀρετήν.

NOTES

1. Induction and intuition of principles have been the objects of numerous studies and interpretations. A recent discussion is by W. F. R Hardie in his *Aristotle's Ethical Theory* (Oxford, 1968), esp. ch. III, "The Nature of the Inquiry," and with exhaustive bibliography.

2. W. F. R. Hardie is critical of the way Aristotle tries to relate these two doctrines. He writes: "What is unsatisfactory in Aristotle's treatment is his failure to make explicit the distinction between the comprehensive plan and the paramount end." (ibid., 23)

3. Ibid., 31. Hardie refers the reader to *EN* X. 9, 1181b 20-23.

TIMELY OBSERVATIONS ON ARISTOTLE'S ARCHITECTONIC OF *POLITIKE TECHNE*[1]

...ἐν ἁπάσαις [τέχναις καὶ ἐπιστήμαις] δὲ τὰ τῶν ἀρχιτεκτονικῶν τέλη πάντων ἐστὶν αἱρετώτερα τῶν ὑπ' αὐτά· τούτων γὰρ χάριν κἀκεῖνα διώκεται. *Nicomachean Ethics* I, 1094a15-16.

1. *Introduction*

Other speakers, I am confident, will present careful analyses on the diverse topics in Aristotle's *Politics*. My own address has a somewhat different concern. Assuming that Aristotle's conception of the Architectonic Principle of arts and sciences of civilized life is sound on the whole and correctly formulated, the issue I will try to explore is this: What problems confront us when the cohesion of the principle is challenged and its relevance is doubted? No problem is more central to the on-going "battle of the Ancients and the Moderns" today than that of the foundations and ends of the political life in organized societies. At least this much is true about the Architectonic Principle: its supreme importance as the science and art of the political life.

Pericles, the great governor of Athens, assured the Athenians in 430 BC, when he gave his famous "Funeral Oration", that they were privileged to be free to philosophize by example and education. Still, it took great thinkers to explicate the meaning of *philosophein* as a political responsibility, to connect it to a theory of human nature and tie it to the concept of *bios politicos* as the most desirable way of life.

When the classical city declined so did the theoretical task of preserving the meaning of this *bios*. However, neither the experience of Athens nor the political reflections of the Greek philosophers were forgotten. At least the model, though not the substance, of this heritage was invoked centuries later when the practice of feudalism had to be stripped of intolerance. Socio-economic changes made possible the birth of the modern state. Once the age of liberty had begun in Europe, attendant political doctrines emerged through considerable effort and bloodshed. Lessons that could be learned from the Greeks were scrutinized more for critical picking than for renaissance of ideas. Given this distinction, my address is an attempt to re-assess Aristotle's relevance to the complex problems of the modern state as a case of *bios politicos*. Hence the title "timely observations" as they relate to modern states.

My remarks deal with three comparative issues: (1) the function of the architectonic principle that makes *politike techne* (poliscraft) the highest art in *politeia* and its denial in the modern state; (2) the structural and functional differences in political axiology between the classical "common good" and the modern "general will"; and (3) the responsibility of the classical *politicos* vis-a-vis that of the modern statesman. In the conclusion I try to draw certain implications these differences have for the function of *philosophein* itself concerning the problematic of the values of the changing character of the states in the contemporary world vis-a-vis the classical view of political *eudaimonia* or happiness.

2. *Politikē*: the Principle of the Architectonic

For Aristotle, ethics as well as the other arts and sciences that pertain to the civilized life, derive their meaning and value from the purpose and good of the science and art of politics.[2] What makes *politikē* the leading art is the end it seeks to attain, the end being the *koinon agathon*. In a key passage of the *Politics*, Aristotle refers to the *politikē dynamis*.[3]

Aristotle's Architectonic of Politike Techne   271

This faculty or *dynamis*, to bring about a determinate effect, is present in all human beings. Its actualization is necessary to effect the *agathon* which is its *telos*, the greatest of all goods and which coincides with the *eudaimonia* of all individuals; it requires for its physical setting a *koinonia* that can be transformed into a *polis*, i.e. to become a political whole self-sufficient and consisting of free citizens who are equal and alike (ἴσοι καὶ ὅμοιοι).[4]

The *agathon* for each art needs to be identified and understood as related to the highest good which is also the common good.[5] The *agathon* is not be taken as that of the individual qua *idiotēs*, but qua *politēs*.[6]

The *politicos*, we are told, must have studied psychology in order to understand the end or purpose of human life.[7] He must also have a firm grasp of the difference between correct and deviant types of government. The leaders in the correct (*orthai*) types pursue the common cause and that which is conducive (*sympheron*) to the happiness of the citizens; those of the deviant ones (*parekbatikai*) invariably tend to serve their own interests, of their cohorts and of the party they lead.[8] For Aristotle, the deviant constitutions have compromised *nous* and have thereby risked *homonoia*.

Human beings have two traits that distinguish them from the rest of the animate world. The first is rational speech (ζῷον λόγον ἔχον) and life endowed with intelligence (καὶ τῷ ἀνθρώπῳ δὴ ὁ κατὰ τὸν νοῦν βίος, εἴπερ τοῦτο μάλιστα ἄνθρωπος. οὗτος ἄρα καὶ εὐδαιμονέστατος).[9] The second is the possession of social drive (ὁρμὴ κοινωνικότητος). In fact, νοῦς (mind, reason, intelligence) is a principle rooted in nature, and whereas nature is intelligible, only in human beings does *nous* attain knowledge of itself. Therefore, *nous* must also be recognized as the *arche* of *politicos bios* and related to the end and good of community life. Stated this way, the principle defines the structure of the correct types of constitutions or *politeiai*, besides being the prime mover in political life.[10] *Nous* is assumed in the definition of the species; it is embedded in *logos*, it is the source of consistency and agreement of true statements. As *homonoia*, it is the principle that lies at the foundation of interpersonal agreement and the settling of disputes.

This *koinonia* of *nous*, *homonoia*, provides the basis for political normalcy and the criterion of the common good. Since other conference speakers will touch on this subject I will say no more except to stress two points: (a) *nous* and not the desires of the *epithymētikon*, provides the criterion of community agreements, of common values and shared standards; and (b) *nous* as the *logos* of nature or cosmic intelligibility, is the ultimate sustainer of reasonableness. Hence Aristotle's insistence on the continuity from individual to *koinonia* to the *kosmos*.

It is one thing for human beings to be by nature logical and political animals, quite another to develop their potential, their dispositions, to perform excellently. Two institutions are needed for this task, laws and education. The latter enables the citizen to establish excellent habits beyond those of special and professional skills, i.e. the *aretai* that contribute to the common good. For Aristotle, it is impossible for citizens to be happy, i.e. *eudaimones*, without possessing the appropriate excellences or virtues.[11] External conditions, especially leisure, are needed to pursue virtue and perform political actions[12]

The point is that while every instance of human conduct, individual and collective, is value-directed, it is not the case that all valued objectives are of the same quality, or to put the issue differently, are in line with the supreme objective of human life: happiness or *eudaimonia*. The correlation of ethics and politics is such that it allows us to view these fields as continuous and, in a sense, as one field: human action, involving at once *epistēmē* (although short of being of the demonstrable sort) and *technē*.[13]

Aristotle's Architectonic of Politike Techne 273

3. *Politeia vs. State*[14]

A distinction is needed at this point to show the difference between the organic character of the classical *polis* and the molecular structure of the modern state.[15] Unlike what took place in the classical *polis*, in modern times individual and state are polarized entities, often in conflict and more as adversaries rather than partners in a common pursuit. Every reform movement that sought to reconcile the antagonists has failed. Hidden forces of oppression continue to show up just as unexpected acts of violence against the tyranny of the state become unavoidable. The *polis* is absent from the operations of the modern state. The state is not a *polis*, cannot be. At best, it is a benevolent despot, and has found a place in all of us, who in vain believe ourselves to be its citizens. If we are its citizens, we relate to the state in radically different ways from what the citizens of the *polis* thought their function to be. They sought justice in order to secure *eudaimonia*, whereas we want justice to deliver rights to satisfy the cravings of the will.

This calls for a special note about the place of ethics in recent philosophy. It is commonplace nowadays to insist that ethics is a dominant field of philosophy and that political philosophy must be taken over by the social sciences. It seems that the rise of individualism and the related theories of value in modern thought gave ethics its central role in philosophy. In contrast, political theory has all but given up the quest of the common good. This divorce is not Aristotle's doing. Anyway, the emergence of individualism has made the idea of liberty or freedom the centerpiece of ethics. As a result, the moderns frequently find it easy to accuse the ancients of having absorbed the individual within the institutions of the *politeia*.[16]

The *polis*, being an organic and telic association, could not and did not become a state. The difference between the two is of the essence for what I have to say. It would be a serious anachronism to try to treat the *polis* as though it was either a special sort of state, a "city-state" or the precursor of the modern state. Since the *polis* differs in structure and objectives from the state, the theoreticians of the latter often become eager critics in trying to expose its limitations.

B. Bosanquet once noted the following: "I am convinced that the ancient theory of state can only be strengthened and amplified by the wealth of modern experience."[17] Aside from being an underhanded compliment, the statement is typical of the modern evaluation of the classical political theories. Bosanquet has stated a widespread and prevalent conviction, namely that the modern, while continuous with the classical, has superseded the latter in scope and efficacy.

In his *Politeia*, Plato insists that the individual as citizen is a microcosmic *politeia*, and the difference between the *polites* and the *politeia* is that while the citizen orders his own *psyche* after the model of the perfect *politeia*, the actual *politeia* is (a) an organization of just citizens and (b) an organization of institutions in accordance with the logic of the ideal values.

Aristotle, following Plato on the relation of citizens and *politeia* in light of the common good, declared the bonds indissoluble. This special sense of loyalty to a constitution did not survive the demise of the classical *polis*. Social and individual ends did not coincide in the emergence of the modern states as they did in Aristotle's accounts of constitutions. The overlapping, where it takes place, is partial.[18] The antagonism between government as the tool of the state and the citizen as subject lingers on as part of social dynamics. The government itself struggles to maintain a balance between license and stricture, freedom and order, private ends and public security. The modern individual citizens are constantly engaged in a battle over securing rights and privileges to satisfy special interests.

The ancient philosophers were convinced that the common good is discoverable through the faculty and the use of *nous*; but *nous*, the faculty of rational intuition (*An. Post.* II 18, 100b5-16), is neither the common sense of the moderns nor the modern concept of the Will, be it individual or general. Actually, the Greeks would have found this

Will a peculiar and unfathomable entity, if an entity at all. *Nous*, according to Aristotle, the real principal element of the soul, has the fundamental property by virtue of which human life, ensouled as it is, is distinguished from all other beings. Whereas *nous* enables us to assert and ascertain the common good, no such conception of the *koinon agathon* is forthcoming from the concept of the Will. What the modern Will demands and seeks to secure from inimical agencies is an ever-expanding freedom. Still, the freedom that the modern Will demands has been seen as the basis for the relentless pursuit of rights. Thus the major problem in political thought is dealing with the pursuit of rights; in practical terms, it is the securing of conditions of freedom for the will (whatever its membership) to exercise its power. In this on-going struggle, the pursuit of power has become the centerpiece of political conduct.[19] In view of these differences one wonders to what extend one can distinguish today between correct and deviant types of states.

The criteria Aristotle used for the ancient constitutions have changed radically as have the ends. Clearly then the state is not a harmonizer of ends as is the case of the *politeia*, for it has no natural teleology nor a comparable view of human nature. The domain of ends is parcelled out to special interests to act as they see fit within the limits of the law, the latter being subject to change. The state, not being a *politeia*, is forced to grant too much in freedom and nothing in the harmony of ends. Its motive is neither *harmonia* nor the *eu zên*. The latter is not its responsibility.[20] As MacIver has noted, "Social protection and the ambition of power — these two are the most diverse but most mingled motives which stimulated the formation of state-institutions."[21] The thesis does not apply to the Aristotelian assessment of the model of *politeia*, especially to the principles of *eu zên* and *homonoia* as the formal, final and efficient causes. From Aristotle's view of *politeia*, on the contrary, the modern model of state, if further developed and its telic course corrected, would be regarded as the prelude to the return to the model of *politeia*. MacIver, however, can still identify weaknesses in the practice of politics of the Greek city-states, as he calls them.[22]

For the *polis* to function properly it must secure the conditions of *politicos bios* for all citizens in accordance with the constitution. Philosophical *bios*, however, may suffer serious setbacks or take the wrong turn when seeking ends not suitable to the ends of the political function, even if such ends seem advantageous to those who are interested in personal gain or survival in times of crisis. The disconnection between the philosophical and the political types of *bios* and the changes that have taken place in their respective pursuits throughout the emergence of the modern state, have seriously affected the manner in which we have been philosophizing and thinking of the place of reason in politics.

4. Implications

The recent demise of the communist states as political systems is too obvious to need comment and the same holds for the relentless dogmatism on which it rested its theoretical premises. There is, however, a subtle narrowness and covert intolerance built into the modern practice of democracy whereby this form of government is declared today to be the only one that merits recognition as the *orthē politeia*, to use a Greek expression. One suspects that the narrowness is a function of the sacrosanct status of individuality in the name of absolute freedom and unlimited rights. But what if democracy should fail, for reasons as yet unforeseen? We seem to have no viable alternatives. When crises deepen, people paradoxically turn to dictatorships in hope of salvation.

There are two ways in which post-classical movements altered the Greek conception of the *logikon* of the architectonic principle: The first is the *hyperlogon* of theology. The second is the subordination of the *logikon* to the *epithymētikon* of the moderns. In both cases the idea of the common good was changed beyond recognition and became undefined and vague. So did the idea of happiness, of *eudaimonia*. Witness the famous dictum of the American Declaration of Independence, "life, liberty and the pursuit of happiness." Again, the classical *nous* was replaced with the pursuit of power, be it the power of the church or the power of the state.[23] Hence, there is good reason why the history of ethics must be re-written as the history of politics and ethics.

Once the divorce between ethics and politics takes place, the *politikon telos* moves in a different direction from that of the *ēthikon telos*. What this means is that the Architectonic no longer obtains in practice although still defensible in theory. Once divorced from political action, ethics rarely succeeds in promoting the autonomy of its ends. This explains why so many people today seem convinced that it is not possible for ethical values to be self-supportive unless they are sanctioned by religious beliefs. In modern times, unlike the middle ages, philosophers and intellectuals repeatedly tried to cast off the authority of religion over ethics. However, most of the attempts did not succeed despite the critique of the authoritarian rule of religious institutions. The cause of their failure must be sought in the commitment to the separate status of ethics from politics and the reluctance to re-examine the tradition that had established ethical action as a distinct personal performance of the individual. Briefly stated, Aristotle's Architectonic principle was discarded as irrelevant to the art and science of ethics. We have yet to re-unite ethics and politics. In this regard, Aristotle's position on political theory and its relevance to the study of contemporary political affairs, has been underestimated.[24]

5. Conclusion

The return of the *polis* type of community organization is no longer feasible, given the present conditions of socio-economic determinants. There are theorists who now hold the same verdict for the future of the "nation-state". The question that puzzles us now is "What Next?" Is a synthesis of the polis and the nation state possible? I have doubts about it just as I do about the possibility of a world state, or if you prefer, a world *polis*. The real issue in all these contingencies, as Aristotle would say, is the formulation of the principle of the Architectonic: how to conceive of the art and science of politics as the overarching source of value and conduct, for without it human dignity is compromised and peace becomes short-lived, as it has happened repeatedly in the past.

The powerful states today do not bring small nations to their senses, they bring them to their knees. Their geopolitical diplomacy and the use of perfected manipulative techniques of intimidation, are now the real weapons of traditional brutal force. This practice allows for the conclusion that the old civilizing arts no longer serve humanity. This is where the modern states have brought humanity and education with the cultivation of the acquisitive urge. The responsibility of making the citizens civilized is left to institutions other that those that normally comprise the backbone of the state. Paradoxically, every time the modern states tried to become the educator, their policies ended in disaster. Yet, the states have functioned as best they could, even without the benefit of the Architectonic Principle. As H. Schneider (1974) has said somewhat charitably, "Government and industry are, according to our traditions responsible primarily for making us secure and prosperous, rather than civilized and happy. They are essentially insurance for peace and security. Unfortunately our investment in this insurance is not yielding the intended benefits; instead, we have collective insecurity."[25]

We are all familiar with the recent political failures and ethical crises. The sense of alienation has never been deeper and indeed more intense. The state is our great political sick man and we have no idea how to restore his health or whether the restoring is possible.

But try we must for the sick man is all we have. The citizen in the modern state is indeed the *homo economicus*, demanding the steady rise of standards of living to the largest number of social units. In seeking to provide liberty and security, the modern state forgot to use *nous* to tie rights to happiness. Whether this modern state can humanize its constituents through technology and consumerism, remains to be seen. In the meantime, it might help to keep a copy of Aristotle's *Politics* in our personal and public libraries, just in case. One never can tell whether and when even the best and most progressive of modern states may become deviant. Some say that this is already happening right under our noses.

Today, the most important branch of philosophy is political theory, and the most urgent problem is the preservation of democracy in the service of the common good. In democracy, *as a way of life*, to be citizen is a privilege to be cherished, an honor to be celebrated and a responsibility to be exercised in justice, in truth and in trust in the universal dignity of all human beings. Humanity never had a better opportunity and a more urgent need to put new life into the Greek ideal of democracy. This heritage is vital to the future goal of the art of politics and the best means of our survival. Hence, it is the responsibility of all nations to guard the integrity of Greece and preserve its cultural tradition, including the language in which the great ideas of civilized existence found their fullest expression.

NOTES

1. Presented at the Sixth International Conference on Greek Philosophy, "Aristotelian Political Philosophy," Ierissos, Greece. August 19-26, 1994.

2. The architectonic principle is related to the arrangement of the arts, the *technai*, whereby it is argued that the leading art is the *politikē technē*. Plato in the *Gorgias* argued for an architectonic of crafts. For *technai* provide the best, ἀεὶ πρὸς τὸ βέλτιστον θεραπεύουσαι, and they differ from the pseudo-crafts that offer pleasure, not caring whether the pleasure is *beltiston* or not. The principle for arranging the architectonic is the pursuit of the best whereby each craft is prepared to give the *logos* concerning the how and the that the craft serves the best. Given the duality of body and soul, there correspond two crafts to each, one maintaining health and the other restoring health. Thus, with respect to the body gymnastics aim at maintaining it while medicine aims at restoring its health.

3. ' Ἐπεὶ δ' ἐν πάσαις μὲν ταῖς ἐπιστήμαις καὶ τέχναις ἀγαθὸν τὸ τέλος, μέγιστον δὲ καὶ μάλιστα ἐν τῇ κυριωτάτῃ πασῶν, αὕτη δ' ἐστὶν ἡ πολιτικὴ δύναμις. *Pol.* III, 1282b14-16.

4. *Pol.* 1328a35-38: ἡ δὲ πόλις κοινωνία τίς ἐστι τῶν ὁμοίων, ἕνεκεν δὲ ζωῆς τῆς ἐνδεχομένης ἀρίστης. ἐπεὶ δ' ἐστὶν εὐδαιμονία τὸ ἄριστον, αὕτη δὲ ἀρετῆς ἐνέργεια καὶ χρῆσίς τις τέλειος.

5. In the opening chapter of *E. N.* bk. I, Aristotle gives a partial example of subordinate crafts that come under πολιτική: στρατηγική, οἰκονομική, ἰατρική, ναυπηγική, ῥητορική, ἠθική (?), and under strategike come ἱππική, χαλινοποιητική.

6. He uses the same expressions in *E. N.* I. 13, 1102a5-10: ' Ἐπεὶ δ'ἐστὶν ἡ εὐδαιμονία ψυχῆς ἐνέργειά τις κατ' ἀρετὴν τελείαν, περὶ ἀρετῆς ἐπισκεπτέον ἂν εἴη· τάχα γὰρ οὕτως ἂν βέλτιον καὶ περὶ τῆς εὐδαιμονίας θεωρήσαιμεν. δοκεῖ δὲ ὁ κατ' ἀλήθειαν πολιτικὸς περὶ ταύτην μάλιστα πεπονῆσθαι· βούλεται γὰρ τοὺς πολίτας ἀγαθοὺς ποεῖν καὶ τῶν νόμων ὑπηκόους. Fisch (1974) has correctly explained that Aristotle in the *E. N.*

Aristotle's Architectonic of Politike Techne 281

is not addressing the issue of praxis as it pertains to individuals as *idiotai* but as *politai*, citizens. In this sense, praxis is at once individual and social.

7. *E.N.* I. 13, 1102a 18-26; for the *telos* of human life see also *Pol.* VIII. 13, 1331b24-50.

8. On *orthai* and *parekbatikai politeiai*, see *Pol.* II. 13, 1284b22-25; 6, 1279a19-21. According to Fisch (1974), "It is only the arts and crafts as institutionalized in the *polis* that are in question, and the argument moves toward the conclusion that the poliscraft is the architectonic art to which all the rest are subordinate, and that their several ends are subsidiary directly or indirectly to its end, the architectonic end, which is human good, the good for man." (39-40)

9. *E. N.* X. 7, 1178a6-7; IX. 9, 1170a16-17.

10. The concept of the principle is gathered from a close reading of such major works as the *De Anima, Politics, Nicomachean Ethics,* and *Metaphysics.*

11. *Pol.* VIII. 9, 1328b 39-40: τὴν εὐδαιμονίαν ὅτι χωρὶς ἀρετῆς ἀδύνατον ὑπάρχειν εἴρηται.

12. *Pol.* VIII. 9 1329a 1-2: ὅτι ἄρα σχολῆς καὶ πρὸς τὴν γένεσιν τῆς ἀρετῆς καὶ πρὸς τὰς πράξεις τὰς πολιτικάς; also, VIII. 15, 1334a 1-14.

13. Fisch (1974) has aptly explained it as *poliscraft*, "the art or craft of creating a polis, keeping it going, guiding it into change for the better, guarding it from change for the worse" (26).

14. The definition of *politeia* is given in *Pol.* IV. 1, 1289a 15-18: πολιτεία μὲν γάρ ἐστι τάξις ταῖς πόλεσιν ἡ περὶ τὰς ἀρχάς, τίνα τρόπον νενέμηνται, καὶ τί τὸ κύριον τῆς πολιτείας καὶ τί τὸ τέλος ἑκάστης τῆς κοινωνίας ἐστίν; also, III. 6, 1278b8-11; III. 1, 1274b38; 4, 1276b29. Compare R. M. MacIver's definition of the modern state (1962 [1926]): "The state is an association which, acting through law as promulgated by a government endowed to this end with coercive power, maintains within a community

territorially demarcated the universal external conditions of social order." (22)

15. Aristotle's conception of the organic character of the *polis* is given descriptively in the following passage in Book III. 11, 1281b 4-7: πολλῶν γὰρ ὄντων ἕκαστον μόριον ἔχειν ἀρετῆς καὶ φρονήσεως, καὶ γίνεσθαι συνελθόντων, ὥσπερ ἕνα ἄνθρωπον τὸ πλῆθος, πολύποδα καὶ πολύχειρα καὶ πολλὰς ἔχοντ' αἰσθήσεις, οὕτω καὶ τὰ ἤθη καὶ τὴν διάνοιαν.

16. G. Vlachos (1981) in his article. "Φρόνησις Πολιτική", (78 and n. 33), draws attention to the late nineteenth century French thinker, Benjamin Constant, who argued that the concept of liberty in the ancients recognized only the citizen and ignored the human being (*De la liberté des Anciens compareé à celle des modernes*, [Labouaye, Paris 1872]). Vlachos' article has persuasively refuted the so-called antinomy "individual vs. citizen" other theorists have claimed to be a noxious problem in the *Nicomachean Ethics*, by showing that the basic excellence of *phronesis* is a qualification of the citizen as individual and as political agent. See also Vlachos (1994, 14-24, 25 n5).

17. Bosanquet (1910), in the Introduction to the second edition (xxxix).

18. Kitto (1967) has drawn attention to the difference between the Greek city and the modern state. The opening statement of his essay touches directly on the problem: "The Greek *polis*, the "city-state", was oftener than not something that we should hardly recognize as a city, and something very different in conception from our `state': therefore it seems better to use the Greek word instead of so misleading a translation" (161). Fisch (1974), following Kitto, points out that the Greeks lacked the concept of the state, that `state' is a mistranslation of `polis', and in fact it was Machiavelli who made the state "the central concept of modern European political theory" (34). On the modern use of the term "state" in the expression "city-state", see M. I. Finley (1982, 3ff.). The point I am raising in this connection is that using the modern expression to cover the Greek *politeia* as well becomes a serious anachronism when issues of interpretation remain unattended.

19. See R. M. MacIver, (1962 [1926]). Referring to the idea of the general will he notes that "This is not so much the will *of* the state as the will *for* the state, the will to maintain it" (11). Of special interest to us is his definition of the modern state: "The state, because of its rigid, unbroken, coercive framework of political law, has a permanence and fixity that distinguishes it from all other institutions" (18). And further down he writes: "The state serves best when it provides the liberty and order on which other associations can build and by which they seek more intimate or more particular ends. The state cannot possibly fulfil the purpose of the family or the church or the trade union or the cultural organizations. Its attempts to usurp the place of any of these have been historically futile." (21)

20. MacIver writes: "There are many interests which are shared by only a part of the citizen body. All cultural interests are exceedingly diversified, and the advance of culture seems to involve an ever greater differentiation of human purposes and ideals. For this reason, as for another to be mentioned presently, the state is unfitted to comprise these within its own organization. It must stand for what is recognized, by the political consciousness of the times, as the *common concern of the people*. No doubt the determination of what is the common concern must be arrived at by (at most) a majority-decision and is liable to be consciously perverted by particular dominant interest." (20)

21. *Op. cit.*, 46.

22. Most pertinent is the following comment: "In respect of social forms, our world has become differentiated far beyond the Greek or even the Roman. The self-government of the city-community was a great achievement but it could only be a step towards the solution of the great problem of liberty and order, of the union of individuals within society, until the sphere of political government began to be discovered. The failure to distinguish the state from the community left 'Athenian liberty' itself a monument broken and defaced." (87)

23. R. Aron (1968) notes: "The will to power and wealth has carried the day. The demand for equality has gone beyond the formalism of equal

rights, or the opening of all occupations to everyone, only as a direct result of the increase in the collective resources. Even today most criticism of the so-called affluent society stems from this realization. The becoming of these societies is not subject to a conscious social will. It proceeds in accordance with the unforeseeable vicissitudes of history and in many respects still appears to be immoral and irrational. What is the major charge which may legitimately be brought against all developed societies of whatever regime? Not one of them makes use of its resources in the way an all-purposeful sage would have them do; not one of them respects the priorities that seem obvious to men of good will." (248)

24. See also C. Lord and D. K. O'Connor (1991), where related issues are discussed in the essays of S. G. Stalkover, "Aristotle's Social Science", C. Lord, "Aristotle's Anthropology", J. Ober, "Aristotle's Political Sociology", D. K. O'Connor, "The Aetiology of Justice", and R. Bodéüs, "Law and the Regime in Aristotle".

25. "The American Establishment, the Civilizing Arts and Philosophy," (1974, 434) in Walton and Anton. According to Schneider, "the responsibility and the privilege of making us more civilized falls more directly on our so-called *cultural* institutions than on our political, legal and commercial systems." (437)

BIBLIOGRAPHY

Ackrill, J. L., tr. 1963. *Aristotle's Categories and De Interpretatione.* Oxford: Clarendon Press.

Anton, John P. 1957. *Aristotle's Theory of Contrariety.* London: Routledge and Kegan Paul. New York: Humanities Press.

_____. 1975. "Some Observations on Aristotle's Theory of Categories," *Diotima* 3, 67–81.

_____. 1976. "Plotinus' Approach to Categorial Theory." In *The Significance of Neoplatonism*, ed. by R. B. Harris, 83–99. New York: State University of New York Press.

_____. 1981. "Aristotle's Theory of Categories in Post-Classical Ontologies," *Proceedings of the World Congress on Aristotle* (1977). Thessaloniki, Greece. 214–220.

_____. 1982. "Aspects of Ancient Ontologies." In *Philosophies of Existence: Ancient and Medieval*, ed. by P. Morewedge, 60–77. New York: Fordham University Press.

Apelt, O. 1891. *Beiträge zur Geschichte der griechischen Philosophie.* Leipzig: Teubner. Reprint 1975, Aalen: Scientia Verlag.

Arnauld, A. 1964. *The Art of Thinking: Port-Royal Logic*, translated, with an Introduction, by J. Dickoff and P. James, and a Foreword by C. W. Hendel. New York: The Library of Liberal Arts.

Aron, Raymond. 1968. *Progress abd Disillusion: The Dialectic of Modern Society.* New York and Toronto: The New American Library. Mentor Book.

Barker, E. 1925 [1918]. *Greek Political Theory: Plato and His Predecessors.* London Methuen University Paperbacks.

_____. 1959. *The Political Theory of Plato and Aristotle.* DoverPublications.

_____. 1960. *Greek Political Theory: Plato and His Predecessors.* London and New York: Barnes and Noble. University Paperback.

_____. 1962. *The Politics of Aristotle.* Translated with an Introduction, Notes and Appendices. New York: Oxford University Press. A Galaxy Book.

Bloom, A. tr. 1968. *The Republic of Plato.* New York: Basic Books.

Bosanquet, Bernard. 1919. *The Philosophical Theory of the State.* London: Macmillan.

Brandis, C. 1862. *Geschichte der Entwinklungen der griechischen Philosophie und ihrer Nachwirkungen in Roemischen Reiche.* I. Hälfte. Berlin.

Brentano, F. 1975. *On the Several Senses of Being in Aristotle,* ed. and tr. Rolf George. Berkeley: University of California Press.

Cairns, H. 1949. *Legal Theory from Plato to Hegel.* Baltimore: The Johns Hopkins University Press. For a discussion on Aristotle see pp. 77-126.

Calhoun, G. M. 1944. *Introduction to Greek Legal Science.* Oxford: Oxford University Press.

Categoriae. Ed. L. Minio-Paluello. 1974. Oxford Classical Texts. Oxford: Clarendon Press.

Cherniss, H. 1944. *Aristotle's Criticism of Plato and the Academy.* Baltimore: Johns Hopkins University Press.

Cornford, F. M. tr. 1945. *The Republic of Plato*. Oxford: Oxford University Press.

Dancy, R. M. 1975. *Sense and Contradiction: A Study in Aristotle*. Dortrecht, Holland: Reidel. Synthese Historical Library.

_____. 1975. "On Some of Aristotle's First Thoughts about Substances," *Philosophical Review*, 84, 338-73.

De Rijk. L. M. 1952. *The Place of the Categories of Being in Aristotle's Philosophy*. Assen: Van Gorcum.

De Lacy, Phillip. 1958. "Οὐ μᾶλλον and the Antecedents of Ancient Scepticism," *Phronesis* 3, 59-71; reprinted in *Essays in Ancient Greek Philosophy*, edited by J. P. Anton with G. L. Kustas. Albany: SUNY Press. 1971, 593-606; references to this edition.

Demos, Raphael. 1959. "Partly So and Partly Not So," *Mind 69 (N. S.), 51-56*.

Edel, A. 1967. *Aristotle*. New York: Dell Publishing Co.

Elders, Leo. 1961. *Aristotle's Theory of the One: A Commentary on Book X of the Metaphysics*. Assen: Van Gorcum.

Finley, M. I. 1982. *Economy and Society in Ancient Greece*. Edited with an Introduction by B. D. Shaw and R. P. Seller. New York: Viking Press.

Fisch, Max. 1974. "Poliscraft," in Walton C., and J. P. Anton, pp. 24-48.

Fortenbaugh, W. W. "Aristotle on Prior and Posterior, Correct and Mistaken Constitutions," in *TAPA* 106 (1976),

Frede, Michael. 1987. *Essays in Ancient Philosophy*. Minneapolis: University of Minnesota Press.

Friedrich, C. H. 1955. "Two Philosophical Interpretations of Natural Law," *Diogenes*, 10.

_____. 1958. *The Philosophy of Law in Historical Perspective*. Chicago. 2nd edition. Chapter III, "Law as Participation in the Idea of Justice. Plato and Aristotle," pp. 13-26.

Fritz, Kurt von, and Ernst Kapp. 1950. *Aristotle, The Constitution of Athens*. New York: Hafner.

Guthrie, W.K.C. 1981. *A History of Greek Philosophy*, Vol. 6, *Aristotle: An Encounter*. Cambridge: Cambridge University Press.

Hamburger, M. 1951. *Morals and Law: The Growth of Aristotle's Legal Theory*. New Haven: Yale University Press.

Hardie, W.F.R. 1968. *Aristotle's Ethical Theory*. Oxford: Oxford University Press.

Harter, Edward. 1975. "Aristotle on Primary *Ousia*." *Archiv für Geschichte der Philosophie*, 57, 1–20.

Hicks, R. D., ed. and tr. 1907. *Aristotle: De Anima*. Cambridge: Cambridge University Press.

Kant, I. 1920. *Kant's Inaugural Dissertation and Early Writings on Space*, trans. by J. Handyside London: Open Court.

_____. 1933, 1952. *Critique of Pure Reason*. Tr. Norman Kemp Smith. London: Methuen; MacMillan.

_____. 1950. *Critique of Pure Reason*, translated by N. K. Smith, 2nd impression with corrections. London: Macmillan.

Kapp. E. 1942. *Greek Foundations of Traditional Logic*. New York: Columbia University Press.

Kitto, H. D. F. 1967. "The City," in *The Living heritage of Greek Antiquity*. European Cultural Foundation. The Hague: Mouton & Co., pp. 161-76.

Konvitz, M.R. 1973. "Equity and Law in Ethics," in *The Dictionary of the History of Ideas*, ed. P. Wiener, ed. Vol. II, 148. Scribner's.

Kort, F. 1952. "The Quantification of Aristotle's Theory of Revolution," *American Political Science Review*, 46, 486-93.

Kyle, G. 1965. "Categories", *Proceedings of the Aristotelian Society*, Second Series (1938/9); reprinted, *Logic and Language*, ed. with Introductions by A. Flew. N.Y.: Doubleday, 281–98.

Leyden, W. von. 1967. "Aristotle and the Concept of Law," *Philosophy*, 42, 1-19.

Lord, Carnes and David K. O'Connor, edd. 1991. *Essays on the Foundation of Aristotelian Political Science*. Berkeley: University of California Press.

Lukasiewicz, Jan. 1970–1971. "On the Principle of Contradiction in Aristotle," (tr. by V. Wedin), *Review of Metaphysics* 24, 485–509.

MacIver, R. M. 1964 [1926]. *The Modern State*. Oxford University Press.

Maguire, J.P. 1947. "Plato's Theory of Natural Law," *Yale Classical Studies*, 171-78.

Maridakis, G.S. 1973. "Σκέψεις ἐπὶ τῆς θεωρίας τοῦ ᾽Αριστοτέλους περὶ ἐπιεικείας," in E. von Caemmerer et al., edd. *Festschrift für Pan. J. Zepos*. Athens. Katsikalis (Zabakis) Verlag.

Mesthene, E. 1950. "On the Status of the Laws of Logic," *Philosophy and Phenomenological Research* 10, 354–373.

Μιχαηλίδης-Νουάρος, Γ. [n.d]. "Οἱ αἰτίες τῶν ἐπαναστάσεων κατὰ τὸν 'Αριστοτέλη," *Πρακτικὰ Παγκοσμίου Συνεδρίου 'Αριστοτέλους*, v. IV.

Moody, E. A. 1935. *The Logic of William of Ockham*. London: Sheed and Ward.

Morrow, Glenn R. 1948. "Plato and the Law of Nature," *Essays in Political Theory*, edited by M.R. Konvitz and A.E. Murphy.

Ockham. 1974. *Ockham's Theory of Terms: Part I of the Summa Logicae*, translation and Introduction by Michael J. Loux. Notre Dame, Indiana: Univ. of Notre Dame Press.

Porphyry. 1975. *Isagoge*, translation and Introduction and notes by E. W. Warren. Toronto: The Pontifical Institute of Medieval Studies.

Preus, Anthony "*Eidos* as Norm in Aristotle's Biology," *Nature and System* 1 (1979), 79–101.

Robinson, R. 1962. *Plato's Earlier Dialectic*. Oxford: Oxford University Press.

Ross, W. David, ed. 1924. *Aristotle's Metaphysics*. 2 vols. Oxford: Oxford University Press. (Revised Text with introduction and commentary.)

_____. 1928. *The Works of Aristotle*. Vol. I.Oxford: Oxford University Press. *Categoriae and De Interpretatione*, tr. Edgehill, E. M.

Schneider, H. W. 1974. "The American Establishment," in Walton and Anton, pp. 433-45.

Shorey, Paul and H. D. P. Lee, trs. 1955. *Plato, The Republic*. Baltimore: Penguin Books.

Vinogradoff, P. 1922. *Outlines of Historical Jurisprudence*. London. Vol. 2, esp. chapter iii. See also P. Shorey's review of this work in *Classical Philology* XIX (1924), "Universal Justice in Aristotle's Ethics."

Vlachos, G. 1981. "Φρόνησις Πολιτική. Ἡ ἀντινομία τοῦ ἀνθρώπου καὶ τοῦ πολίτης τὰ "Ἠθικά Νικομάχεια"", Ἐπιστημονικὴ ἐπετηρίδα τῆς Παντείου Ἀνωτάτης Σχολῆς Πολιττκῶν Ἐπιστημῶν. Ἐπιμ. Παν. Δ. Δημάκη: *Ἀριςτοτέλης καὶ Πολιτική*. Ἀθήνα, pp. 67-80.

_____. 1994. *L'Idée d'homme libre dans la république des Athéniens: Le témoignage de Démosthène*. Athens and Komotini: Editions Sakkoulas.

Vlastos, G. 1947. "Justice and Equality in Early Greek Thought," *Classical Philology*, 42, 156-78.

Walton, C., and Anton, J. P., edd. 1974. *Philosophy and the Civilizing Arts. Essays Presented to Herbert W. Schneider on his Eightieth Birthday*. Athens, Ohio: Ohio University Press.

INDEX

A
Accidental beings, 63-65
Account, 20, 34, 54, 55, 57, 73, 74, 109, 112, 114, 119, 121, 123, 125, 134, 141, 147, 148, 162, 164, 202, 239, 249, 266, 267
Ackrill, 57, 73, 77, 285
Ajaxes, 105, 109, 116, 118, 124, 125
Ammonius, 59, 78, 100, 104, 110-114, 117, 124, 168
Archery, 261, 262
Aristotle, 7, 12-25, 27, 28, 31, 33, 36-48, 53-67, 69, 76, 70-85, 100, 101, 103-106, 108-111, 113-127, 132-137, 139-142, 144, 145, 147, 148, 152-161, 163-168, 175-182, 185, 186, 188-192, 195-198, 202, 205-213, 215-234, 236, 237, 239-242, 245-252, 254, 257-267, 271-273, 275, 276, 278, 286-291
Arnauld, 180, 182, 286

B
Boethius, 58
Biology, 19, 41, 192, 200, 291
Botany, 13, 14, 239

C
Cherniss, 36, 73, 75, 76, 84, 287
Circularity, 41, 42
Contraries, 17, 18, 35, 37, 47
Co-incidental properties, 20, 194, 196-198
Copula, 161, 165
Cratylus, 10, 36
Critias, 8

D
Dexippus, 59, 78, 100, 104, 108-110

E
Empedocles, 7
Entelecheia, 15, 16, 24, 147, 205, 250
Epieikēs, 247, 249, 250
Epistemological relativism, 33
Ethics, 10, 13, 14, 19, 21, 24, 25, 32, 41, 216, 222, 235, 238, 241, 245-247, 254, 257, 260, 263-265, 267, 269, 271-274, 277, 278, 289, 291
Eudaemonistic ethics, 238
Eudoxus, 257
Euthyphro, 11

Existents, 15, 18-20, 42, 43, 46, 53, 111, 163, 164, 194, 195

F
Frede, 152-155, 157, 168, 288

G
Gorgias, 8, 9, 247, 271
Greek, 7, 8, 13, 14, 18, 21, 27, 28, 36, 53, 55, 57, 66, 82, 100, 133, 135, 140, 151, 160, 185, 217, 224, 240, 245, 259, 269, 270, 275-277, 280, 286-289, 291

H
Hellenic ideal of conduct, 21
Hellenistic movements, 182
Heraclitus, 7, 10, 259
Herminus, 59, 78, 123, 158
Hippias, 8
Homonyma, 55, 56, 58-62, 64-67, 70, 72-76, 78-85, 100-128, 157
Homonymy, 53, 54, 56, 58-60, 66, 71-73, 80, 83, 85, 104-111, 115, 116, 165

I
Iamblichus, 108, 120-123, 128, 132, 158
Inherence, 143, 146, 164, 166, 168, 198
Inherence of properties, 198
Institutions, 21, 24, 25, 208, 224, 230, 233, 245, 272, 274-276, 278, 279
Intelligence, 11, 16, 20, 189, 195, 219, 272
Interest, 12, 46, 54, 76, 80, 104, 107, 113, 115, 117, 118, 123, 124, 136, 152, 153, 168, 178, 182, 198, 206, 275, 276

K
Kant, 156, 180, 181, 289
Kapp, 133, 229, 242, 288, 289
Kategorein, 120, 133, 135, 144, 145, 154, 156, 158, 161, 163-166
Kategoria, 108, 133-139, 146, 147, 152, 156-169, 177, 179

L
Lawgiver, 227, 248, 250, 251, 253
Law of contradiction, 36, 38

Index 295

Legetai, 118, 135, 143-145, 163, 166, 167

M
MacIver, 275, 276, 290
Metaphysics, 13, 14, 18, 19, 25, 33, 36, 38-46, 48, 63, 64, 69, 73, 134, 135, 139, 140, 158, 168, 181, 188, 190, 222, 241, 260, 272, 288, 290, 291

N
Negations, 165, 180
Neoplatonic, 123-125, 128
Neoplatonic theory, 123
Nicomachean Ethics, 14, 21, 25, 216, 222, 235, 245-247, 254, 257, 263, 264, 269, 272, 274
Nicostratus, 59, 78, 121, 123
Nominalism of Ockham, 182
Nous, 15, 20, 41, 57, 179, 265, 272, 275, 277, 279

O
Ockham, 179, 180, 182, 290
Oligarchies, 212, 213, 229
Olympiodorus, 59, 78, 100, 107, 118, 119, 124, 132

Ontological, 31, 33, 37, 38, 40, 42, 43, 47, 48, 62, 63, 101, 102, 106, 127, 132, 144, 158, 166, 169, 177, 178, 186, 188, 193
Ontology, 37, 40, 42-44, 47, 52, 54, 57, 59, 60, 73, 76, 81, 84, 85, 114, 123, 127, 133, 138, 146, 151, 167, 176-179, 181, 182, 190, 192, 193
Ousia, 14, 19, 20, 45, 53-57, 59-66, 74, 75, 78, 79, 81, 84, 85, 101, 104, 106-108, 110, 111, 117, 119, 121-123, 127, 128, 133, 140, 141, 144-146, 160, 163, 165, 166, 168, 169, 177, 178, 182, 194-202, 259, 289
Ousiai, 15, 62, 63, 67, 111, 141, 161, 166, 177, 179, 186, 190, 193, 195-198
Owens, 69

P
Parmenides, 7, 10, 32, 35, 73
Pericles, 270
Peripatetic School, 12, 260
Philoponus, 58, 59, 61, 77, 78, 100, 115-118, 168

Plato, 9-13, 24, 25, 28, 31-40, 43, 47, 48, 71-76, 84, 100, 115, 119, 120, 126, 146, 148, 189, 216, 217, 223-225, 229, 231, 233, 240, 241, 247, 266, 268, 271, 274, 275, 286-288, 291
Plotinus, 108, 179, 182
Polis, 11, 21-24, 206, 207, 212, 217, 219, 224, 236, 241, 242, 271-276, 278
Politeia, 25, 207, 215, 235, 236, 270, 273-277
Political theory, 23, 208, 220, 231-233, 235, 274, 275, 278, 279, 286, 290
Porphyry, 54, 57, 59, 77, 78, 85, 103-113, 121, 123, 124, 126, 128, 158, 176, 179, 180, 182, 291
Prodicus, 8
Properties, 20, 35, 45, 46, 53, 60, 61, 63-65, 72, 75, 79, 81, 84, 101, 102, 106, 109, 111-113, 117, 119, 120, 122, 125, 141, 147, 161, 164, 186, 194-199, 219, 250
Protagoras, 8, 31, 32, 40, 46, 47
Pythagoras of Samos, 7

R
Reducible, 46, 63, 124, 193, 251
Regularities, 187, 189, 190, 192, 196-200
Religion, 8, 11, 278
Ross, 57, 63, 64, 77, 134, 135, 137-141, 158, 266, 291

S
Simplicius, 58, 59, 71, 75, 76, 77, 78, 80, 100, 108, 120-124, 158, 168
Socrates, 8, 9, 11, 74, 119, 121, 122, 221, 247
Sophistic movement, 8, 9
Speusippus, 58, 60, 75, 76, 80, 81, 84, 100, 101, 105
Symbebēkota, 53, 133, 177, 186, 194-200

T
Theaetetus, 31, 33-36, 71, 74
Thrasymachus, 8
Timaeus, 11, 36, 73

U
Utility, 12, 47, 195, 232, 236

W

Wholes, 186-188, 190-199
Will, 7, 21, 22, 31, 34-36, 39, 45, 47, 59, 66, 74, 81, 82, 104, 110, 132-135, 138-141, 144, 152, 153, 155, 158, 163, 164, 176, 178, 180, 181, 210, 202, 205-207, 209, 219-224, 226, 229, 232, 235, 237, 250, 251, 253, 258, 259, 261, 263, 264, 266, 269-272, 274, 275, 277

Z

Zoology, 13
Zoon, 66, 83

ABOUT THE AUTHOR

Dr. John P. Anton (Ph.D. Columbia University, Doctor of Philosophy *Honoris Causa* University of Athens), is Distinguished Professor of Greek Philosophy and Culture at the University of South Florida. His expertise is in the Philosophy of Aristotle, the History of Philosophy, Aesthetics, Ancient, Medieval and Contemporary Greek Thought, Language and Literature. He has lectured extensively at universities in the United States of America and in Greece. Dr. Anton has served as Trustee of the *American Society for Aesthetics*, President of the *Georgia Philosophical Association*, President and Secretary-Treasurer of the *Society for Ancient Greek Philosophy*, Board Member of the *Society for the History of Philosophy* and of the *Society for the Advancement of American Philosophy*, and it is currently Chairman of the Executive Committee of the *International Society for Neoplatonic Studies*. He is an Honorary Member of Phi Betta Kappa and Corresponding Member of the Academy of Athens. Dr. Anton is the author, editor, and translator of over seventy five articles and fifteen books including:

Aristotle's Theory of Contrariety. London: Routledge and Kegan Paul. New York: Humanities Press. 1957. New Edition, University Presses of America. 1987.

Critical Humanism as a Philosophy of Culture: The Case of E. P. Papanoutsos. Minneapolis: North Central Publishing Co. 1981.

Philosophical Essays (in Greek). Athens: Makrides and Co. Publishers. 1969.

The Poetry and Poetics of Constantine P. Cavafy. London: Harwood Academic Publishers. 1995.

Essays in Ancient Greek Philosophy. Volume I. Edited by J. P. Anton and G. Kustas. Albany: State University of New York Press. 1971.

Essays in Ancient Greek Philosophy. Volume II. Edited by J. P. Anton and A. Preus. Albany: State University of New York Press. 1983.

Essays in Ancient Greek Philosophy. Volume III. Edited by J. P. Anton and A. Preus. Albany: State University of New York Press. 1989.

Essays in Ancient Greek Philosophy. Volume IV. Edited by A. Preus and J. P. Anton. Albany: State University of New York Press. 1991.